AN INTRODUCTION TO THE STUDY OF

SOUTHWESTERN ARCHAEOLOGY

An introduction to the study of Southwestern archaeology with a preliminary account of the excavations at Pecos

by
ALFRED VINCENT KIDDER

and a summary of
Southwestern archaeology today

by
IRVING ROUSE

New Haven and London
YALE UNIVERSITY PRESS

Table of Contents

List of Illustrations

PAGE

FIGURES

Southwestern Archaeology Today

The Southwest occupies a special place in American archaeology. Its large masonry ruins, called pueblos, have attracted constant attention and, as a result, it has become perhaps the most intensively excavated part of the New World. Much of the present generation of American archaeologists was trained in the Southwest, and many innovations in method and theory originated there.

Not the least of the achievements of Southwestern archaeology was the publication of the present volume in 1924. It was the first detailed synthesis of the archaeology of any part of the New World and, as such, set the pattern for much subsequent work in other areas. Kidder's approach to synthesis, whereby he divided the Southwest into regions and, within each region, arranged the remains chronologically, working back from the historic pueblos to the prehistoric pueblos and then to the pre-pueblo remains, has been copied in many other parts of the New World.

But Southwestern archaeology has not stood still since 1924. There have been many new discoveries, new conclusions, and new innovations in method and theory. It is the purpose of this summary briefly to sketch the new developments, in order that the reader may obtain a better knowledge of the present status of archaeology in the area.

An Introduction to the Study of Southwestern Archaeology was originally published in 1924 as Number 1 of the Papers of the Southwestern Expedition, Department of Anthropology—now the R. S. Peabody Foundation for Archaeology—Phillips Academy, Andover, Massachusetts. Subsequent numbers in the series are:

2. *Pueblo Pottery Making,* by Carl E. Guthe, 1925.
3. *The Pueblo of Jemez,* by Elsie Clews Parsons, 1925.
4. *The Indians of Pecos Pueblo, a Study of Their Skeletal Remains,* by Earnest Albert Hooton, with appendices on the dentition by Habib J. Rihan and on the pelves by Edward Reynolds, 1930.
5. *The Pottery of Pecos, Volume I, Dull Paint Wares,* by Alfred Vincent Kidder, together with a section on black-on-white wares by Charles Avery Amsden, 1931.
6. *The Artifacts of Pecos,* by Alfred Vincent Kidder, 1932.
7. *The Pottery of Pecos, Volume II, the Glaze Wares,* by Alfred Vincent Kidder and Anna O. Shephard, 1936.

All were published under the imprint of the Yale University Press and all except Number 6 are now out of print.

Kidder had intended also to publish a final report on the Pecos excavations, but in 1929 he joined the staff of the Carnegie Institution of Washington to direct its research in the Maya area and thus was diverted from the task. After his retirement from the Carnegie Institution, he was able to prepare only a monograph of miscellaneous studies, *Pecos, New Mexico: Archaeological Notes,* which has been published as Volume 5 of the Papers of the Robert S. Peabody Foundation for Archaeology (Andover, 1958).

In the original *Introduction,* with characteristic breadth of interest, Kidder made a number of statements relating Southwestern archaeology to that of the New World as a whole. Many of the terms he used and the theories to which he referred have changed; e.g., the term "Archaic" is now applied to the pre-Sedentary peoples of Middle America rather than to the Sedentary peoples, as it was when he wrote. Since my summary is limited to the Southwest, it does not deal with changes like these, but the reader who is interested in them may consult one or more of the following general syntheses, which are listed in the bibliography on pp. 49 ff.: Kroeber, 1948, pp. 772–839; Kroeber (ed.), 1953, pp. 211–64; Rouse, 1960; Willey, 1960; and Willey and Phillips, 1958, pp. 61–205.

Those who wish to obtain additional bibliographic information on Southwestern archaeology may consult Douglas W. Schwartz' "Southwestern Archaeological Bibliography." This has so far appeared only in a preliminary mimeographed edition, circulated privately by the author from the Museum of Anthropology, University of Kentucky, but a final printed edition is planned. For additional sources on the modern Southwestern Indians, I would suggest George Peter Murdock's *Ethnographic Bibliography of North America,* second edition, published by the Human Relations Area Files (New Haven, 1953).

My summary is built around two chronological charts which I presented at the annual meeting of the Society for American Archaeology in Columbus, Ohio on May 4, 1961 (figs. 1 and 3). I am grateful to the following archaeologists for suggesting revisions in these charts, either at the meeting or in subsequent correspondence: Douglas S. Byers, Emil W. Haury, Erik K. Reed, Raymond H. Thompson, and Joe Ben Wheat. The manuscript has been read by Haury, Thompson, and by Kwang-chih Chang, William D. Lipe, and William W. Wasley, who have contributed much helpful criticism. I am also indebted to Richard F. Flint for advice on geological problems and to Paul S. Martin and H. Marie Wormington for assistance with my illustrations. Permission to reproduce the latter has been granted by the Chicago Natural History Museum, Denver Natural History Museum, the Society for American Archaeology, and John Wiley and Sons, Inc.

Kidder's *Introduction* is one of the classics of American archaeology. The Yale University Press is rendering a real service by undertaking this reprint, and I am honored to be associated with it. I am also pleased to have had the opportunity to work with Dr. Kidder and greatly appreciate his advice and encouragement.

IRVING ROUSE

CULTURAL TRADITIONS

In 1924, Southwestern archaeology was concerned almost exclusively with the Pueblo Indians, who built the great masonry structures of historic and prehistoric time, and with their ancestors, the Basket Makers. Kidder, therefore, wrote almost entirely about the Anasazi tradition, to use the modern term which covers both Basket Maker and Pueblo cultures. Subsequent archaeologists have discovered a number of other traditions, which are more or less distinct from the Anasazi. These may be characterized as follows.

ANASAZI TRADITION

The Anasazi tradition is centered in the high plateau country of the San Juan, Little Colorado, and upper Rio Grande valleys (fig. 11). The modern Pueblo Indians and their ancestors have inhabited this general region since about the time of Christ, relying mainly upon natural runoff from springs and the heads of streams to water their crops. They have far surpassed the other Indians of the Southwest in architecture, developing not only the large, multistory masonry pueblos but also unique religious structures known as kivas. The Anasazi buried their dead in the ground, often accompanied by vessels and ornaments.

The Anasazi tradition made a sharp distinction between painted and culinary wares. The former is typically black on white and the latter, decorated with corrugations. Some of the kivas contain mural paintings, but there is relatively little carving in stone, bone, and shell; apparently, the Anasazi were too preoccupied with architecture and pottery to pay much attention to the other arts. Their designs were almost entirely geometric before they came under foreign influence.

HOHOKAM TRADITION

In the late 1920's, Harold S. Gladwin, working through his own private research organization, the Gila Pueblo, began to investigate the ruins of the Lower Gila area, i.e., of the desert lowlands southwest of the Anasazi center (fig. 11). He was encouraged to do so by Kidder, who had been impressed by the aberrance of many Lower Gila remains and by their Mexican resemblances and had urged study of the chronological position of these remains relative to the more typically Pueblo sites (see pp. 298–302). Gladwin found that the aberrant remains belonged to a different tradition, to which he gave the name Hohokam. The Hohokam Indians typically lived in pit houses and did not construct multiroom dwellings until they came under the influence of the Anasazi. On the other hand, they developed an elaborate system of ditches to irrigate the desert, many of which have been cleared out and are being re-used by modern farmers. The Hohokam were likewise more advanced than the Anasazi in art. They painted, carved, engraved, and even etched both human and animal figures on pottery, stone vessels and palettes, and upon ornaments of stone and shell (fig. 5).

The Hohokam also depicted life forms on their pottery, in red designs painted on a buff background, and modeled figurines of clay in Mexican fashion. Other evidences of Mexican influence include large oval courts, in which a ceremonial ball game was presumably played, mosaic mirrors made from iron pyrites, copper bells, and platform mounds, built as substructures for temples (Wasley, 1960). Burial was by cremation, and the ashes were typically placed in the ground with a number of grave objects (Gladwin et al., 1937; Wormington, 1947, pp. 118–47).

The authorities disagree about the origin and fate of the Hohokam tradition, as will be discussed later. According to the most widely accepted theory, the tradition developed locally during the first millennium A.D., reached a climax at the end of that time, and then declined. An invasion of Anasazi Indians at about 1300 A.D. undoubtedly hastened the decline. Thereafter, the fate of the Hohokam Indians becomes obscure, but they most probably survived as the present-day Pima and Papago Indians of the Lower Gila area (fig. 3).

MOGOLLON TRADITION

Since 1930, a number of Southwestern archaeologists, including Emil W. Haury, of the University of Arizona, and Paul S. Martin, of the Chicago Natural History Museum, have turned their attention to the mountainous territory which Kidder terms the Upper Gila and Mimbres areas (fig. 11). They have been attracted there by the presence of a third major tradition, the Mogollon. Though not so advanced as either the Anasazi or the Hohokam tradition, this one deserves attention because it has yielded the earliest evidences of intensive agriculture, pottery, and a settled form of life. It was apparently in existence from about 300 B.C. to 1100 A.D., when the Mogollon Indians became acculturated to the Anasazi tradition— with the result that their descendants are to be found in the modern pueblos (fig. 3).

Like the Anasazi, the Mogollon Indians relied upon natural runoff of water from the mountain streams to grow their crops. On the other hand, they built simple pit houses, like those of the Hohokam tradition (fig. 4). They buried their dead unburned in pits or beneath cairns, frequently accompanied by mortuary offerings. Their pottery was typically polished, smudged, or painted red on brown. Tubular pipes attest the use of tobacco, and there were some ornaments of Hohokam type (Wheat, 1955; Martin, 1959).

CULTURAL TRADITIONS 7

ATHAPASKAN TRADITION

Interspersed among the modern Pueblo Indians are a series of tribes, such as the Navaho and Apache, which are descended from a fourth major tradition, the Athapaskan (fig. 3). This takes its name from the languages spoken by the surviving representatives of the tradition. The Athapaskan family of languages centers in western Canada, whence some of its speakers apparently migrated into the American Southwest shortly before the arrival of Europeans. They brought with them a nomadic form of life based upon hunting and a northern type of pottery, having conical bases and surfaces roughened by scoring the wet clay. Studies of Navaho remains indicate that for a while these Indians adopted the painting of pottery from the Anasazi and even experimented with walls and towers of masonry, but they never ceased to live in their typical log, brush, and earth lodges, known as hogans, and to make sweat houses (Riley, 1954).

DESERT TRADITION

To the north and west of the present-day Athapaskan speakers, in the San Juan area and the Northern Peripheral district (fig. 11), live another group of nonagricultural tribes, the Ute, Paiute, and Shoshoni. These appear to be survivors of a Desert tradition, so-called because it was adapted to the dry conditions of the early postglacial time when it began (Jennings et al., 1956). The Desert tradition is important because it seems to have been the root from which subsequent Southwestern traditions, such as the Anasazi, Hohokam, and Mogollon, branched off in more recent times (fig. 1).

Sayles and Antevs (1941) were the first to document the Desert tradition archaeologically. It lacks agriculture, pottery, and permanent houses, its sites consisting simply of hearths and refuse, i.e., of remains of camps, situated in caves or in the open. The typical implements are metates and manos, the bottom and top stones which were used to grind wild vegetable foods. Projectile points are also present, indicating that the people were hunters as well as foragers. Baskets, sandals, and other perishable materials are common in the cave sites.

PALEO-INDIAN TRADITION

In 1926, a party of paleontologists from the Colorado Museum of Natural History discovered projectile points in association with the bones of an extinct animal, the *Bison taylori,* at Folsom in northeastern New Mexico. Other such finds, comprising different kinds of projectile points and the bones of other extinct animals, such as the mammoth, followed; and as a result it is now possible to distinguish a sixth major tradition, called Paleo-Indian. It is known primarily from "kill sites," containing the bones of the extinct animals the Paleo-Indians hunted and butchered at the scenes of their kills, apparently because they were ill equipped to carry such large animals back to the places where they lived. Among the bones are remains of the hunting weapons, especially lance heads, which are more finely made than the points of the Desert tradition. The Paleo-Indian kill sites, interspersed with a few places of habitation, are most common in the high plains of eastern New Mexico and Colorado but extend also into the basin country of southern Arizona, where they antedate the sites of the Desert tradition (fig. 1). (See Wormington, 1957, for detailed summaries of the Paleo-Indian and Desert traditions, which she terms Paleo-Eastern and Paleo-Western respectively.)

OTHER TRADITIONS

The foregoing enumeration does not exhaust the list of "basic cultures," as the traditions are frequently called. Others are included in Figures 1 and 3 and will be discussed later.

Some archaeologists believe that the trend toward distinguishing traditions has gone too far: Daifuku (1961), for example, recognizes only the Anasazi and Hohokam; and Reed (1951, 1955) similarly considers Anasazi and Mogollon to be but branches of the same basic tradition. In effect, these authors raise the question of which kinds of remains are to be considered "basic" to Southwestern archaeology. The question is avoided here by treating all of the traditions impartially, regardless of their importance or distinctness.

Another problem is caused by the fact that a tradition may be conceived in two different manners: as a group of people (a sort of prehistoric tribe) or as a way of life (i.e., a pattern of culture). The two are not necessarily the same, since a people can change their way of life. For example, Jennings and others (1956, fig. 1,e) identify the early historic Indians of the lower Rio Grande as Mogollon, whereas Kelley (1952, fig. 1) considers them to be Pueblo. Both are right, in that these Indians were descendants of people who originally had Mogollon culture but who became acculturated to the Pueblo way of life. In the following pages, such conflicts have been resolved by treating the traditions as ways of life rather than as groups of people.

CHRONOLOGICAL TECHNIQUES

In the absence of a native form of writing, which could have provided a record of the ages of the sites and traditions, Southwestern archaeologists have found it difficult to date them, as Kidder notes in this volume (pp. 139, 158–63, 345–51). Great strides have been made toward the resolution of this problem since he wrote in 1924, however.

DEVELOPMENTAL CLASSIFICATION

Kidder used a relatively gross method of establishing chronology (pp. 166 ff.) He simply arranged the sites in order of increasing complexity, especially of pottery: (1) "Basket Maker" sites, which lacked pottery and ruins; (2) "post-Basket Maker" sites, which contained the crudest pottery and the simplest house ruins; (3) "pre-Pueblo" sites, with more advanced pottery and the beginnings of religious as well as residential buildings; (4) Pueblo ruins, with the most advanced pottery and architecture; and (5) modern Pueblo culture. This classification has since been modified and comparable classifications have been set up for the Mogollon and Hohokam traditions, as shown in Figure 3.

The three classifications do not, of course, take into account local variations in the rate and direction of development. To express these, some archaeologists (e.g., Gladwin, 1957) have divided each tradition into a series of "branches," or local sequences of development, but these are too detailed to be discussed in the present summary.

CULTURAL CHRONOLOGY

In his Pecos excavations (pp. 89–129), Kidder himself was pioneering a new, more precise, and more purely chronological method of dating. By concentrating on Pecos, he was able to work out a sequence which is not subject to the factor of local variation. Other archaeologists were establishing similar sequences in other parts of the Southwest, and it was their hope, which has since been realized, eventually to synthesize these local sequences over the entire Southwest.

As Kidder notes herein (pp. 161–62), the approach is
based upon the fact that Southwestern pottery is a most
sensitive indicator of changes in time. Like our modern
automobiles, it was constantly being modified by the
Indians in accordance with the dictates of fashion, so that
it can now be easily classified into types. By comparing the
pottery types which occur in various levels of the refuse
heaps into which the Indians obligingly piled their trash,
archaeologists have been able to work out a series of local
successions of types. They have found, too, that each level
in the trash heaps has its own distinctive frequencies of
types, reflecting the fact that, at all sites within a local
area, the types tended to have the same relative popularity
at any one period of time. To determine the age of a newly
excavated ruin, therefore, it is only necessary to compare
its types and their frequencies with the master sequence
which has been built up for the area (Spier, 1931; Woodbury, 1960). Each of the columns in Figure 3 has largely
been set up on this basis.

In the preceramic sites of the Paleo-Indian and Desert
traditions, projectile points provide similar evidences of
chronology. Though not so complex as pottery vessels,
they too have changed markedly from time to time, as
fashions changed. Studies of stratified sites have established
local sequences of projectile-point types comparable to the
sequences of pottery types in the ceramic sites. Thus when
a new, Paleo-Indian site is discovered, it can be dated by
comparing its projectile points with the master sequence
for the area. The individual columns of Figure 1 are based
upon these master sequences.

To cross-date the various local sequences is a more difficult task. The simplest procedure is to arrange the sequences in parallel series, extending back from historic
time or from some other known datum point, as in the
columns of Figure 3, and to assume that all phases, i.e.,
the members of each series, have had approximately the

same duration, so that the third phase in the first sequence is of the same age as the third in the second sequence, etc. Unfortunately, this assumption is frequently wrong, as Figure 3 will indicate, since changes take place more rapidly in some areas than in others. Another approach is to assume that phases of two local sequences which have similar pottery or projectile-point types are contemporaneous. This method is more reliable but, again, types sometimes change more rapidly in one area than in another. It is also possible to look for pottery which has been traded from one area to the other or for evidences of mutual influence, such as a design style which the people of one tradition have adopted from another.

Kidder (pp. 349–51) suggested that the process of cross-dating local chronologies might eventually be carried from the Southwest down through Mexico into Yucatan, so as to apply the hieroglyphically inscribed dates of the Maya calendar to Southwestern archaeology. This has not yet been accomplished. The difficulties of cross-dating local chronologies are great, and other methods of making broad-scale correlations have been developed which promise better results (cf. Jennings et al., 1956, pp. 93–94).

GEOCHRONOLOGY

One of these is geochronology, so called because it is based upon the chronology of the environment, as worked out by geologists and other students of natural history. Kidder notes (p. 348) that his generation had no way of applying this to Southwestern archaeology. However, recent advances in geochronological techniques and the discovery of the Paleo-Indian and Desert traditions, to which these techniques are particularly applicable, have changed the picture (Smiley, 1955). Southwestern archaeological sites can now be referred to either of the two latest divisions of geological time: (1) the final, Wisconsin glaciation, when ice was widespread in the uplands, pluvial (moist) conditions prevailed in the lowlands, and animals such as the mammoth, mastodon, horse, and camel were common; and (2) postglacial time, when temperature and moisture began to approximate modern conditions and the glacial-age mammals gradually became extinct (fig. 1).

Most geologists agree that the ice advanced and retreated several times during the Wisconsin glacial period, but the number and time of these advances is still uncertain. The formulation of Flint and Brandtner (1961, fig. 1) has been adopted here. During the latter part of the Wisconsin, according to their formulation, the ice advanced to, and then retreated from, three successive maxima, which are known in the Great Lakes region as the classical Wisconsin, Port Huron, and Valders respectively (fig. 1).

It is difficult to identify these changes in Southwestern sites since they were not in glaciated areas. The correlation is better made by looking for evidences of pluvial conditions, which presumably developed in the inhabited areas at the times when the glaciers were advancing in the uplands, and for bones of the glacial-age mammals.

Postglacial time likewise has at least three subdivisions, but the specialists have not yet been able to agree upon the exact nature, time, and names of these subdivisions either. In Figure 1 we have followed the version of Antevs (1955), as it has been modified by Martin, Schoenwetter, and Arms (1961), in preference to an alternative version by Deevey and Flint (1957), because the former has been more generally accepted by Southwestern archaeologists. Antevs' first subdivision, the Anathermal, is characterized by warming and drying conditions and by gradual extinction of the glacial-age mammals; his Altithermal, by the warmest climate of postglacial time and by heavy summer rainfall (according to Martin, Schoenwetter, and Arms); and the Medithermal, by somewhat cooler and dryer conditions, which continued until the present time. The Anathermal can best be identified in archaeological sites by the presence of the bones of the surviving glacial-age mammals; the Altithermal, by the extensive arroyos which were cut through the sites at that time; and the Medithermal, by evidences of successive depositions, which are separated by two lesser periods of erosion, one in the thirteenth and fourteenth centuries A.D. and the other beginning in the late nineteenth century A.D. Each of the three periods also has a distinctive pollen spectrum, reflecting the fact that the vegetation of the Southwest changed as the climate became warmer and more moist or vice versa; and it should eventually be possible to date sites by identifying their pollen spectra.

RADIOCARBON DATING

All of the foregoing methods of dating are relative, in the sense that they tell us the age of archaeological remains relative to other remains or to a sequence of geological events and do not provide an absolute date in terms of a scale of years, like our Christian calendar. A reliable method of absolute dating has recently been developed as a by-product of atomic research. Willard F. Libby, the chemist who originated this technique, started with the fact that all living matter contains a radioactive isotope of carbon known as carbon 14. So long as organisms are alive they retain the same relative amounts of carbon 14, and when they die this decomposes at a constant rate, giving of radioactivity in the process. The rate of decomposition has been calculated experimentally and confirmed by measurements of historically dated objects, e.g., Egyptian mummies. To determine how much time has elapsed since an organism died, therefore, it is only necessary to extract its carbon, measure the radioactivity of that carbon, i.e., the amount of carbon 14 left in it, subtract this from the radioactivity of living organisms, and divide the result by the rate of decomposition of carbon 14 (Libby, 1955).

The best material for radiocarbon dating is charcoal from Indian fires. Samples dating from about 15,000 B.C. to 1000 A.D. give the most significant results. Earlier samples have too little radioactivity left for accurate measurement, whereas the statistical error involved in counting radioactivity of more recent samples becomes so large, relative to the date itself, that the latter has little meaning. Earlier dates are, of course, also subject to statistical error, and therefore archaeologists have found it advisable not to rely·upon any radiocarbon date unless it is part of a consistent series and is confirmed by some other method, such as geochronology.

DENDROCHRONOLOGY

For the period since the time of Christ, Southwestern archaeologists are able to use a considerably more precise method of absolute dating, which is not subject to counting errors. This method was already in its infancy when Kidder wrote in 1924, and subsequent developments have fully justified his optimism about it (pp. 162–63, 346–49). A. E. Douglass, an astronomer at the University of Arizona, originated the method as a by-product of research upon the climatic effects of sunspot activity. Needing an indicator of climatic change, he reasoned that tree rings would serve the purpose since trees grow at different annual rates, depending upon the available moisture: a thicker ring indicates a greater amount of annual rainfall than a thinner ring.

Douglass began by making borings in living trees, in order to count the number of annual rings from the present back into the past. By measuring each ring, he was able to determine the climate during the year it was formed. Seeking to extend this record further back into the past, he began to make borings in the beams of historic and prehistoric pueblos. He found that he could match up the innermost rings of the living trees with the outermost rings of the latest pueblo beams by comparing their characteristic patterns of thick and thin rings, representing successions of moist and dry years. Eventually, he and his associates were able to extend these patterns back into the past as far as 59 B.C. and to construct a master chart showing the relative width of each ring from that year up to the present. Now when a beam is brought into the laboratory from an Indian ruin, it can be dated by laying out its rings on a strip of graph paper, moving this strip up and down the master chart until it reaches the part with the same succession of thick and thin rings, and reading off the age of the outermost ring on the beam, which is the time when it was cut (McGregor, 1941, pp. 69–85; Bannister and Smiley, 1955).

Like other dating methods, dendrochronology has weaknesses. It is frequently difficult to match an unknown beam with the master chart because of variations in the growth of individual trees. The outermost rings, from which the date has to be read, are sometimes indistinct or obliterated. Growth patterns in one area differ from those in another, and so it has been necessary to work out separate master charts for different parts of the Southwest. Only the chart for the San Juan and Little Colorado areas in the heart of Anasazi territory (fig. 5) goes back the full distance to the time of Christ. Moreover, the method depends upon the availability of wooden beams, and these are rarely preserved in the sites of any tradition except the Anasazi. Even there the possibility exists that beams were pulled out of abandoned ruins and reused in subsequent constructions, and thus may not date the site in which they are found. Nevertheless, if there is a cluster of tree-ring dates and they are confirmed by some other chronological method, such a ceramic stratigraphy, they can be considered reliable.

MAJOR CULTURAL EVENTS

Figures 1 and 3 summarize the chronology that has been worked out for the Southwest since Kidder wrote in 1924. Along both sides of the two charts are dates in our Christian calendar. Across the top of each, the Southwest is divided into areas. Those for the earliest occupation of the Southwest (fig. 1) are necessarily broad, since we do not yet possess enough information to be able to draw more precise conclusions concerning the distribution of the Indians at that time. For the latter part of the chronology (fig. 3) the areas correspond to Kidder's (see fig. 11), except that it has been necessary to add a new area, the Western Peripheral district, to take care of the lower part of the Colorado Valley. Kidder omitted it because it contained no Pueblo ruins but we must include it because it is the center of one of the recently discovered Southwestern traditions. (The Mexican state of Sonora, west of Chihuahua, might also have been added since it contains Southwestern-like remains, but it has been omitted because it is still so poorly known.) The order in which Kidder discusses the areas has also been changed somewhat to fit the more recent data better.

The geological chronology along the left side of Figure 1 is not continued into Figure 3, since the latter falls entirely into the final glacial period, the Medithermal. Next to it is a listing of the major cultural events, which is continued from Figure 1 into Figure 3. The charts will be discussed in terms of these events, starting with the earliest at the bottom of Figure 1.

ARRIVAL OF MAN (?)

As Figure 1 indicates, there is evidence that the American Indian entered the Southwest before the development of the Paleo-Indian tradition. The evidence consists largely of radiocarbon dates: one of more than 23,800 and another

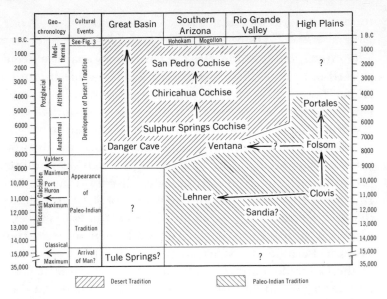

FIG. 1. Southwestern chronology to the time of Christ.

of 28,000 years ago for charcoal from the Tule Springs site in Nevada (Libby, 1955, p. 121; E. S. Deevey, personal communication) and four others ranging from 21,500 to 37,000 years ago for sites in Texas and California (Sellards, 1960). The question is whether these charcoal samples were produced by man, or whether they are the result of fires lit by natural agencies, such as lightning. Some of the sites contain possible stone choppers, flake scrapers, and a bone awl, but the evidence of working by man is likewise inconclusive; the "artifacts," too, may have been produced by natural agencies.

If the finds really are of human origin, then we may assume that the American Indian first reached the Southwest prior to the maximum of the classical Wisconsin advance in the ice (fig. 1), at which time there is supposed to have been a gap between the Rocky Mountain glaciers to the west and the Laurentide ice sheet to the east. (Each time the ice advanced to a maximum, it closed this gap, forming a solid barrier through which man could not have penetrated from the Old World.) It is probable that the earliest Indians originated in eastern Asia, where there is evidence that a similar racial type and similar chopping tools and flake scrapers were in existence at the time. Supposedly, the first Indians migrated north and eastward across the Bering Strait, which was then dry, through Alaska into the Canadian plains, and then southward through the corridor between the western and eastern ice sheets into the central and southwestern United States. It is thought that the migrants subsisted by tapping all possible sources of food, including wild plants as well as game; Willey (1960) has termed this kind of economy "unspecialized food-gathering."

APPEARANCE OF THE PALEO-INDIAN TRADITION

If this hypothesis is correct, the Paleo-Indian tradition must be considered a development of the United States Plains that arose because large game animals were so abundant there that its Indian inhabitants began to specialize in the hunting of large game (fig. 1). If the hypothesis is wrong, then it is probable that the Paleo-Indians were the original migrants into the New World, moving along the route already indicated but during a later retreat in the Wisconsin ice. The first alternative— in situ development on the Plains—is favored by the fact that none of the distinctive Paleo-Indian projectile points has been found in northern Canada, Alaska, or in any part of Asia at a time early enough to be ancestral to the earliest projectile points of the New World.

The crudest, and therefore possibly the first, Paleo-Indian projectile points in the New World are those of the bottom layer in Sandia Cave, near Albuquerque, which was excavated by a party from the University of New Mexico (Hibben, 1941). These are leaf-shaped but occasionally have a hollow base, foreshadowing the subsequent fluted points, which were thinned by removing a flute on either side of the point from the base upwards (fig. 2). The earliest fluted points are those of the Clovis type, named after the bottom layer of the Blackwater Draw site near Clovis in eastern New Mexico (Sellards, 1952, pp. 29–31). Overlying these Clovis-type points at Blackwater Draw and the Sandia-type points at Sandia Cave is a better-made form of fluted points known as Folsom (fig. 2). Above the Folsom-type points at Blackwater Draw, finally, are unfluted, lanceolate points, to which has been given the name of Portales (Sellards, 1952, pp. 72–74).

We have, then, a typological sequence of Sandia-, Clovis-, Folsom-, and Portales-type points for the high plains of the eastern Southwest. All except the beginning of this sequence is supported by stratigraphy. It is also supported by the typology of the game killed at the sites: mammoth bones were associated with Sandia and Clovis points; only *Bison taylori,* with the Folsom points; and there were no bones of extinct animals with the Portales points. The radiocarbon dates are likewise in agreement; dates of more than 18,000 B.C. for the Sandia points are generally considered unreliable, but there are consistent dates for the subsequent types: 11,440 ± 1200 B.C. for the Clovis layer at the Scharbauer site near Midland, Texas; 7,923 ± 350 B.C. for a Folsom deposit near Lubbock, Texas; and ca. 4300 B.C. for the Portales layer at Blackwater Draw (Wendorf and Krieger, 1959, p. 75)—though it should be noted that several additional dates are in conflict with these.

Excavations by the University of Arizona at the Lehner and Naco sites have shown that Paleo-Indians making Clovis-type points penetrated as far westward as southern Arizona (fig. 1), and once again most of the radiocarbon dates are consistent (Haury, 1955; Haury and others, 1959). At Ventana Cave, also dug by the University of

a

b

c   d   e

Fig. 2. Typical projectile points of the Paleo-Indian and Desert traditions: a, Sandia; b, Clovis; c, Folsom; d, Portales-like; e, Gypsum Cave (after Wormington, 1957, figs. 68, 70, 72).

Arizona, evidence was obtained of a similar penetration during the subsequent Folsom period, just as the glacial-age mammals were becoming extinct (Haury, 1950, fig. 115). However, the inhabitants of Ventana Cave were beginning to turn away from the dependence on big-game hunting characteristic of the Paleo-Indians toward the economy of the Desert tradition (fig. 1).

DEVELOPMENT OF THE DESERT TRADITION

Authorities disagree as to whether the Paleo-Indians killed off the game animals by over-hunting or whether these animals became extinct as a consequence of the warming and drying of the climate at the end of the Wisconsin glaciation; possibly both factors were involved. Whatever the reason, only the modern form of bison survived the end of the subsequent Anathermal period, mainly in the high plains to the east, where the Paleo-Indian continued to hunt it (fig. 1).

Farther west, a new form of culture, the Desert tradition, appeared as the big game animals became extinct. Its origin is uncertain; it may be a survival of the earlier "unspecialized food-gathering" form of life, persisting in the western part of the Southwest alongside the Paleo-Indian intrusion from the east, or it may be a development of the Paleo-Indians themselves. In any case, the first Desert Indians did not completely ignore big game; bones of mammoth, horse, and camel, for example, have been found at the earliest sites of the Cochise sub-tradition in southeastern Arizona, where there are radiocarbon dates from 6240 to 4240 B.C. (Haury, 1960). Most other Desert-tradition sites contain only the bones of smaller, modern mammals.

It is curious that the earliest Cochise sites, belonging to the Sulphur Spring stage, contain no projectile points. Points begin to appear in the next stage, known as Chiri-cahua, but in such small numbers that they are considered intrusive (Sayles and Antevs, 1941, p. 28). Only the final, San Pedro stage of the Cochise sub-tradition has an appreciable number of stone projectile points (fig. 1). On the other hand, Desert-tradition sites elsewhere in the Southwest are well supplied with projectile points; they are common, for example, in Gypsum Cave, near Las Vegas, Nevada, and in Danger Cave, near Great Salt Lake, with radiocarbon dates of 8495–6567 and 8320–2050 B.C. respectively (Harrington, 1933; Jennings, 1957). The points are characteristically stemmed or notched and lack the flutes typical of the Paleo-Indians (fig. 2). They were hafted to lances, for the bow and arrow had not yet reached the Southwest.

The Desert Indians were foragers, utilizing all available sources of food in the environment, vegetable as well as meat. Metates and manos are common in their sites, testifying to the importance of wild vegetable foods in their diet. Excavators from Harvard University have also found corncobs. in Bat Cave, southwestern New Mexico, with radiocarbon dates ranging from 3970 B.C. to past the time of Christ (Dick, 1954; Libby, 1955, p. 112). These indicate that maize agriculture was spreading northward from Mexico into the Chiricahua stage of the Cochise sub-tradition during the Altithermal period (fig. 1), but it apparently did not reach more remote parts of the desert tradition, e.g., at Danger Cave. Even in Cochise, it seems to have been of minor importance; the type of corn planted was too primitive for effective agriculture.

In caves where perishable materials have survived, Desert-tradition remains include a rich variety of baskets, sandals, mats, netting, etc. There are no permanent houses, except in the latest Cochise sites, though the Indians did dig pits and line them with stones for use as hearths. They buried their dead in simple graves or under stone cairns, accompanied by mortuary offerings (Jennings et al., 1956; Kelley, 1959; Martin, 1959).

RISE OF THE SEDENTARY TRADITIONS

The Desert tradition persisted through both the Altithermal and Medithermal climatic periods in the Northern Peripheral district of the Southwest, i.e., the Great Basin (fig. 1). There it maintained its original, nonagricultural form and was ancestral to the modern foraging tribes of the area, such as the Ute and Paiute (fig. 3). To the south and east, however, other groups of Desert Indians began, shortly before the time of Christ, to acquire new crops from Mexico, including beans, squash, and better forms of corn. They also learned to manufacture pottery from the Mexican Indians. With these innovations as a base, they produced a series of new traditions, which we may call Sedentary, because they are characterized by more or less permanent villages of farmers.

Mogollon tradition. Priority in the development of the new traditions is apparently due the Indians of the San Pedro stage of the Cochise sub-tradition, i.e., the descendants of the Chiricahua Cochise who had originally acquired corn during the previous Altithermal period (fig. 1). In the first millennium B.C. a group of San Pedro Indians living in the mountain valleys along the southern part of the border between Arizona and New Mexico began to obtain the new crops and, later, to construct pit dwellings. Still later, about 300 B.C., they learned how to make pottery, and thus a new tradition, the Mogollon, was born (Haury, 1957, p. 27; Martin, 1959, pp. 13–16).

The antiquity of the Mogollon tradition is well attested by a series of five radiocarbon dates, averaging 194 ± 160 B.C., and by 35 tree-ring dates, ranging from 280 to 320 A.D. (Wheat, 1955, pp. 169–74). The tradition persisted until 1100 A.D., passing through five stages of development, which are numbered from 1 to 5 (fig. 3). Mogollon 1 to 3 were concentrated in the Upper Gila and Mimbres areas and in the adjacent part of the Lower Gila area

FIG. 3. Southwestern chronology from 500 B.C. to the present.

(fig. 11). Mogollon 4 and 5 extended into the nearby parts of the Rio Grande Valley and the Eastern Peripheral district as well (figs. 3, 11).

The pit houses of the Mogollon 1 stage vary from roundish to quadrangular in plan (fig. 4). They range from 2 to 5 feet deep and are usually provided with a ramp on one side for easier entrance. The walls were of plain earth, and the roofs consisted of logs covered by small branches which were coated with mud plaster. Pits dug into the floors of the houses served for the storage of food or as fireplaces. There were as many as 26 of these houses in each village, and the bigger villages also had larger pit structures, which are thought to have been built for religious purposes. The burial practices of the Desert tradition continued, though some graves were now dug inside houses.

Mogollon 1 pottery is predominantly plain or a polished

red ware (fig. 4). Stone manos and metates, mortars and pestles, and grooved mauls persist from the Desert tradition, along with notched and stemmed projectile points. Tubular pipes of stone came into use for smoking tobacco, and ornaments were cut out of stone, bone, and shell. Balls and disks of stone are also found in the sites; their purpose is unknown. The bow and arrow made its first appearance at this time and gradually replaced the spear and thrower as the principal weapon.

Subsequent stages of the tradition are distinguished mainly by their ceramics, for the Mogollon Indians, like

Fig. 4. Pit house and pottery of the Mogollon tradition (after Martin, 1959, pp. 60, 64).

our own hillbillies, changed their culture relatively little during the 1,300 years of its existence. In stage 2, the potters began to decorate their vessels with broad-line, geometric designs painted red on a brown background. Mogollon 3 pottery is marked by thin-line, red-on-brown painting with more refined designs. Red-on-white painting becomes predominant during Mogollon 4 and black-on-white painting during Mogollon 5, both probably as a result of influence from the Anasazi tradition, where the white background has a much longer history. The Mimbres branch produced unusually fine black-on-white pottery during Mogollon 5, with designs depicting animals, people, and even scenes, as Kidder illustrates in Plate 45.

The Mogollon Indians also came under the influence of Anasazi architecture during stage 5. They began to make masonry pueblos along with their typical pit dwellings and intermediate forms. Other elements of Anasazi culture, such as kivas, became popular, and by the end of stage 5 the Mogollon Indians had shifted completely to the Anasazi tradition (Wheat, 1955; Martin, 1959).

Hohokam tradition. Only slightly later (if at all) than the beginning of the Mogollon tradition, a second group of San Pedro Cochise, in the Lower Gila area, began to develop a new tradition, the Hohokam (figs. 3, 11). The event is well documented at Ventana Cave, where refuse of the San Pedro type gradually gives way to refuse of the earliest Hohokam (Haury, 1950, pp. 543–48). Like the Mogollon, the Hohokam probably obtained agriculture and pottery from Mexico, but the route is uncertain.

The Hohokam developed through four stages, Pioneer, Colonial, Sedentary, and Classic (fig. 3). These stages are not so well dated as those of the other Sedentary traditions. Both radiocarbon and tree-ring dates are lacking, and only the later stages have been well correlated by cultural means with the Mogollon and Anasazi chronologies. It is thought that the Hohokam tradition began about the time of Christ, some 300 years after the beginning of Mogollon (fig. 3).

The Indians of the original, Pioneer stage carried on agriculture without recourse to irrigation, utilizing the natural floodwaters of the Gila River. They built single-room, quadrangular pit houses, similar in construction to the Mogollon dwellings but shallower and larger (fig. 5). They practiced cremation rather than inhumation, depositing the ashes in trenches or pits, frequently accompanied by grave objects. They already painted their pottery red on buff and occasionally also yellow, portraying geometric designs, and also made crude human figurines of clay, which are Mexican in appearance.

The Pioneer Hohokam were skilled workers of stone. They made not only metates, manos, mortars, and pestles, like the Mogollon, but also polished, grooved axes. They likewise fashioned jars and palettes of stone. The latter bear traces of pigment, and it is believed they were used to grind and mix cosmetics, since they frequently occur as grave objects, for use of the deceased in the afterlife. Projectile points and ornaments were not very different from those of the Mogollon (fig. 5).

In the subsequent, Colonial stage, the Hohokam began to construct artificial irrigation ditches. Their houses became smaller and had rounded corners. There is some evidence that cooking was done in outdoor brush kitchens, like those the Pima and Papago Indians use today. The Hohokam began at this time to make large Mexican-type ball courts—flat, oval areas, up to 200 feet long, with earthen embankments along the sides. The game was played with a rubber ball and probably had some religious significance, as in Mexico. From Mexico, too, the Hohokam obtained mirrors made by setting bits of iron pyrites into stone disks. The source of these Mexican influences has been identified as the Chalchihuites culture of the state of Durango (Jennings et al., 1956, p. 93).

FIG. 5. Pit house and artifacts of the Hohokam tradition: a, pottery; b, arrowheads; c, clay figurines; d, stone bowls; e, pit house; f, stone palette (after Mc-Gregor, 1941, pp. 140, 148, 152, 153, 155, 161).

Colonial-stage pottery was still painted red on buff; the designs consisted of small repeated figures, some of which were geometric and others life forms (fig. 5). Figurines were better made and truer to life. Stone bowls and palettes and stone and shell ornaments were incised or carved in life forms; these objects occur most commonly with the ashes of cremations.

The climax of the Hohokam development came in the Sedentary phase. At this time, the people of the tradition withdrew from some outlying territory, but they also expanded northward up the Verde Valley to the Flagstaff region, coming into contact there with the Sinagua tradition, which will be discussed later (fig. 3). In the Lower Gila area, the Hohokam enlarged and improved their irrigation system. Houses and burials continued as before. Ball courts became smaller. The red-on-buff pottery reached its greatest elaboration, being decorated with complicated interlocking patterns of geometric and life forms (fig. 5). Huge shouldered jars were made with a capacity of up to 30 gallons; the ashes from cremations were sometimes buried in these jars. The clay figurines now consisted solely of heads, which were presumably placed on fiber bodies. True representation of human beings was attempted.

Stone vessels and palettes are, if anything, less ornate than during the Colonial stage, but carving of ornaments in stone and shell reaches its climax. Shell bracelets are especially well made. The Hohokam learned to etch designs on shell by applying an acid solution made from the juice of the giant cactus—this some 300 years before Europeans invented the technique of etching. Copper bells also made their appearance in Colonial time, and analysis has shown that they were probably imported from Mexico.

The fourth, Classic stage of the Hohokam tradition is misnamed, since many of the distinctive traits of the tradition were on the decline at that time. The stage is only

"classic" in the sense that the Hohokam Indians, like the
Mogollon before them, had now come under the influence
of the Anasazi. But whereas the Mogollon Indians seem
to have adopted Anasazi culture, the Hohokam maintained their own identity; the purely Anasazi remains in
their territory which appear at this time are believed to
have been constructed by invaders from the north and
east.

According to Schroeder (1947), the invaders came in
two waves. The first arrivals were former Sinagua Indians
from the Flagstaff area, who had become acculturated to
the Anasazi tradition about 1100 A.D. and 50 years later
began to move down the Verde Valley, pushing back the
Hohokam people who had previously moved up the valley
during the Sedentary period. Next came the Salado branch
of the Anasazi, a people who had moved from the Little
Colorado area into the Tonto Basin, on the northeastern
edge of Hohokam territory, in 1100 A.D. and who continued south into the Lower Gila area about 1300 A.D.
There the Salado built thick-walled, multistoried pueblo-
like structures of adobe; buried their dead instead of
cremating them; and introduced polychrome pottery. It
was these Indians who produced Casa Grande and the
polychrome pottery illustrated by Kidder in Plates 48–49.

The invasions were apparently peaceful, for they did
not affect the irrigation system; indeed, it seems to have
been expanded to take care of the influx of population.
The Hohokam themselves began, under Anasazi influence,
to build multiroom surface houses, no more than a single
story high, which were enclosed within compound walls.
They also made platform mounds. Cremation continued
alongside the Anasazi practice of inhumation. The pottery
was still painted red on buff but was more poorly decorated; life designs were on the way out. Figurines became
scarce, and the carving of stone, bone, and shell declined.
Stone vessels, palettes, and pyrites mirrors were no longer

being made (e.g., McGregor, 1941, pp. 131–88; Wormington, 1947, pp. 118–47).

The Classic stage came to an end about 1400 A.D., as
part of a general withdrawal of Anasazi peoples, which
will be discussed later. The fate of the Hohokam Indians
is uncertain, but most authorities believe that they continued in the Lower Gila area and eventually became the
modern Pima and Papago Indians. The latter live in a
manner very similar to the original, Pioneer stage of the
Hohokam tradition, with single-room huts, flood-plain
rather than irrigation agriculture, and without the distinctive Hohokam ball courts, mounds, and arts. Hence,
it would appear that the Hohokam tradition gradually developed to a climax during the Sedentary stage, then began
to decline because of (or perhaps despite) the Anasazi invasions of the Classic stage, and that the modern Pima
and Papago Indians are the end product of this decline
(Gladwin et al., 1937, p. 18; Jennings et al., 1956, pp.
91–96).

DiPeso (1956) has recently proposed an alternative interpretation of the sequence in the Lower Gila area. He
distinguishes the Pioneer phase as a separate Ootam tradition and suggests that the Hohokam of the remaining
stages, Colonial, Sedentary, and Classic, were the result
of an invasion from Mexico. According to this hypothesis,
it was the Ootam, rather than the Hohokam, who developed out of the Desert tradition in the Lower Gila area.
When the Hohokam arrived from Mexico at the end of
the Pioneer stage, they pushed the Ootam back into the
fringes of the area, where the latter survived as a group
known in the more orthodox interpretation as the Desert
branch of the Hohokam. Meanwhile, the Hohokam invaders, developing an irrigation system in the heart of the
area, were able to progress through the Colonial, Sedentary, and Classic stages, after which they disappeared, leav-

ing the area in the possession of the surviving Ootam Indians, who became the modern Pima and Papago.

Schroeder (1960) has offered a slightly different interpretation. He would group the Pioneer phase of the Hohokam with the Patayan and Sinagua traditions, described below, as a basic Hakataya tradition; and, like DiPeso, he treats the Colonial and Sedentary stages as the result of a Hohokam invasion from Mexico. Gladwin (1957, pp. 81–88) also favors the migration theory. We shall have to obtain a better knowledge of the local sequences in the Lower Gila area, especially during the Pioneer and Colonial stages, before we can make a final choice among these theories.

Patayan tradition. According to more generally accepted theory, this tradition, also known·as Yuman, arose independently in the Western Peripheral District, i.e., in the lower Colorado Valley, at some time during the first millennium A.D. Again, the earliest stages of the tradition are obscure; it may have issued directly from the Desert tradition or it may be an offshoot of the Pioneer stage of the Hohokam, as suggested in Figure 3. Once established, the Patayan tradition persisted with little change until historic time. It is probably ancestral to the modern Yuman-speaking tribes of the lower Colorado and lower Gila valleys.

Patayan is the only "Sedentary" tradition which lacks permanent house structures. The Indians built brush huts on the surface of the ground, of which only the traces of posts survive. They cooked in pits lined with stones and cremated their dead. The pottery is brownish in color and only occasionally painted red. Some sherds are found in scattered heaps, said to be trail shrines. Farming was dependent upon inundation of the flood plains, in the absence of irrigation. Percussion-flaked choppers took the place of the ground stone axes prevalent elsewhere in the

Southwest. Sea shells from the Gulf of California were made into ornaments and many were traded to the Hohokam and other inland peoples (Jennings et al., 1956, p. 91; Schroeder, 1957, 1960).

Sinagua tradition. Another Sedentary tradition, the Sinagua, arose in the lower part of the Little Colorado Valley, centering around the modern town of Flagstaff (fig. 11). It lay between the Verde Valley, which was the northernmost outpost of the Hohokam Indians, as already noted, and the southwesternmost concentration of Anasazi Indians in the Kayenta area (fig. 12). The origin of the Sinagua tradition is unclear. According to present evidence, it came into existence locally about 400 A.D. and lasted until 1100 A.D. (fig. 3).

The Sinagua Indians practiced runoff agriculture, like the Anasazi and Mogollon. They lived in unusually deep pit houses with long side entrances. Their pottery was a brown ware, typically polished and smudged like Mogollon pottery. On the other hand, when painting came into fashion later on, the designs reflected Hohokam and Anasazi influences (Wheat, 1955, pp. 204–05; Schroeder, 1960).

These influences became particularly strong after an eruption of a volcano known as Sunset Crater, which has been tree-ring dated between September 1064 and June 1065 (Smiley, 1957, p. 13). The eruption spread over the surrounding countryside a fine volcanic ash which was so fertile that it attracted not only the Sinagua but also groups of Hohokam and Anasazi Indians. The Hohokam introduced their typical dwellings and ball courts, but did not remain long, as already noted. From the Anasazi Indians, the Sinagua adopted stone masonry, first lining their pit houses and then constructing typical pueblos on the surface of the ground. As a result, the Sinagua Indians passed over from their own tradition to that of the Anasazi, and they carried it with them when they subsequently invaded Hohokam territory in the Verde Valley (Wormington, 1947, pp. 166–67).

Transitional cultures. Between Patayan and Sinagua territory are two lesser known "branches," the Cohonina and the Prescott, which are not significant enough to show in Figure 3. They are best regarded as blends of the neighboring traditions (Jennings et al., 1956, p. 91). This corner of the Southwest is fascinating because so many of the Sedentary traditions impinged on it.

DOMINANCE OF THE ANASAZI TRADITION

Since Kidder's conclusions cover Anasazi prehistory in detail, it need be only briefly discussed here. Like the other Sedentary traditions, Anasazi probably developed out of Desert culture, but a complete transition has not yet been found, as Figure 3 will indicate.

Thanks to dendrochronology, which has been applied to all stages of the Anasazi tradition, its chronology is much better known now than when Kidder wrote in 1924. According to the tree-ring dates, Anasazi began appreciably later than either Mogollon or Hohokam. It did not arise until some 300 years after the start of Mogollon, as the two traditions are currently defined, or until 700 years later, if the Anasazi tradition be redefined to start with the beginning of pottery and intensive agriculture, as the Mogollon tradition does. Its climax came later too: whereas the Mogollon tradition may be said to have reached maturity by 500 A.D. and the Hohokam by 900 A.D., it was 1100 A.D. before the Anasazi tradition attained its full development.

As Anasazi reached its climax, it literally overwhelmed all of the other traditions except the Patayan (fig. 3). Kidder, therefore, was correct in saying (p. 140) that the distribution of pueblo ruins is practically coincident with the limits of the Southwestern culture area. We may speak of the period when the Anasazi tradition had its broadest distribution, between 1100 and 1600 A.D., as the time of dominance of the Anasazi tradition.

As already noted, Kidder used a developmental classification in discussing the Anasazi tradition in the present volume. This proved to be too gross, and in 1927 he invited the leading Southwestern archaeologists to meet at Pecos in order to draw up a new terminology, which has become known as the Pecos classification. This, however, is somewhat overelaborate, and Frank H. H. Roberts, Jr. (1935, p. 32) has proposed a simpler version, which will be used here. The three classifications may be compared as follows:

Kidder's classification (pp. 323 ff.)	Pecos classification	Roberts' modification
	Basket Maker I	
Basket Maker	Basket Maker II	Basket Maker
Post-Basket Maker	Basket Maker III	Modified Basket Maker
Pre-Pueblo	Pueblo I ⎱	Developmental Pueblo
Prehistoric Pueblo ⎰ Early Period	Pueblo II ⎰	
⎱ Great Period	Pueblo III	Great Pueblo
⎰ Late Prehistoric Period	Pueblo IV	Regressive Pueblo
Modern Pueblo	Pueblo V	Historic Pueblo

The first stage in the Pecos classification, Basket Maker I, was purely hypothetical and can therefore be disregarded. If remains of this type are ever found in the Anasazi area, they can more properly be assigned to the Desert tradition. Pueblo I and II are better combined as Developmental Pueblo because they are too variable to differentiate easily.

It is necessary at this point to discriminate periods of time from stages of development. There is so much local variation within the Anasazi tradition and our chronological control is so good that we are able to distinguish survivals of earlier stages alongside later ones. In order to take these survivals into account, the following summary of Anasazi prehistory is organized according to periods of time, though the stage names are used as headings for the periods. Each heading refers to the time when the designated stage first appeared and does not preclude the possibility that a previous stage may have survived into the same period. In each case, Roberts' terminology is given first and Kidder's equivalents follow in parentheses.

Basket Maker (Basket Maker). The Basket Maker stage is actually transitional between the Desert tradition and the Anasazi, resembling in this respect the San Pedro stage of the Cochise sub-tradition. Like the latter, it lacks pottery and intensive agriculture. It does have a primitive form of corn, squash, slab-lined cists, and, in one locality, houses made of pieces of wood set into mud mortar, which were constructed over saucer-shaped depressions. The cists were used both for storage and for burial, with accompanying grave objects. Much perishable material has been preserved in the caves; as in the Desert tradition, it includes baskets, bags, sandals, nets, and cords. As in the Desert tradition, too, the atlatl was still used in place of the bow and arrow.

Kidder's map of the distribution of Basket Maker sites (fig. 28) is still essentially correct; they are limited to the San Juan area and to the adjacent part of the Northern Peripheral district. The stage probably developed in this region out of an as yet undiscovered Desert culture by the acquisition of agriculture. It has been suggested that this came from the east, since Basket Maker crops differ significantly from those of the Mogollon and Hohokam traditions to the south (Carter, 1945, p. 120; Jennings et al., 1956, pp. 74–75). One possible source is the Woodland peoples who were moving out onto the Plains from the Mississippi Valley at the time.

Modified Basket Maker (Post-Basket Maker). In this period, the Basket Maker Indians really achieved a Sedentary status. They acquired beans and new varieties of corn, which presumably made possible a greater dependence upon agriculture, and began to build pit dwellings, lined with stone slabs. They also made their first pottery, which was gray with an occasional black-painted design. The bow and arrow came into use toward the close of the period.

Sites of the period are presently known not only from the San Juan and Little Colorado areas, where Kidder plots them (fig. 29), but also from the Northern Peripheral district and the Rio Grande area (figs. 11, 3). This indicates an expansion westward and southward, which must have brought the Basket Makers into contact with the Mogollon Indians, from whom they apparently acquired pit houses and pottery (Jennings et al., 1956, pp. 86, 79). The origin of their new crops is unclear.

Developmental Pueblo (Pre-Pueblo and Early Period). This was a time of experimentation in houses. Some dwellings continued to be dug into the ground; others were constructed on the surface. Some were still made of slabs; others, of adobe bricks, wattle-and-daub construction, masonry, or various combinations of these techniques. Shapes varied from round to rectangular, and multiple- as well as single-room dwellings were built. But the trend was toward single-story, multiroom pueblos, built of masonry. The first kivas made their appearance, circular in shape and completely underground. The pottery was now painted black on white, and there was also simple corrugated cooking pottery. Cotton fabrics began to be made. Basketry declined; burial was in the refuse outside the houses. The Developmental Pueblo Indians were the first to practice cranial deformation.

The distribution of the Anasazi tradition at this time is shown by the unshaded area in Kidder's Figure 31, which needs to be corrected only by cutting off its southeastern lobe, now recognized as the Mogollon tradition. This was the time of maximum extension of the Anasazi tradition into the Northern Peripheral district, where it largely displaced the Desert tradition (fig. 3). Whether Anasazi Indians actually invaded the Great Basin or whether the Desert Indians adopted agriculture and other Anasazi customs is unclear; both processes may well have taken place (Jennings and Norbeck, 1955, p. 6).

To the south, there was a reversal of relations with the Mogollon tradition, which now began to adopt Anasazi traits, whereas it had previously contributed its own customs to the Anasazi development (Wheat, 1955, p. 229). Contact opened up with the Mississippi tradition to the east, and a number of traits, such as wattle-and-daub construction, effigy vessels, stirrup-spout bottles, and hollow-ring vessels, are thought to have reached the Anasazi from this source. On the other hand, the Anasazi were apparently too remote to have been affected by the Mexican influences which appear among the Hohokam at this time (Jennings et al., 1956, pp. 82–86).

Great Pueblo (Great Period). Pueblo architecture now reached maturity, and large, multistoried masonry buildings were constructed in the cliffs and on the valley floors. Great circular kivas as well as the smaller, regular-sized structures were also built in the valleys. Black-on-white and corrugated pottery reached the peak of their elaboration, and polychrome pottery made its appearance in the south. Ornaments were highly developed in several areas, but there were relatively few life forms. Mosaic work in turquoise became widespread. Burial continued as before.

This was a time of great regional specialization in Anasazi culture, and Kidder well illustrates the specializations in the present volume. As he points out (fig. 12), there were three districts of highest development, all within the San Juan area: Chaco Canyon, Mesa Verde, and Kayenta. Surface pueblos reached their greatest complexity in Chaco Canyon and cliff dwellings in Mesa Verde.

The Anasazi tradition as a whole now had its broadest distribution. Kidder's Figure 31, where oblique shading refers to the Great Pueblo stage, does not do justice to this distribution, since it includes only the areas in which the Anasazi Indians built great pueblos. There were also Indians on a Developmental Pueblo level in much of the Northern Peripheral district and in the southern part of the Rio Grande area (Kelley, 1952; Jennings and Norbeck, 1955).

The population did not remain stable. The Northern Peripheral district was gradually abandoned at this time, and its former inhabitants probably helped to swell the population of the larger pueblos in the San Juan area to the south—if some of them did not revert to the status of Desert Indians. The Anasazi expansion southward was also gradual, as we have seen, taking place partially by a process of acculturation, in the case of the Mogollon and Sinagua peoples, and partially through migration into the territory of the Hohokam. Archaeologists are beginning to think that the further extension of Anasazi culture across the Mexican border into the Chihuahua basin may also be a matter of acculturation (Jennings et al., 1956, p. 58), but final word on this point must await completion of the research currently being undertaken there by the Amerind Foundation, under the direction of Charles C. DiPeso.

The Anasazi now came under the influence of the so-called Meso-American civilizations, either directly or by way of the Hohokam tradition. It is from Meso-America that the people of the great pueblos obtained the custom of making mosaics, copper bells, and, increasingly, the use of life forms in art (Jennings et al., 1956, pp. 96–98).

Regressive Pueblo (Late Prehistoric Period). This period is misnamed; it might better be termed the "Golden Age" since, despite further withdrawals from outlying regions, the Anasazi built their largest pueblos at the time and produced some of their best pottery. The pueblos now tend to have central courts and the kivas become rectangular. Corrugated cooking pottery dies out, but painted wares are more elaborate. In the east they are characterized by lead glaze paint and in the west by an unglazed ware of highest artistic quality, known as Sikyatki polychrome (pl. 42). Both the polychrome pottery and mural paintings in the kivas show a number of new life forms, such as birds, mythological beasts, and masked dancers, which Brew (1944, pp. 242–45) attributes to influence from the Tlaloc religion of central Meso-America. He suggests, further, that this is the source of the Katchina cult among the modern Pueblo Indians.

At this time the Pueblo Indians withdrew into the horizontally shaded area shown in Figure 31, abandoning most of the southern part of the Southwest, into which they had so recently expanded, as well as their original homeland and previous culture center in the San Juan area to the north. Kidder (pp. 340–42) attributes the withdrawal to pressures from nomadic tribes. These tribes were in the area upon the arrival of European explorers, but archaeologists have not yet succeeded in demonstrating that they go back far enough to be responsible for the withdrawals, as will be discussed in the next section. An alternative theory, which would account equally well for the withdrawals, assumes a deterioration of the climate. Kidder rejects this theory (pp. 337–38), but some evidence has since accumulated in its favor. Tree-ring studies have revealed that there was a period of severe drought between 1276 and 1299 A.D., and geologists have identified this as a time of extensive arroyo cutting (Bryan, 1954, p. 47; Martin, Schoenwetter, and Arms, 1961, fig. 1). The two must have combined to lower the water table and thus to make agriculture more difficult. Nevertheless, authorities still disagree as to whether it was the pressure of nomads or difficulties in agriculture which caused the Anasazi to abandon so much of their territory; possibly both factors were involved (cf. Kelley, 1952; Jennings and Norbeck, 1955, p. 7).

Historic Pueblo (Modern Pueblo). European civilization has had relatively little impact upon Pueblo culture. Though the more progressive Indians have begun to build individual houses and have adopted such European innovations as glass windows, most still live in traditional pueblos. Kivas survive as the centers of Pueblo religion, and the churches Spanish missionaries constructed in the hope of Christianizing the Indians lie abandoned and in ruins. The Indians continue to make native pottery, though glazing has gone out of fashion.

At the beginning of the Historic period, the Pueblo Indians occupied the areas shown in black on Figure 31, to which must be added a group around La Junta below El Paso in the Rio Grande Valley (Kelley, 1952, fig. 1). Subsequently, they withdrew into the localities marked by white dots, where they still live. Indians of the several Nomadic traditions took their places in the abandoned districts, only to be displaced in turn by the modern Mexican- and Anglo-American populations.

EXPANSION OF THE NOMADIC TRADITIONS

As Kidder points out (p. 336), nomadic tribes must have roamed the Southwest throughout the period of development of the Sedentary traditions; and their remains therefore comprise an important part of the archaeological record. Nevertheless, archaeologists have been too preoccupied with the task of working out the nature and history of the Sedentary traditions to pay much attention to the Nomadic remains, and so we still know relatively little about them. They constitute one of the great unsolved problems of Southwestern archaeology (Reed, 1955, p. 58).

The nomads fall into at least two groups: (1) local,

Desert-tradition Indians who rejected agriculture and a settled form of life or who reverted to nomadism; and (2) Athapaskan speakers who migrated into the Southwest from western Canada.

Desert tradition. Research on the recent part of the Desert tradition has centered in the Northern Peripheral district, where archaeologists have been able to demonstrate an unbroken line of development beginning well before the time of Christ and culminating in the modern Ute, Paiute, and Shoshone Indians (Steward, 1940; Taylor, 1961). The principal additions to the earlier Desert remains, which have already been described, are the bow and arrow and, among some tribes, a crude form of pottery.

As more research is done in this area and in California, it should be possible to break down the Desert culture into a series of distinct traditions. Meighan (1959) has tentatively named five of them: Basic Seed Gatherer, Big Game Hunter, Specialized Lake Dweller, Coastal Desert, and Horticultural Desert. The last is simply another way of looking at the Anasazi intrusion into the Northern Peripheral district.

Our concern at the moment, however, is with the nature of the nomads who invaded the Anasazi homeland in the San Juan basin, i.e., with the ancestors of the Ute and Paiute who lived there in early historic time. The obvious procedure would be to identify historic sites of these tribes and then to work back into prehistory in an effort to determine whether the tribes go back to the time of the Pueblo withdrawals. So far as the writer is aware, this has not yet been done.

Athapaskan tradition. The earliest known occurrence of Athapaskan-like pottery in the Southwest is among the culinary ware of the Rosa phase in Gobernador Canyon at the headwaters of the San Juan River, with tree-ring dates running from 710 to 875 A.D. This phase is Developmental Pueblo, though in a modified form, and is thought to have obtained the pottery from a foreign source. The occurrence of stockades and evidence that many of the sites were burned suggest that the source was hostile. Athapaskan nomads would be a possibility, but a more likely one is the Woodland peoples of the eastern United States, who made similar conical-based pottery with roughened surfaces (Hall, 1944a, pp. 62–67).

After a gap of some 200 years the Rosa phase is succeeded in the San Juan headwaters and along the adjacent tributaries of the Rio Grande by a Largo-Gallina phase, which is tree-ring dated between 1106 and 1254 A.D. This phase is also Developmental Pueblo, though contemporaneous with the beginning of the more advanced Great Pueblo culture in the heart of the San Juan basin (Lange, 1956). It, too, has Athapaskan-like pottery; and there are again evidences of the burning of houses, possibly by hostile nomads. Hall (1944b, p. 103) and Gladwin (1957, pp. 216–17) have identified the nomads as Navaho and have suggested that they were responsible for the subsequent abandonment of the San Juan headwaters by the Anasazi Indians. Hall (1944b, p. 103) adds, "The inference is that the same aliens who caused abandonment of the Governador, and presumably brought in pointed bottom pottery, also caused Pueblo people in the adjoining area to move from small settlements and build the large pueblos in Chaco Canyon for their own protection."

Notwithstanding these theories, there is a gap of another 250 years before the first definitely identified Athapaskan sites. They are again in the Gobernador Canyon and have a series of tree-ring dates beginning with 1491 (plus x) and 1541 A.D. and extending through 1771 ± 5 A.D. (Riley, 1954, pp. 51–52). They consist of typical Navaho hogans, built of logs, brush, and earth; sweat houses; and culinary vessels with pointed bottoms and scored surfaces. But there are also evidences of Pueblo influence, such as masonry walls and towers, polychrome pottery, and corncobs. Kidder (1920) has attributed these influences to Pueblo Indians who took refuge among the Navaho after their revolt against the Spaniards in 1680 (see this volume, pp. 81–83).

Other Navaho remains have been excavated by Dittert, Hester, and Eddy (1961) in the San Juan Valley proper, to the north of Gobernador Canyon, and by Keur (1941) on Big Bead Mesa to the south (fig. 6). Dittert et al. (pp. 245–46) recognize three successive phases: Dinetah, dating from 1550 to 1698 A.D., which is pristine Navaho; Gobernador, from 1698 to 1775, which shows strong Pueblo influence probably resulting, as already noted, from the Pueblo revolt of 1680; and Cabezon, from 1745 to 1812, during which the Navaho cast off some Pueblo influence and attained their present form of life.

The Navaho, then, may have entered the Southwest either in the time of the Rosa phase, ca. 700 A.D.; the Largo-Gallina phase, ca. 1100 A.D.; or the Dinetah phase, ca. 1550 A.D. Various authors (e.g., Gladwin, 1957, pp. 216–17) have speculated that they moved down through the high plains into southeastern Colorado and then turned westward into the mountains of southern Colorado and northern New Mexico. This would account for the concentration of their remains astride the Continental Divide, as just described, and is consistent with the direction of movements during the historic period (Harrington, 1940, pp. 530–31).

Other Athapaskan Indians may have entered the Southwest further west via the Northern Peripheral district. The Huschers (1942) have found a series of hogan-like structures in western Colorado with coarse black pottery of unknown shape (see also this volume, pp. 248–49). Several sites have yielded Anasazi trade sherds, which indicate habitation during the Developmental Pueblo period, about 1100 A.D. One wonders whether the builders of these sites could have been responsible for the with-

FIG. 6. Hogan and pottery of the Athapaskan tradition (after Keur, 1941, pls. 4, a; 3, a).

drawal of the Developmental Pueblo people from the Northern Peripheral district.

Linguistic studies have also shed some light upon the time when the Athapaskan Indians entered the Southwest. The amount of time that has elapsed since two languages split apart can now be calculated with a fair degree of accuracy by measuring the amount of divergence in their basic vocabulary. Using this technique, which is known as glottochronology, Hoijer (1956) has determined that the Navaho and Apache separated from the northern Athapaskans between 900 and 1300 A.D. This eliminates the possibility that the Navaho are responsible for the intrusive pottery in the Rosa phase, but would permit arrival either in the time of the Largo-Gallina or Dinetah phases, i.e., ca. 1100 or 1550 A.D.

SUMMARY

Let us assume for the sake of this summary that the earliest "unspecialized food-gatherers" really did exist and that these Indians were ancestral to the subsequent Desert Indians. Then we may say that there has been a continuous cultural development in the Southwest, starting with the earliest gatherers and extending through the Desert tradition to the various Sedentary traditions: Mogollon, Hohokam, Patayan, Sinagua, and Anasazi. This has been termed the "Southwestern co-tradition," because it is the only series of traditions indigenous to the Southwest (Martin and Rinaldo, 1951).

If the earliest finds are valid, the Southwestern co-tradition began about 30,000 B.C. The Desert tradition was the first of its members to acquire agriculture, about 4000 B.C., but only in a very rudimentary form. The subsequent Mogollon tradition pioneered intensive agriculture, pottery making, and permanent houses shortly before the time of Christ. Though the earliest Sedentary tradition, it was by no means the most highly developed. The Hohokam tradition surpassed it in the first millennium A.D. by developing an extensive system of irrigation, as well as elaborate carving, engraving, and etching of bowls, palettes, and ornaments. Hohokam is also notable for its Mexican influences, such as ball courts, copper bells, and pyrites mirrors. The Anasazi tradition subsequently produced the most advanced architecture in the Southwest, with its great masonry pueblos and kivas, and the best pottery. This tradition spread throughout the Southwest in the period between 1100 and 1400 A.D., overwhelming the other members of the co-tradition, including the Hohokam.

But this is not the whole picture of Southwestern archaeology. A number of foreign traditions have intruded into the area, affecting the local co-tradition in one way or another. The first of these was the Paleo-Indian tradition, which presumably developed in the Plains about 14,000 B.C. and which emphasized hunting of the big game animals that abounded there. It appears to have been limited to the eastern and southern parts of the Southwest, so far as our present evidence goes. The Hohokam could be a second intrusion rather than part of the co-tradition, if DiPeso, Schroeder, and Gladwin are right in concluding that it results from a migration of Mexicans into the Southwest. More certain is the arrival of the Athapaskan Indians from the north, which took place between 1000 and 1600 A.D. These tribes replaced the Anasazi over most of the Southwest and have come to constitute a majority of the Indian population in the area. Mexican-Americans and Anglo-Americans are thus only the latest in a series of intruders upon the territory of the Southwestern co-tradition.

References

Antevs, Ernst
  1955   Geologic-climatic dating in the West. *American Antiquity*, vol. 20, no. 4, pp. 317–35. Salt Lake City.
Bannister, Bryan, and Terah L. Smiley
  1955   Dendrochronology. In "Geochronology," edited by T. L. Smiley, *University of Arizona Bulletin, Physical Science Bulletin*, no. 2, pp. 177–95. Tucson.
Brew, J. O.
  1944   On the Pueblo IV and on the Katchina-Tlaloc relations. In "El norte de Mexico y sur de Estados Unidos," *Sociedad Mexicana de Antropología*, no. 3. Mexico City.
Carter, George F.
  1945   Plant geography and culture history in the American Southwest. *Viking Fund Publications in Anthropology*, no. 5. New York.
Colton, Harold S.
  1946   The Sinagua: A summary of the archaeology of the region of Flagstaff, Arizona. *Museum of Northern Arizona, Bulletin* no. 22. Flagstaff.
Daifuku, Hiroshi
  1961   Jeddito 264: A report on the excavation of a Basket Maker III-Pueblo I site in northeastern Arizona with a review of some current theories in Southwestern archaeology. *Papers of the Peabody Museum of Archaeology and Ethnology, Harvard University*, vol. 33, no. 1. Cambridge.
Deevey, Edward S., and Richard Foster Flint
  1957   Postglacial hypsithermal interval. *Science*, vol. 125, no. 3240, pp. 182–84. Washington.
Dick, Herbert W.
  1954   The Bat Cave-pod corn complex: A note on its distribution and archaeological significance. *El Palacio*, vol. 61, no. 5, pp. 138–44. Santa Fe.
DiPeso, Charles C.
  1956   The Upper Pima of San Cayetano del Tumacacori: An archaeo-historical reconstruction of the Ootam of Pimeria Alta. *The Amerind Foundation*, no. 7. Dragoon, Arizona.
Dittert, Alfred E., Jr.; Jim J. Hester; and Frank W. Eddy
  1961   An archaeological survey of the Navaho Reservoir district, northwestern New Mexico. *Monographs of the School of American Research and the Museum of New Mexico*, no. 23. Santa Fe.

Flint, Richard F., and Friedrich Brandtner
1961 Climatic changes since the last interglacial. *American Journal of Science*, vol. 259, pp. 321–28. New Haven.

Gladwin, Harold Sterling
1957 A history of the ancient Southwest. Portland, Me.

Gladwin, Harold S.; Emil W. Haury; E. B. Sayles; and Nora Gladwin
1937 Excavations at Snaketown: Material culture. *Medallion Papers*, no. 25. Globe, Arizona.

Hall, Edward Twitchell, Jr.
1944a Early stockaded settlements in the Governador, New Mexico: A marginal Anasazi development from Basket Maker III to Pueblo I times. *Columbia Studies in Archeology and Ethnology*, vol. 2, pt. 1. New York.
1944b Recent clues to Athapaskan prehistory in the Southwest. *American Anthropologist*, vol. 46, no. 1, pp. 98–105. Menasha.

Harrington, J. P.
1940 Southern peripheral Athapaskawan origins, divisions, and migrations. In "Essays in Historical Anthropology of North America," *Smithsonian Miscellaneous Collections*, vol. 100, pp. 503–32. Washington.

Harrington, M. R.
1933 Gypsum Cave, Nevada. *Southwest Museum Papers*, no. 8. Los Angeles.

Haury, Emil W.
1950 The stratigraphy and archaeology of Ventana Cave, Arizona. University of Arizona Press. Tucson.
1955 A mammoth hunt in Arizona. *Archaeology*, vol. 8, no. 1, pp. 51–55. Brattleboro, Vt.
1957 An alluvial site on the San Carlos Indian Reservation, Arizona. *American Antiquity*, vol. 23, no. 1, pp. 2–27. Salt Lake City.
1960 Association of fossil fauna and artifacts of the Sulphur Spring stage, Cochise culture. *American Antiquity*, vol. 25, no. 4, pp. 609–10. Salt Lake City.

Haury, Emil W.; E. B. Sayles; and W. W. Wasley
1959 The Lehner mammoth site, southeastern Arizona. *American Antiquity*, vol. 25, no. 1, pp. 2–30. Salt Lake City.

Hibben, Frank C.
1941 Evidences of early occupation of Sandia Cave, New Mexico, and other sites in the Sandia-Manzano region. *Smithsonian Miscellaneous Collections*, vol. 99, no. 23. Washington.

Hoijer, Harry
1956 The chronology of the Athapaskan languages. *International Journal of American Linguistics*, vol. 22, no. 4, pp. 219–32. Baltimore.

Huscher, Betty H. and Harold A.
1942 Athapaskan migration via the intermontane region. *American Antiquity*, vol. 8, no. 1, pp. 80–88. Menasha.

Jennings, Jesse D.
1957 Danger Cave. *Memoirs of the Society for American Archaeology*, no. 14. Menasha.

Jennings, Jesse D., and Edward Norbeck
1955 Great Basin prehistory: A review. *American Antiquity*, vol. 21, no. 1, pp. 1–11. Salt Lake City.

Jennings, Jesse D., et al.
1956 The American Southwest: A problem in cultural isolation. In "Seminars in Archaeology: 1955," edited by Robert Wauchope, *Memoirs of the Society for American Archaeology*, no. 11, pp. 59–127. Salt Lake City.

Kelley, J. Charles
1952 Factors involved in the abandonment of certain peripheral Southwestern settlements. *American Anthropologist*, vol. 54, no. 3, pp. 356–87. Menasha.
1959 The Desert cultures and the Balcones phase: Archaic manifestations in the Southwest and Texas. *American Antiquity*, vol. 24, no. 3, pp. 276–88. Salt Lake City.

Keur, Dorothy Louise
1941 Big Bead Mesa: An archaeological study of Navaho acculturation, 1745–1812. *Memoirs of the Society for American Archaeology*, no. 1. Menasha.

Kidder, Alfred Vincent
1920 Ruins of the historic period in the Upper San Juan Valley, New Mexico. *American Anthropologist*, vol. 22, no. 4, pp. 322–29. Menasha.

Kroeber, A. L.
1948 Anthropology. New York.

Kroeber, A. L. (editor)
1953 Anthropology today, an encyclopedic inventory. Chicago.

Lange, Charles H.
1956 The Evans site and the archaeology of the Gallina region, New Mexico. *El Palacio*, vol. 63, no. 3, pp. 72–92. Santa Fe.

Libby, Willard F.
1955 Radiocarbon dating. (Second edition.) Chicago.

Martin, Paul S.
1959 Digging into history: A brief account of fifteen years of archaeological work in New Mexico. *Chicago Natural History Museum, Popular Series, Anthropology*, no. 38. Chicago.

Martin, Paul S., and J. B. Rinaldo
1951 The Southwestern co-tradition. *Southwestern Journal of Anthropology*, vol. 7, no. 3, pp. 215–29. Albuquerque.

Martin, Paul S.; James Schoenwetter; and Bernard C. Arms
1961 Southwestern palynology and prehistory: The last 10,000 years. Mimeographed report from the Geochronology Laboratories, University of Arizona, Tucson.

McGregor, John C.
  1941   Southwestern archaeology. New York.
Meighan, Clement W.
  1959   Varieties of prehistoric cultures in the Great Basin region. *The Basketmaker*, vol. 33, no. 2, pp. 46–59. Los Angeles.
Reed, Erik K.
  1951   Cultural areas of the pre-Spanish Southwest. *New Mexico Quarterly*, vol. 21, no. 4. Albuquerque.
  1955   Trends in Southwestern archeology. In "New Interpretations of Aboriginal American Culture History," *75th Anniversary Volume of the Anthropological Society of Washington*, pp. 46–58. Washington.
Riley, Carroll L.
  1954   A survey of Navaho archaeology. *University of Colorado Studies, Series in Anthropology*, no. 4, pp. 45–60. Boulder.
Roberts, Frank H. H., Jr.
  1935   A survey of Southwestern archaeology. *American Anthropologist*, vol. 37, no. 1, pp. 1–35. Menasha.
Rouse, Irving
  1960   Recent developments in American archaeology. In "Selected Papers of the Fifth International Congress of Anthropological and Ethnological Sciences, Philadelphia, September 1–9, 1956," edited by Anthony F. C. Wallace, pp. 64–73. Philadelphia.
Sayles, E. B., and Ernst Antevs
  1941   The Cochise culture. *Medallion Papers*, no. 29. Globe, Arizona.
Schroeder, Albert H.
  1947   Did the Sinagua of the Verde Valley settle in the Salt River Valley? *Southwestern Journal of Anthropology*, vol. 3, no. 3, pp. 230–46. Albuquerque.
  1957   The Hakataya cultural tradition. *American Antiquity*, vol. 23, no. 2, pp. 176–78. Salt Lake City.
  1960   The Hohokam, Sinagua and the Hakataya. *Archives of Archaeology*, no. 5. Madison, Wis.
Sellards, E. H.
  1952   Early man in America: A study in prehistory. Austin.
  1960   Some early stone artifact developments in North America. *Southwestern Journal of Anthropology*, vol. 16, no. 2, pp. 160–173. Albuquerque.
Smiley, Terah L. (editor)
  1955   Geochronology, with special reference to Southwestern United States. *University of Arizona Bulletin, Physical Science Bulletin*, no. 2. Tucson.
  1957   Climate and man in the Southwest. *University of Arizona Bulletin, Program in Geochronology, Contribution*, no. 6. Tucson.
Spier, Leslie
  1931   N. C. Nelson's stratigraphic technique in the reconstruction of prehistoric sequences in Southwestern America. In "Methods in Social Science," edited by Stuart A. Rice, pp. 275–83. Chicago.

Steward, Julian H.
1940 Native cultures of the intermontane (Great Basin) area. In "Essays in Historical Anthropology of North America," *Smithsonian Miscellaneous Collections*, vol. 100, pp. 445–502. Washington.

Taylor, Walter W.
1961 Archaeology and language in Western North America. *American Antiquity*, vol. 27, no. 1, pp. 71–81. Salt Lake City.

Wasley, William W.
1960 A Hohokam platform mound at the Gatlin site, Gila Bend, Arizona. *American Antiquity*, vol. 26, no. 2, pp. 244–62. Salt Lake City.

Wendorf, Fred, and Alex D. Krieger
1959 New light on the Midland discovery. *American Antiquity*, vol. 25, no. 1, pp. 66–78. Salt Lake City.

Wheat, Joe Ben
1955 Mogollon culture prior to A.D. 1000. *American Anthropological Association, Memoir* no. 82. Menasha.

Willey, G. R.
1960 New World prehistory. *Science*, vol. 131, no. 3393, pp. 73–86. Washington.

Willey, Gordon R., and Philip Phillips
1958 Method and theory in American archaeology. Chicago.

Woodbury, Richard B.
1960 N. C. Nelson and chronological archaeology. *American Antiquity*, vol. 25, no. 3, pp. 400–01. Salt Lake City.

Wormington, H. M.
1947 Prehistoric Indians of the Southwest. *The Colorado Museum of Natural History, Popular Series*, no. 7. Denver.
1957 Ancient man in North America. (Fourth edition.) *Denver Museum of Natural History, Popular Series*, no. 4. Denver.

AN INTRODUCTION TO THE STUDY OF

SOUTHWESTERN ARCHAEOLOGY

Preface

In 1915 the Trustees of Phillips Academy, at the suggestion of Dr. Roland B. Dixon of Harvard University, and Dr. Hiram Bingham of Yale University, acting as Advisory Committee to the Trustees, for the Department of Archaeology of the Academy, on the foundation of the late Robert Singleton Peabody, determined to undertake excavations in the Pueblo area. It was desired to select a field of operations large enough, and of sufficient scientific importance, to justify work upon it for a number of years. The author was invited to carry out the investigation and to submit proposals as to a site. After the consideration of a number of ruins, Pecos was recommended.

The Pecos ruins lie on the headwaters of the Pecos River in San Miguel County, New Mexico (see map, fig. 10, p. 143); they are the remains of a large Pueblo Indian town, whose people figured prominently in New Mexican history from the time of the first arrival of the Spaniards in 1540, down to the final abandonment of the place in 1838. There was thus a recorded occupation of practically three centuries; and the archaic type of much of the broken pottery that lay scattered about the mounds indicated that Pecos had been inhabited for a great many years before the coming of Europeans. There is, indeed, no known ruin in the Southwest which seems to have been lived in continuously for so long a period. This was a most important consideration, because it gave rise to the hope that remains would there be found so stratified as to make clear the development of the various Pueblo arts, and thus enable us to place in their proper chronological order many other Southwestern ruins whose culture had long been known, but whose time-relations one to another were still problematical. Furthermore, Pecos had been a very large pueblo, and had occupied a commercially strategic position near the edge of the buffalo plains; for this reason it might be expected to have attracted to itself a part at least of any trade which entered the Southwest from other areas, and objects characteristic of those areas were likely to be found in the graves or in the stratified rubbish heaps at Pecos, thus providing evidence as to the chronology of cultures well outside the Pueblo region. From the point of view of specimens also the site was a favorable one, because its large cemeteries had never been despoiled, and the graves promised a rich harvest skeletal material and mortuary offerings. Lastly, the survivors of Pecos had taken refuge at the pueblo of Jemez, where their immediate descendants were still living; and investigations among these people could hardly fail to reveal much of value as to the language, customs, and ceremonies of the old town.

Title to the land upon which the ruins lie had been held for many years by Gross-Kelley and Company of Las Vegas. In 1915 Mr. Harry Kelley of this firm, believing that so important a monument of antiquity should become public property, very generously arranged for the deeding of the ruins to the State Museum of New Mexico. The application of Phillips Academy for permission to excavate was promptly and cordially approved by Dr. E. L. Hewett, Director of the Museum, and on his recommendation was granted by the Board of Regents. No hampering conditions were imposed, but the Regents requested that the old mission church, greatly damaged by the weather and by vandalism, and in immediate danger of entire collapse, be so repaired and protected that no further harm should ensue. They also requested a representative collection of specimens from the ruin. These obligations were gladly assumed, and work was begun in June, 1915.

Excavations were carried on in 1915 and 1916. From 1917 to 1919 operations were suspended, but were resumed in 1920, and have continued to the present time. When the work was started, it was thought that five or six field-seasons would be sufficient to clear the site, and that a final report would be ready for publication about the year 1924. It has now become evident, however, that even without the long interruption of the war, the original schedule could not have been adhered to; for the site has proved to be of vastly greater extent than had been supposed, and the archaeological problems encountered have turned out to be so complex in themselves, and so far-reaching in their application, that it is not yet possible to set even an approximate date for the completion of the field-work. Thus the preparation of a single final report, covering the entire investigation, would be unconscionably delayed, and experience has shown that for one reason or another long-deferred reports often fail to appear at all. Hence it seems wiser to bring out from time to time shorter contributions, dealing with such parts of the work as may be ready for publication. While in some cases they may fail in completeness and finality, they will have, at least, the virtue of freshness.

The present paper, the first of this contemplated series, is designed to give a brief description of Pecos and of its history, to outline the work so far accomplished, and to provide a background, so to speak, for the more specialized monographs which are to follow. The bulk of the work, however, is devoted to a general account of Southwestern archaeology. Because of the vastness of the field and the paucity of our knowledge, this is necessarily far from complete; but it seems worth while to present even so inadequate a summary, because the true value of the excavation of such a site as Pecos cannot properly be appreciated without some knowledge of its bearing on the broader problems of the history of man in the Southwest. The description of the work at Pecos has been placed first in order that those not familiar with this particular field may be better able to visualize the conditions under which archaeological evidence is gathered at a pueblo ruin. The reader who is interested only in the wider aspects of the subject may turn at once to the third section; or, for an even briefer summary, to the conclusions (p. 323), where the results of the investigation are presented in the form of a tentative reconstruction of Southwestern history.

Where everyone concerned has been so helpful it is difficult to single out individuals for thanks, but I cannot let slip this occasion for acknowledging my deep indebtedness to Drs. Dixon and Bingham, who conceived the project of an intensive excavation at a large Southwestern site, and who gave me the opportunity of directing it; nor to Dr. James Hardy Ropes, Chairman of the Committee on Archaeology, whose sympathetic cooperation and support have made my connection with the Department a thoroughly congenial one. Dr. Charles Peabody, Director, and Mr. Warren K. Moorehead, Curator, welcomed me most cordially to the Department, and have placed every facility of the Museum unreservedly at my disposal.

Dr. Carl E. Guthe joined the staff in 1916, and remained with us until 1920, when he was called by the Carnegie Institution of Washington to undertake excavations of great importance in Central America. Whatever success the Pecos expedition may have achieved is in large measure due to Dr. Guthe's scientific acumen, ready resourcefulness, untiring industry, and unquenchable enthusiasm.

Dr. and Mrs. S. K. Lothrop, Dr. E. A. Hooton, and Messrs. G. C. Vaillant and S. K. Moorehead have all worked at Pecos, and each one has contributed assistance of great value. During every field-season, my wife has been with me and has taken practically entire charge of the important and laborious task of cleaning and sorting the hundreds of thousands of potsherds recovered during the

digging. My secretary, Miss Ida Sanford, has been indefatigable in the Museum, and during the summer of 1922
accompanied the expedition in the field.

Without the cooperation of the authorities of the State
Museum of New Mexico nothing, of course, could have
been done; and to the Regents of that Institution, together
with its Director, Dr. Hewett, and the members of his
staff: Messrs. K. M. Chapman, W. Bradfield, and L. B.
Bloom, the hearty thanks of the Department are due. I
wish also to express my appreciation of the many services
rendered by Messrs. G. D. Hughes, J. F. Miller, J. W.
Harrison, Charles Earickson and S. Gray, residents of the
Pecos Valley, all of whom have done everything in their
power to further the purposes of the expedition.

ALFRED VINCENT KIDDER

History of Pecos

The Pecos River rises in the Santa Fe range in north-central New Mexico, and flows in a generally southerly direction for nearly 600 miles before it empties into the Rio Grande in Texas. Not more than twenty miles from its source it breaks out of its narrow mountain canyon into a wide, rugged valley, the average elevation of which is about 7,000 feet. To the north the bare summit of Pecos Baldy rises above timberline and is only clear of snow for a few weeks in midsummer; to the east are the lower crests of the Tecolote chain; and to the west the red-cliffed barrier of the Pecos Mesa. Most of these higher lands are covered with fine forests of large yellow pines, and along the river are thick groves of cottonwoods and willows, but the valley itself is a typical bit of the arid Southwest; its soil is red adobe, gashed with deep, dry arroyos; its sandstone ledges are barren; its adobe flats clothed with stunted junipers, pinyons, and cactus (pl. 1, a). About a mile west of the river lies the ruined pueblo. It occupies the flat top of a long, narrow tongue of rock which stands well above the surrounding land and from which one can look out over the whole country. In the broad, sandy bed of an arroyo that swings by the base of the rocks, is a never-failing spring of pure, cold water. Such an ideal combination of easily defensible building site and abundant water supply could not fail to appeal to the ancient village Indian, and the Pecos *mesilla* was settled in very early times. It eventually grew from a small town to a very large one, and at the time of the coming of the Spaniards it contained, without much doubt, more human beings than any other permanent community in what is now the territory of the United States.

Pecos was discovered by the first Spanish expedition that entered the Southwest.[1] The exploration of that country was brought about by rumors of rich cities in the unknown lands to the north of New Spain, circulated by one Cabeza de Vaca, a survivor of an expedition to Florida under Pamfilo de Narvaez. Wrecked on the Gulf coast in 1528, the majority of Narvaez's men lost their lives, but de Vaca, accompanied by a negro called Esteban and two other Spaniards, succeeded after eight years of great hardship in making his way westward from tribe to tribe. He crossed southern Texas, and finally reached the Spanish settlements on the Pacific coast of Mexico. During his wanderings de Vaca had heard stories of large and opulent cities in the north; and these stories so interested Mendoza, then governor of New Spain, that he sent out a Franciscan monk, Fray Marcos de Nizza, to investigate them.

Nizza, with the negro Esteban as interpreter, started north in 1539. On the way he was temporarily delayed; and Esteban, sent ahead to reconnoiter, exceeded his instructions, pushed through to what is now New Mexico, and reached the first of the "cities." Just what occurred there will never be known, but Esteban was doubtless overbearing and arrogant; at all events he was promptly imprisoned and very shortly killed. When Nizza, following a few days' journey behind, arrived in the neighborhood, he was met by some survivors of Esteban's Indian escort in full flight southward, and was told by them of the death of the negro. Not daring to enter the country openly, yet hesitating to return without some definite information, the friar ventured to the edge of the valley in which the

1. Material for the present brief historical sketch has been derived almost entirely from the writings of Bandelier, Bolton, Bancroft, Twitchell, and Winship. References to the original Spanish sources can be found in the copious footnotes of those authors. See Bolton, 1916; Bancroft, 1889; Winship, 1896; Twitchell, 1911, 1914; Bandelier, 1881, 1890a, 1892a. The full titles of works quoted will be found in the bibliography at the end of this volume.

"cities" lay, and obtained a view of one of them from a
long distance off. He was much impressed by its apparent
size, and by the tales which Esteban's Indians told him;
and when he had succeeded at last in making his way back
to Mexico, he set the capital on fire with glowing accounts
of the "Seven Cities of Cibola." [2]

It must be remembered that at this time the Spanish
in Mexico were in just the proper state of mind to be in-
flamed by stories of golden lands. The glories of the
Montezumas were fresh in everyone's memory, and Pizarro
had recently dazzled the world with his discovery of the
riches of the Incas. Only too willing to believe in the
wonders in the north and wishing to profit by them at
once, Mendoza immediately equipped a large expedition,
placed it under the command of Francisco Vasquez de
Coronado, and in the spring of 1540 despatched it upon
its journey of discovery and conquest.[3]

After a long and difficult march, hindered by failure of
provisions, and the attacks of savage tribes, the army
reached the fabled cities. The disappointment of all hands
is most graphically expressed by Castañeda, the chronicler
of the expedition:

> When they saw the first village, which was Cibola,
> such were the curses that some hurled at Friar Marcos
> that I pray God may protect him from them. It is
> a little unattractive village, looking as if it had been
> crumpled all up together. There are mansions in New
> Spain which make a better appearance at a distance.[4]

After overcoming some resistance by the inhabitants,
the Spaniards entered the town and took possession of it
and the surrounding country in the name of the King.

2. For an account of the wanderings of Cabeza de Vaca see Bandelier,
1890a, chap. 2; Nizza's journey is discussed at length in chap. 4 of the
same work.
3. The Coronado expedition is exhaustively treated in Winship, 1896.
4. Winship, 1896, p. 483.

This first pueblo to fall into the power of the white man was Hawikuh, one of the Zuñi villages in western New Mexico (see map, fig. 10, p. 143).[5] Hawikuh was typical of all the other pueblos of that time. They were really huge apartment houses with hundreds of small living rooms grouped closely together, and often terraced to a height of four or five stories. The women built the walls of stone and adobe mud, the men cut and set the roof beams. The women owned the houses, and the unmarried men lived, for the most part, in round, subterranean rooms located in the yards and courts of the town. The people supported themselves by growing corn, beans, and squashes; made fine pottery, raised cotton and wove it into serviceable garments, and kept numbers of domesticated turkeys. The Spanish admired the cleanliness and order of the pueblos, and were struck by the simple democratic form of government, administered by the older men. They were, however, deeply chagrined at the lack of the expected riches of gold and silver, and determined to continue their explorations in the hope of finding better things further on.

They stayed in Cibola for a time to rest themselves and to allow their horses to recuperate. Coronado, in the meantime, instructed the Cibolans to let it be known among all the other Pueblos that he wished them to come to confer with him and render allegiance. There shortly arrived a deputation from Cicuye, as Pecos was called by the earlier conquistadores. Castañeda describes the visit and its results as follows:[6]

> Some Indians came to Cibola from a village which was seventy leagues east of this province, called Cicuye. Among them was a captain who was called Bigotes (Whiskers) by our men, because he wore a long moustache. He was a tall, well-built young fellow,

5. Hodge, 1895.
6. Winship, 1896, narrative of Castañeda. The quotations are literal, but have been pieced together to make a consecutive account.

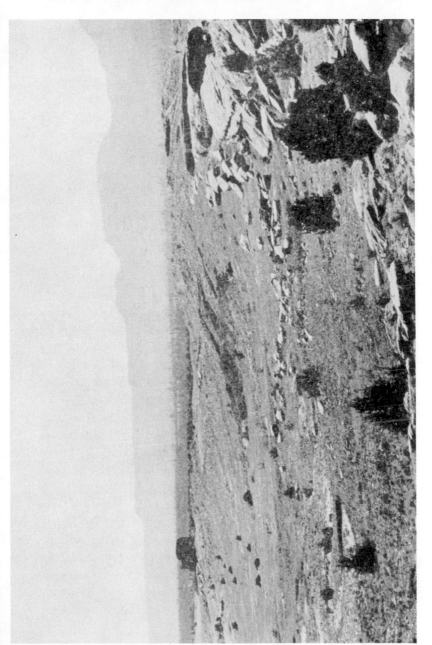

PLATE 2. General view of Pecos from the north.

with a fine figure. He told the general that they had
come in response to the notice which had been given,
to offer themselves as friends, and that if we wanted
to go through their country they would consider us
as their friends. They brought a present of tanned
hides and shields and head-pieces, which were very
gladly received, and the general gave them some glass
dishes and a number of pearls and little bells which
they prized highly, because these were things they had
never seen. They described some cows which, from a
picture that one of them had painted on his skin,
seemed to be cows, although from the hides this did
not seem possible, because the hair was woolly and
snarled so that we could not tell what sort of skins
they had.[7] The general ordered Hernando de Alvarado to take twenty companions and go with them,
and gave him a commission for eighty days, after
which he should return to give an account of what he
had found. Captain Alvarado started on his journey
and in five days reached a village which was on a
rock called Acuco [Acoma, see map, fig. 10, p. 143]
having a population of about two hundred men. . . .
From here they went to a province called Triguex,
three days distant.[8] The people all came out peacefully, seeing that Whiskers was with them. Alvarado
sent messengers back from here to advise the general
to come and winter in this country. The general was
not a little relieved to hear that the country was
growing better. Five days from here he came to Cicuye
[Pecos, see map, fig. 10, p. 143], a very strong village
four stories high, a village of nearly five hundred
warriors, who are feared throughout that country. It
is square, situated on a rock, with a large court or
yard in the middle, containing the estufas. The houses

7. This refers, of course, to the buffalo.
8. Probably near the present site of Bernalillo on the Rio Grande.

are all alike, four stories high. One can go over the top of the whole village without there being a street to hinder. There are corridors going all around it at the first two stories, by which one can go around the whole village. These are like outside balconies, and they are able to protect themselves under these. The houses do not have doors below, but they use ladders, which can be lifted up like a drawbridge, and so go up to the corridors which are on the inside of the village. As the doors of the houses open on the corridor of that story, the corridor serves as a street. The houses that open on the plain are right back of these that open on the court, and in time of war they go through those behind them. The village is inclosed by a low wall of stone. The people of this village boast that no one has been able to conquer them and that they conquer whatever villages they wish. The people and their customs are like those of the other villages. The people came out from the village with signs of joy to welcome Hernando de Alvarado and their captain, and brought them into the town with drums and pipes something like flutes, of which they have a great many. They made many presents of cloth and turquoises, of which there are quantities in that region. The Spaniards enjoyed themselves here for several days and talked with an Indian slave, a native of the country toward Florida.[9] This fellow said that there were large settlements in the farther part of that country. Hernando de Alvarado took him to guide them to the cows; but he told them so many and such great things about the wealth of gold and silver in his country that they did not care about looking for cows, but returned after they had seen some few, to report the rich news to the general. They called the Indian "Turk" because he looked like one. . . . The general

9. This, of course, merely means the country to the east.

sent Hernando de Alvarado back to Cicuye to demand some gold bracelets which this Turk said they had taken from him at the time they captured him. Alvarado went, and was received as a friend at the village, and when he demanded the bracelets they said they knew nothing at all about them, saying the Turk was deceiving him and was lying. Captain Alvarado, seeing that there were no other means, got the captain Whiskers and the governor to come to his tent, and when they had come he put them in chains. The villagers prepared to fight, and let fly their arrows, denouncing Hernando de Alvarado, and saying that he was a man who had no respect for peace and friendship. Hernando de Alvarado started back to Tiguex, where the general kept them prisoners more than six months. This began the want of confidence in the word of the Spaniards whenever there was talk of peace from this time on, as will be seen by what happened afterward.

Coronado had in the meantime moved his army into winter quarters at Tiguex, near the present site of Bernalillo on the Rio Grande. Here the overbearing conduct of the Spaniards soon resulted in difficulties with the Indians, resulting in the siege of a pueblo and the massacre of its inhabitants. To quote again from Castañeda:

> During the siege of Tiguex, the general decided to go to Cicuye, and take the governor with him, in order to give him his liberty and to promise them that he would give Whiskers his liberty and leave him in the village, as soon as he should start for Quivira. He He was received peacefully when he reached Cicuye, and entered the village with several soldiers. They received their governor with much joy and gratitude. After looking over the village and speaking with the natives he returned to his army, leaving Cicuye at

peace, in the hope of getting back their captain Whiskers.

In the spring of 1541 Coronado set out with high hopes for the land called Quivira, so glowingly described to him by the Turk.

> The army left Tiguex on the 5th of May, and returned to Cicuye, which, as I have said, is twenty-five leagues from there, taking Whiskers with them. Arrived there, he gave them their captain, who already went about freely with a guard. The village was very glad to see him, and the people were peaceful and offered food. The governor and Whiskers gave the general a young fellow called Xabe, a native of Quivira, who could give them information about the country. This fellow said that there was gold and silver, but not as much of it as the Turk had said. The Turk, however, continued to declare that it was as he had said. He went as a guide, and thus the army started off from here. The army started from Cicuye, leaving the village at peace and, as it seemed, contented, and under obligations to maintain the friendship because their governor and captain had been restored to them.

This journey out into the great buffalo plains was another series of disappointments. Week after week the adventurers traveled across the level wastes, and the further they went the more certain it became that the Turk had been lying to them, undoubtedly prompted thereto by the people of Pecos. He said, indeed, just before he was finally garroted by the exasperated Spaniards

> that the people at Cicuye had asked him to lead them off onto the plains and lose them, so that the horses would die when their provisions gave out, and they

would be so weak if they ever returned that they could be killed without any trouble, and thus they could take revenge for what had been done to them. This was the reason why he had led them astray, supposing that they did not know how to hunt or to live without corn, while as for the gold, he did not know where there was any of it.

Worn out by their wanderings, and despairing of any success in this direction, the army turned back, and after nearly a month came again to Pecos. Here the advance party was unpleasantly surprised to find the people actively hostile; so they pushed on to Tiguex without stopping. Pecos was, however, reduced to submission by Arellano before the arrival of the main body, and when Coronado reached the place he was well received.

The winter of 1541–42 was spent at Tiguex, and in the spring Coronado decided to return to New Spain. Two devoted Franciscans, however, elected to stay and endeavor to convert the natives to Christianity. Castañeda says:

Friar Juan de Padilla, a regular brother of the lesser (Franciscan) order, and another, Friar Luis, a lay brother, told the general that they wanted to remain in that country, Friar Juan de Padilla in Quivira, because his teachings seemed to promise fruit there, and Friar Luis at Cicuye. The general sent a company to escort them as far as Cicuye, where Friar Luis stopped, while Friar Juan went on back to Quivira. He was martyred a short time after he arrived there. Friar Luis remained at Cicuye. Nothing more has been heard about him since, but before the army left Tiguex some men who went to take him a number of sheep that were left for him to keep, met him as he was on his way to visit some other villages, which were fifteen or twenty leagues from Cicuye, accompanied

by some followers. He felt very hopeful that he was
liked at the village and that his teachings would bear
fruit, although he complained that the old men were
falling away from him. I, for my part, believe that
they finally killed him.

Thus Pecos was doubtless the scene of one of the first
Christian martyrdoms to take place in the United States;
and it was certainly the first place in the United States at
which livestock was introduced.

After the withdrawal of the Coronado expedition, no
Spaniard set foot on New Mexican soil for nearly
forty years. In 1581, however, Fray Rodriguez and two
other priests, with a small escort of soldiers under Francisco Sanchez Chamuscado, pushed up the Rio Grande to
the neighborhood of Bernalillo, and later turned east,
where they visited three pueblos and heard of others. One
of the three may have been Pecos, but the meager accounts
give us no information about it. At the close of the year
Chamuscado and his men withdrew to the south, re-
luctantly leaving the Franciscans to their work of prosely-
tizing among the people of the Rio Grande.

Late in 1582 Antonio de Espejo and Friar Bernadino
Beltran led an expedition into the north to determine the
fate of the three missionaries. On their arrival at the
pueblo of Puara (in the neighborhood of the present town
of San Marcial, New Mexico), they learned that Rodriguez and his companions had all been killed by the
Indians. Although the real object of the expedition had
now been accomplished, Espejo determined to take advantage of the opportunity to make further explorations.
With a mere handful of men he set out upon one of the
most remarkable journeys on record. He stopped at Acoma,
Zuñi, and the Hopi towns, and swinging south passed
through what is now central Arizona. He then returned to
the Rio Grande via Zuñi and visited the pueblos north of

a

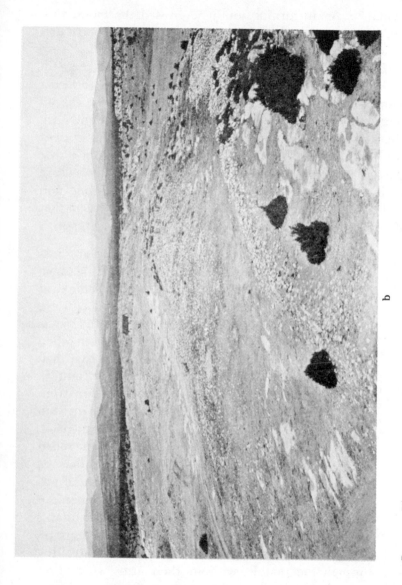

b

PLATE 3a. View northwest across the Arroyo de Pecos. b. The ruin mounds from the top of the church. The remains of the old defense wall may be seen starting in the center foreground and extending along the right edge of the mounds.

Santa Fe. Again turning south he crossed the mountains, and on his way back to Mexico passed through Pecos and followed down the Pecos River.

The next expedition into New Mexico took place in 1590. Its leader was Castaño de Sosa, who took with him a number of Spaniards, both men and women, with the intention of founding a colony. He entered the country via the Rio Grande and the Pecos, traveling up the latter river until he reached the vicinity of the pueblo. A scouting party had preceded him. The events which followed are so interesting, and throw so much light on the condition of Pecos at this time, that I quote the account of them that has been summarized by Miss Hull from de Sosa's report.[10]

On the 23d of the month (December, 1590), Sosa and his secretary, Andres Perez, who were riding somewhat in advance of the rest of the party, descried in the distance a woeful company, ragged and coatless, approaching on foot with arquebuses reversed. On seeing the lieutenant they made no sign, and even when they reached him, the knowledge of how they had come to such a pass made them most reluctant to speak. From the story which was at last drawn from their unwilling lips Sosa learned that, having followed the trail of which Viruega had brought news, they had at last reached a pueblo. This they had entered notwithstanding the lieutenant's orders to the contrary, because it was very cold, the ground was covered with snow, and they were sadly in need of warmth and shelter, as well as of food. The inhabitants had received them kindly, and had given them grain. But the next morning while they were strolling through the pueblo without their arms which they had left outside in order the better to inspire confidence among the Indians, these latter, having sud-

10. Hull, 1916, pp. 316–23.

denly acquired an utterly unexpected and quite alarm-
ing degree of confidence, gave them the war-cry, and
let fly a shower of arrows. Taken by surprise, the
worthy comrades "stood not upon the order of their
going," but fled at once and most precipitately to the
spot where they had heaped up their arms and other
possessions. Here, too, their dusky hosts had been
before them, so that they were able to escape with
only five arquebuses, while the Indians carried off
the honors of war, together with five arquebuses,
eleven swords, the saddles and other trappings for the
horses, and the clothes and bedding. Indeed, they felt
themselves fortunate to have escaped with their lives,
though even life itself, they declared, would have been
lost through starvation, had not God in His infinite
mercy influenced a squaw whom they met on their
way to provide them with food.

In view of their evident distress, the lieutenant did
not inflict on them the punishment which their dis-
obedience well merited. Rather, he endeavored to
comfort them and to overcome their discouragement
by every possible means.

The Indians remained to be dealt with, and he
resolved that, leaving the camp at a place which he
called La Urraca (The Magpie), he himself with an
advance guard of nineteen soldiers and seventeen
servants would go to the pueblo to secure the lost
possessions and to bring the Indians to submission to
his majesty.

On the 26th of December Sosa with this small
company left La Urraca, and proceeding up the river
arrived on the 30th within a league of the pueblo—
evidently Cicuye (Pecos)—where the *maese de campo*
and his party had met with disaster.

The next morning the lieutenant gave his final
orders before entering the village. He besought his

comrades to advance with confidence, believing that they would be kindly received: they had done no harm, so they should fear no evil. But they were to carefully follow the example of the lieutenant, and in no way to depart from his orders. They marched on to the pueblo with lines in order and colors high; but when they reached its environs, they saw all the inhabitants, both men and women, in arms upon the roof, prepared to give battle.

The tactics pursued by Castaño in the face of this crisis are worthy of note. The misfortunes of the *maese de campo* had taught him the value of preparedness. Having pitched his camp within gun-range of the pueblo, he planted his two brass cannon where they would command the strongest position. Thus prepared for all contingencies, he sallied forth with the olive branch in his hand.

He spent five hours in making the rounds of the pueblo, addressing the people with kind words and signs of friendship, and offering them all manner of gifts. But in spite of all these friendly overtures, none would come out from their breastworks and intrench-ments. Rather, they gave the war-cry with increased vehemence, and launched stones and arrows at this unlucky advocate of an armed peace. In the end he deemed it expedient to return to his camp and consult with his comrades as to the best *modus operandi*.

They answered with one voice that he should attack these dogs without more ado. But Castaño was still loath to resort to force, not only from the motives of humanity that at all times animated his breast, but for fear of the disapproval of the authorities to whom he was responsible.

Having stationed two of his men on a height to see that the natives should not withdraw, he once more made a circuit of the pueblo, but only to meet with

greater contumely than ever. For not only were the
cries which heralded his appearance much more de-
risive, but the stones and arrows fell in a heavier
shower; and one squaw went out on a balcony and
threw ashes on his head. At . . . his procedure the
shouts of her dusky compatriots reached deafening
proportions.

Thereupon the lieutenant returned at once to his
camp and ordered his men to mount for the attack,
and to discharge their arquebuses and the two cannon,
to try whether by these means they might affright the
Indians. This stratagem was without visible effect,
for the defenders of the village only made the more
mockery, and hurled the more missiles from behind
their breastworks, while Castaño in vain called to
them with soothing words.

Now the battle began in earnest. Four men were
detailed to ascend with one of the cannon to a quarter
of the roof devoid of people, while the lieutenant
created a diversion by attacking the Indians in front.
Having made the ascent with greatest difficulty because of the desperate resistance offered by the defenders, they proceeded to direct their fire against the
neighboring quarters. The Indians responded with
showers of stones and arrows, and bravely stuck to
their posts, not one showing a sign of fear. The fight
waxed hotter. The excitement spread to the Indian
followers of Sosa. One let fly an arrow; another followed his example. For the first time the defenders
began to show trepidation. Some began to leave their
posts which the besiegers quickly occupied, mounting
by means of ladders, and at frightful risk, because
their arms had to be abandoned before they could
pass through the trap-doors that gave access to the
roof, swords and shields being afterwards passed up
to them by the comrades who remained below. One

after another the defenders fell, and the survivors at last fled from the roof, leaving the Spaniards in possession of the breastworks.

The victory won, the lieutenant marched in triumph through the streets and plazas of the pueblo. And the Indians who were congregated in the wooden corridors which connected all the houses no longer showed hostility, but rather, all made the sign of the cross, indicative of friendship, and cried *"Amigos, amigos, amigos!"* They threw down food from the balconies, but they themselves could not be induced to come down into the streets, nor to approach the Spaniards, though Sosa repeatedly signed to them that he would do them no injury, and they need have no fear.

Having found the captain of the pueblo, the lieutenant demanded the restoration of the property taken from the *maese de campo,* but was answered that all had been either destroyed or taken to other villages save some sword blades without guards which he professed himself willing to return. Sosa, however, doubting the veracity of the wily Indian, secretly sent some of his soldiers to search the other quarters of the pueblo, and if possible to seize some Indian from whom more reliable information might be elicited.

Meantime the captain had mounted to the topmost roof and harangued his people in a loud voice. At the conclusion of the speech they showed great joy, and evinced great friendship for the Spaniards, but without descending from the balconies to the plaza. And now the lost property was brought out—a pitiful heap consisting of two swordblades without guards, a large pouch, some pieces of coarse cloth, and a few other little things. Truly, these seemed little worth the battle! But the lieutenant still hoped that his soldiers would succeed in finding the rest; a vain hope, as it proved, for when he shortly returned to his camp it was only to learn of their failure. They had found in the quarter toward which their search was directed a veritable labyrinth of mines and counter-mines extending underground, with so many little openings and trap-doors that a thorough investigation was impossible at that hour when it was already growing dark.

That night a guard was stationed in the pueblo and all remained quiet. The next morning the lieutenant, having thanked his comrades for their faithful service and having given orders that no injury should be done either to the persons or the property of the conquered Indians, proceeded to explore the pueblo, and to examine its contents. It was found to contain five plazas and sixteen kivas, the latter being underground chambers, well-plastered, which Sosa believed to have been made for protection against the cold. The houses, from four to five stories high, were built in the form of *cuarteles* (garrisons), the entrances all on the outside, and the houses standing back to back. They were all connected by wooden corridors or balconies which ran from house to house throughout the village. Intersecting streets were bridged by wooden beams flung from roof to roof. Access to the houses was had by means of small ladders which could afterward be drawn through trap-doors in the roof.

Each house was found to contain a store of grain —the village as a whole possessing an immense supply, estimated at thirty thousand *fanegas,* evidently the product of several years' harvests. The houses also contained a great deal of pottery, both gaily colored and figured, and black, some of it glazed.

As it was winter, the people were warmly clothed —the men in *mantas* of cotton and buffalo skins, while some wore also gaily figured trousers. The women wore a *manta* fastened at the shoulder with a wide girdle around the waist, and over this another *manta*, gaily colored, and either embroidered or decorated with furs and feathers.

The pueblo had a large amount of land under cultivation, irrigated by two running streams at the side, while the pool which supplied them with water for drinking lay within a gunshot. A quarter of a league from the pueblo, the Rio Salado flowed.

There can be no doubt that the pueblo thus reached by Sosa on December 31, 1590, was the pueblo of Cicuye or Pecos. His description tallies in the main, not only with that of other explorers, but with modern descriptions of the ruins of Pecos.

That night the Indians, taking advantage of the withdrawal of the guard, fled from the pueblo. For several days Sosa remained in the vicinity, hoping for their return. In the meantime provisions were despatched to the rest of the party at La Urraca. As it at last became evident that the Indians would not return to their pueblo as long as it remained in possession of the Spaniards, the lieutenant determined to move on.

After exploring the Tehua country and penetrating as far north as Taos, de Sosa returned to the Cerillos region near Santa Fe, where he was soon after met by a party sent from Mexico with instructions to arrest him for making unauthorized explorations. The entire expedition was recalled, and the first serious attempt at colonization thus met with failure.

The long-planned settlement of New Mexico was actually brought about in 1598 by Oñate, who established his first town at San Gabriel on the Rio Grande, opposite the pueblo of San Juan. Oñate was a very vigorous executive and was accompanied by a small body of no less energetic priests of the order of Saint Francis. The pueblos were quickly and, with the exception of Acoma, peacefully brought into subjection, and were parceled out for religious administration among the monks. Fray Francisco de San Miguel was given the Pecos district, but beyond the fact that that town was his headquarters and that his parish included a number of other pueblos, nothing is known of his pastorate, Oñate himself visited Pecos on the 24th of July, 1598, and received the submission of its people. Santa Fe was founded about 1605.

Of the events which took place in New Mexico during the first three-quarters of the 17th century very little information has come down to us, as all the church and civil records of the province were destroyed in the revolution of 1680. The "Memorial" of Fray Alonzo de Benavides, however, gives us a glimpse of Pecos at about 1620. He says the town "contains more than two thousand souls. Here there is a monastery and a very splendid temple of distinguished workmanship and beauty, in which a Religious put very great labor and care." [11] This, of course, proves that the great adobe church had already been built, but the exact date of its completion has not yet been established.

The Pueblo revolt took place in 1680. It was caused partly by dissatisfaction with the civil rule of the Spanish, which had been becoming more oppressive year by year, but principally, it would seem, by a deep-rooted hatred of Christianity and a desire to return to the unhampered practice of the ancient native religion. Trouble had evidently been brewing for a long time, and there had been a few minor outbreaks, but it was not until 1680 that real unanimity among the Pueblos was reached under the leadership of one Popé, a medicine man of San Juan. A carefully thought-out plot was hatched; the towns were to rise simultaneously on a given day and every Spaniard in

11. Ayer, 1916, p. 22.

the country was to be exterminated. In spite of the most elaborate precautions to preserve secrecy, the plans of the Indians leaked out at the last moment. But warning came too late to save the Spanish from a most terrible disaster, and on the day of the rising, August 10th, there were killed no less than four hundred men, women, and children. Among this number were twenty-one priests. Those who escaped the first onslaught fled to the capital at Santa Fe, where they were organized for defense by the governor, Otermin.

The priest of Pecos, Fray Fernando de Velasco, a veteran of thirty years' service in New Mexico, was warned by Juan Gé, one of his Indian converts, apparently during the night of August 9–10. He set out at once to notify his superior, who was stationed at Galisteo, a short distance to the west. He crossed the high Pecos mesa, traversed the long pine-covered slopes on the other side, and had almost reached his destination when he was killed within sight of the pueblo of Galisteo. Whether he was pursued and over-taken by his own parishioners, or intercepted by the Indians of Galisteo, is not certain.

At Santa Fe, Governor Otermin and the other sur-vivors were immediately attacked by five hundred warriors from Pecos and the eastern pueblos, shortly reinforced by large numbers of Indians from the north. After being be-sieged for five days, and having their water supply cut off, the Spaniards determined to abandon the town and attempt a retreat. The Indians fortunately did not oppose them, they made their way to the Rio Grande, and eventually succeeded in reaching the undisturbed settle-ments north of where the city of El Paso now stands. The victory of the Pueblos was complete; no Spaniard re-mained in the entire country.

During the next ten years Otermin and his successor, Cruzate, made several ineffectual attempts to reconquer the lost province, but only in 1692, when de Vargas had become governor, were any real results obtained. In that year de Vargas marched northward, and by tactful dealing and a strong display of force succeeded without bloodshed in receiving the submission of all the pueblos. He did not spend the winter, however, and when he returned to re-settle the country in 1693, he found his task a very hard one. For the next few years there was almost unceasing war. In spite of the military skill and unflagging energy of de Vargas, revolt followed revolt; quelled in one district, trouble would break out in another, and it was not until 1700 that New Mexico was once more at peace.

While the Spanish were absent from New Mexico, the Pecos, Taos, and Keres had been at war with the Tanos to the west and the Tehua to the north; the hostility of the Pecos, indeed, seems to have been the cause of the abandonment of several of the Tano towns. During the period of the reconquest the Pecos gave no trouble. They fled from their pueblo when de Vargas arrived in 1692, but were not actively hostile; and in 1694 we find their governor, the same Juan Gé who had warned Velasco of the impending revolt, accompanying the army and acting as intermediary between de Vargas and the Indians of Taos.

At the beginning of the eighteenth century Pecos still seems to have held its old position as the largest and strongest of the pueblos, but shortly after 1700 there began a period of decline that ended only with the final abandonment of the town. The chief cause for this was the arrival in the southwestern part of the Great Plains of the Comanche, a warlike, predatory tribe that immediately became the scourge of eastern New Mexico. The Comanche were always, it would seem, particularly hostile to the Pecos, and their raids were a constant source of annoyance and danger. By 1750 the population had shrunk to one thousand. Apparently about this time there occurred a terrible disaster. The Pecos, according to stories still current among the Mexicans in the valley, became infuriated

a

b

PLATE 4: Pecos in 1846. a. Church and monastery. b. Northwest corner of plaza. (Drawn by a member of the American Army of Occupation during the Mexican War. After Emory.)

by the inroads of the Comanche, organized an expedition to carry the war into the enemy's country, and set out with the entire manpower of the pueblo. They would appear to have been ambushed, for they were utterly cut to pieces, only one man escaping. This was the death blow, and when an epidemic of smallpox ravaged the town in 1788, but one hundred and eighty survivors were left. These gradually dwindled away, attacks of mountain fever became more and more severe, until in 1805 the population of the town was reduced to one hundred and four. Gregg in his "Commerce of the Prairies" gives a graphic picture of the dying pueblo:

> This village, anciently so renowned, lies twenty-five miles eastward of Santa Fe, and near the Rio Pecos, to which it gave name. Even so late as ten years ago [i.e. about 1830] when it contained a population of fifty to a hundred souls, the traveler would oftentimes perceive but a solitary Indian, a woman, or a child, standing here and there like so many statues upon the roofs of their houses, with their eyes fixed on the eastern horizon, or leaning against a wall or a fence, listlessly gazing at the passing stranger; while at other times not a soul was to be seen in any direction, and the sepulchral silence of the place was only disturbed by the occasional barking of a dog, or the cackling of hens.[12]

Finally the people of Jemez, a pueblo akin to them in language, invited the remnant of the Pecos to make their home at that place. Accordingly in 1838 the seventeen survivors gave up the struggle, made the eighty-mile journey to the northwest, and abandoned the crumbling ruins of the dwellings that had housed their ancestors for so many centuries.

The town itself, which was doubtless in a ruinous con-

12. Gregg, 1845, vol. 1, p. 272.

dition when it was abandoned, fell quickly into decay, a process aided by the fact that the Mexicans who lived in the vicinity habitually robbed it of beams and timbers for use as firewood. The north building at least kept its form for a few years, as its plaza served for a prison to hold the Texans captured by Armijo in 1841.[13] In 1846 the American army passed through Pecos on its way to the capture of Santa Fe, and in his report Colonel Emory mentions the town and the church (pl. 4, a).[14] One of his pictures (pl. 4, b) shows the kiva in the northwest corner of the plaza; the house walls behind it seem to be still standing to a height of fifteen or twenty feet. Since that time, however, both the church and the pueblo have suffered greatly. The roof beams of the church were removed about 1860, to be used as corral posts, and its adobe walls, unprotected from the rain, have gradually disintegrated. The pueblo went to pieces even faster, the upper walls fell, the timbers below rotted away or were pulled out, and not until a sheltering mound had formed itself over the lower stories was the process of ruin arrested.

13. Kendall, 1844, vol. 1, p. 370.
14. Emory, 1848, p. 30.

Field Work at Pecos

PREVIOUS INVESTIGATIONS

In September 1880, Adolf F. Bandelier visited Pecos and obtained material for a report which was published by the Archaeological Institute the following year.[1] Bandelier, with his usual thoroughness and accuracy, described the ruins as they were at that time, and included a most valuable series of measurements of the house-mounds, the church, and the surrounding defense wall. He also prepared tentative elevations of certain parts of the pueblo, upon which he based estimates as to the former size of the buildings and the number of rooms that they contained. While his work was not accompanied by excavation, which would, of course, have solved many of the problems that puzzled him, Bandelier arrived at remarkably accurate conclusions. The traditional and documentary history of Pecos are also summarized; but, perhaps the most valuable part of the report consists of the information which Bandelier was able to obtain from old residents of the valley, particularly from Mariano Ruiz, a man who in his younger days had been an adopted member of the trible. Ruiz remembered clearly the location of the corrals, fields, and gardens of the pueblo; spoke of the governmental organization; and also had some knowledge of the religious rites of the people.

After Bandelier's work, nothing was done at Pecos for nearly twenty years, but in 1904 Dr. E. L. Hewett published a paper dealing with the general problems of the archaeology of the valley, and presenting much useful ethnological information gathered from the two native Pecos Indians then living at Jemez.[2] Hewett discovered

1. Bandelier, 1881.
2. Hewett, 1904.

that the descendants of the Pecos still visited the ruins of
the pueblo, and made pilgrimages to a sacred cave somewhere in the vicinity.[3]

In 1910, Mr. K. M. Chapman and the writer made a
large collection of potsherds at Pecos. We were very much
struck by the variety of types represented at the site; there
being specimens of all the varieties then known in the
Rio Grande, from the ancient black-on-white to the obviously modern. Accordingly I felt certain that here if
anywhere could be found the stratified remains which were
so badly needed to straighten out the chronological problems of the district. Accordingly, when the chance came
in 1915 to undertake an extensive piece of excavation,
I at once recommended Pecos.

The last work done at the site, prior to the beginning of
the Phillips Academy expeditions, was a survey by Mr.
J. P. Adams, then with the School of American Research
at Santa Fe. He and Mr. Chapman spent some time at the
ruins and gathered data for a large model, a reconstruction
of the pueblo and church, which was made in 1914, ex-
hibited at the San Diego Exposition of 1915, and later
returned to the State Museum in Santa Fe. This model
is about sixteen feet long, and gives an excellent general
idea of what the former appearance of Pecos must have
been (pl. 5).

FIELD WORK OF PHILLIPS ACADEMY

The Pecos ruins occupy the more or less level top of
a long, rocky ridge, which stands boldly up above the
surrounding land. At the north end this *mesilla* pinches
out to a narrow neck of bare sandstone (pl. 12, a); south

3. Mexicans resident in the valley state that the Pecos made such
pilgrimages for many years, but that they discontinued the practice about
1910. In 1915, however, there were found, at a shrine near the pueblo,
two carved wooden prayersticks. Although these lay in the open, they
were so fresh-looking that it seemed as if they could not have been
deposited more than a year earlier.

PLATE 5. Model of the pueblo of Pecos as it appeared about 1700.

of this there is a rise of ground and a great widening of the top, but still further south it is again constricted and falls away in height until it merges with the uplands that stretch off toward the river.

At the extreme southern end lie the ruins of the church and monastery; the latter has crumbled to a low mound, but the massive six-foot adobe walls of the church have resisted time and vandalism, and still stand, at the transepts, to almost their original height (pl. 6). Directly north of the church is a pile of ruins, four hundred feet long by sixty-five or seventy feet wide (pl. 7). Again to the north, and occupying the highest and broadest part of the *mesilla,* is an enormous quadrangular mound five hundred and fifty feet long by two hundred and fifty wide. These two mounds are the remains of pueblo structures which have fallen so completely into ruin that they appear to be nothing but vast heaps of tumbled stones. Closer examination, however, discloses the tops of walls, and here and there the protruding ends of wooden beams. The mounds are overgrown with grass and cactus. In rainy seasons the wild verbena carpets the ruins with brilliant purple.

The remains of the defense wall mentioned by Casteñeda are still easily traceable (pls. 7; 3, b). It starts and ends at the church, hugging the edge of the *mesilla* and surrounding the entire settlement. Outside the wall the ground falls away more or less steeply, the slopes covered with thousands of potsherds and chips of flint.

FIRST SEASON (1915)[4]

Work was started on the east side by opening a trench at the foot of the steep slope that runs from the plain up to the defense wall (pl. 8, a). It disclosed six inches to one

4. During the first year Dr. and Mrs. S. K. Lothrop acted as assistants; Mr. J. P. Adams was surveyor, and Mr. J. L. Nussbaum took charge of the repairs on the church.

a

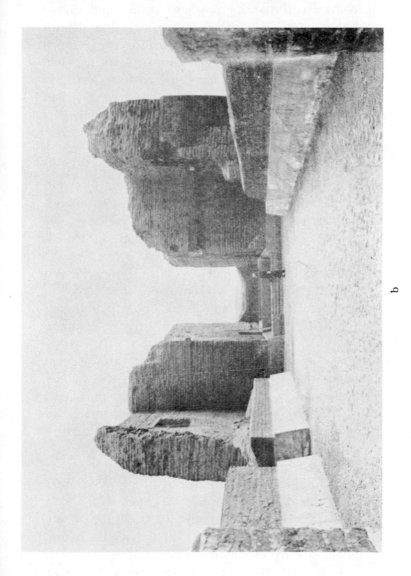

b

PLATE 6. The Pecos church, built about 1617. a. Seen from the ruins of the pueblo. b. Interior after excavation and the reinforcement of the foundations with concrete.

foot of loamy dirt containing potsherds, ashes, and animal bones; below was undisturbed red clay. The deposit deepened as we worked uphill, its surface rising much faster than did the subsoil. When fifty or sixty feet had been covered the depth had increased to four feet, and the nature of the earth began to change. Hitherto it had been featureless mixed stuff, evidently washed down by water from higher up; now ash lenses and firepits appeared, showing that the material was still lying as it had originally been deposited.

Some human bones had been found on the surface, and a few had come from the digging. We were most anxious to discover burials; so a reward of twenty-five cents was offered to the workmen for every skeleton uncovered. The next day one appeared, the following day six; the reward was reduced to ten cents; this brought fifteen more, and in the course of a week or so we were forced to discontinue the bonus or go into bankruptcy. The higher we got uphill the deeper grew the rubbish and the more crowded became the skeletons (pls. 8, b; 11). It was obvious that we were digging in the greatest rubbish heap and cemetery that had ever been found in the Pueblo region; for we were working below the extreme north end of the north building, and the same sort of slope stretched away to the south on the east side alone for nearly a quarter of a mile.

Although we were somewhat overwhelmed by the mere mass of this midden, the conditions it revealed were exactly what we had been hoping for. Such a depth of undisturbed rubbish would be sure to be stratified, the earliest remains at the bottom, later ones above them, and so on up, so that by taking samples from the different levels, we should be able to get evidence as to the exact sequence of the various types of pottery that had been made at Pecos from the time of its foundation down to the beginning of the nineteenth century.

For this reason we gave up all hope of doing any excavation in the building the first year. We confined ourselves to trenching in the rubbish, collecting stratigraphic material, and uncovering and recording skeletons. Our trench was widened to two hundred and fifty feet, and was pushed up toward the defense wall. It was very slow work, for the earth quickly deepened to from ten to twelve feet (pl. 8, b). We soon saw that at our present rate of progress we could not reach the edge of the *mesilla* before snowfall, and concentrated on three narrow salient trenches to explore the deposit ahead and above.

Two of these salients were delayed by skeletons, but the third got on somewhat faster. We had believed that the defense wall was built on the edge of the *mesilla,* and that when we arrived at the wall we should encounter a vertical face of rock. As a matter of fact we reached the defense wall, with a trench twenty feet deep, but no mesa appeared.

After several weeks' digging, rendered very slow by the great depth of the earth and the presence of many skeletons, we found that the whole broad terrace between the ruin mound and the defense wall was made up of nothing but rubbish, and that the rock mesa began directly below the edge of the ruin. We had learned early in the season that the refuse heap was very large, but this latest discovery showed that it was probably at least twice as extensive as had then been estimated (fig. 7). This was the first of the long series of surprises which the Pecos work has furnished. Each one has proved the site to be vastly larger and more complex than had appeared from surface indication.

The earth which has been referred to as rubbish has played so important a part in all the excavations at Pecos, that it merits a brief description. It is a dark, loamy soil, full of charcoal, streaked with thin layers of ashes, and containing an incredible number of potsherds, chips of

FIG. 7.

flint, animal bones, and broken utensils of all sorts. Its dark appearance is due to the high percentage of decayed vegetable matter, principally corn refuse, which has gone into it; but its largest component, its "body," so to speak, consists of fine windblown sand, and of adobe washed from the walls and roofs of the houses. The beds of rubbish were repositories for ashes, house sweepings, table leavings, broken pottery, and discarded implements; they served, as well, for the burial of the dead. The custom of interment in rubbish heaps is a very general one in the Southwest; it was caused, apparently, by no disrespect for the departed, but rather by the fact that the heaps offered as a rule the only soft earth for gravedigging in a land of bare rocks and hard-packed clays.

The first season, as has been said, was spent in working the rubbish. In comparison to the vast amount of it at the site, the progress, when plotted on the map, was not impressive; but the data and specimens secured were highly satisfactory. The most important results were of course those stratigraphic.

In various parts of the digging columns of earth had been isolated, marked out into horizontal sections, and carefully excavated (pl. 9). The material from each cut was kept separate, and shipped in to the Museum for study. When it was cleaned and examined it was found that the commonest, most easily classifiable, and obviously most significant specimens were the fragments of pottery. Work on these potsherds showed that there had been a steady and uninterrupted growth in the ceramic art of Pecos from the days of its founding down to the period of its abandonment in 1838. It was possible to establish eight major pottery types (see pls. 39, 40),[5] and to determine their exact chronological sequence, thus confirming and in many ways amplifying similar results then

5. The eight types are provisionally named as follows: Black-on-white, Glaze 1, 2, 3, 4, 5, 6, Modern. For description, see Kidder, M. A. and A. V., 1917.

being obtained by Nelson at the ruins of the Galisteo basin a few miles to the west.[6]

We must here consider briefly the application of such stratigraphic data. In the Rio Grande, as in other parts of the Southwest, there are great numbers of prehistoric ruins. Some of these contain one type of pottery, some another, still others show two or more types. It had been inferred that these differences in ceramics represented differences in age, but there was no sure method for arranging the types in their proper chronological order, though such an arrangement was of course necessary as a first step toward a study of the history of the region. With the discovery of the stratified deposits at the Galisteo basin ruins and at Pecos we were at once provided with a key to the whole problem; for they disclosed, as has been explained, an orderly superposition of all these types, the oldest naturally lying at the bottom, later ones above, and the latest at the top. With the sequence of the pottery types thus established, it becomes a perfectly simple matter to arrange all sites containing one or more of them in their true chronological order. The same principle is also used in the local work at Pecos: graves, for example, with offerings of Type 3 pottery must be older than graves containing Type 4; rooms filled with Type 6 rubbish must have been abandoned after rooms filled with refuse of Type 5, etc.

During the trenching of 1915 two hundred skeletons were found.[7] These lay in the rubbish at all levels from just under the grass roots (pl. 10, a) to as deep as twenty and twenty-one feet (pl. 9, b). Their general position in regard to the stratigraphic horizons served to date them relatively to each other; many of them, also, were accom-

6. Nelson, 1916.

7. Exclusive of about one hundred and fifty burials that came to light during Mr. Nussbaum's repair work on the church. A great mass of skeletal material of the historic period still awaits excavation in and near the mission.

WEST TERRACE

NORTH TERRACE

NORTH BUILDING

EAST TERRACE

MAIN EAST RUBBISH HEAP

DEFENSE WALL

SOUTHWEST RUBBISH HEAP

SOUTH BUILDING

SOUTHEAST RUBBISH HEAP

DEFENSE WALL

SCALE
0   50   100

MISSION CHURCH

PLATE 7. Sketch plan of the Pecos ruins.

panied by mortuary offerings of pottery, which allowed us to fix their chronological position with even greater accuracy. Although a considerable percentage of the skeletons were in very bad condition, it was possible by careful work to save a large number of them.

The specimens, aside from potsherds and human and animal bones, numbered about three thousand; they included pottery vessels, effigies, pipes; objects of stone such as arrowheads, scrapers, knives and drills; bone and antler tools in great abundance; and much miscellaneous material in the way of ornaments, fetishes, objects of European manufacture, etc.

Second season (1916)[8]

During the winter of 1915–16 much time was spent in studying the pottery recovered in the stratigraphic tests. It was found that the early types were very poorly represented, and that the later types, which there was no reason to suppose had been made for any greater length of time than the early ones, were present in disproportionately large quantities. It was decided that this was due to the fact that our tests had been made too far downhill and that the thickest deposits of early material must lie at the base of the heavy rubbish close against the mesa. For this reason it was felt that several deep tests must be made. One gang of men, accordingly, was kept testing in the main east diggings all summer, and the rest were used in an attempt to run out the extent of the other rubbish deposits that were thought to surround the pueblo.

Narrow exploratory trenches were cut at intervals of 100 feet or so all along the east slope, and pits were sunk on the terrace east of the north building. These showed

8. In this year Dr. C. E. Guthe acted as assistant, and Mrs. Kidder took charge of the cleaning and sorting of the thousands of potsherds recovered.

that the rubbish heaps extend over these entire areas, but that they are in most places not as deep as they are below the north building.

Trenches were next opened on the west slopes. Here there was found to have been little or no dumpage, a condition undoubtedly due to the strong west winds which prevail in the Pecos Valley, and which would naturally have induced the people to throw their refuse to leeward over the east side.

There now remained to be investigated an area that we called in our field notes the "North Terrace," a smooth, gently sloping surface running from where the defense wall cuts across the narrowing neck of the *mesilla* up to what appeared to be the foundations of the north wall of the main north quadrangle (pls. 7; 12, a). Here there were no signs whatever of house structures except a single low mound, and the place seemed to contain nothing but shallow rubbish and material washed down from the decaying pueblo.

We now received our second annual surprise. The first day's work disclosed house walls; we followed them up, and eventually laid bare, in this innocent-looking place, forty rooms, a kiva, and no less than two hundred burials. Although the actual digging progressed in the opposite direction, it will be simpler to describe the buildings from north to south.

Just within the defense wall, but obviously erected at a very much earlier time, was found a series of chambers, whose walls stood only about eighteen inches high (pls. 1, b; 12, a). These ancient foundations date from the period of the first occupation of the Pecos mesa, a fact that was proved by finding piled *against* them rubbish containing only black-on-white pottery, the type shown by stratigraphy to be the oldest of all. This dwelling, which we may for convenience call the Black-on-white house, extended from the western edge of the mesa across to the eastern; it there turned south and traces of it could be made out here and there under later structures.

Near the northwestern end of the main quadrangle was found a large Black-on-white rubbish heap and cemetery, so that we were led to suspect that the Black-on-white houses turned somewhere near the northeast corner and ran out to the western edge of the mesa, thus forming a three-sided pueblo open to the west and partly surrounding a large courtyard or plaza.

Debris of the Black-on-white period is scanty or even absent at the bottom of most parts of the rubbish deposits along the rest of the Pecos mesa; it is, however, comparatively heavy below the North Terrace, on both east and west sides. I believe, accordingly, that on the North Terrace lay the nucleus of the Pecos pueblo. As to the date of its founding or the length of its occupation we can say little or nothing as yet, but from the fact that at Rowe, and across the Arroyo de Pecos at "Bandelier Bend" and at "Loma Lothrop," there are ruins of what were larger and, in some respects, apparently earlier Black-on-white villages, we can hazard the guess that this mesa settlement was erected toward the close of the Black-on-white period and not long before the beginning of the next, or Glaze 1, stage. At all events the northern wing of the oldest pueblo was abandoned and presumably in ruins during Glaze 1 times, for skeletons accompanied by Glaze 1 pottery were found buried above the floor levels in several of its rooms (fig. 8).

The bulk of the Glaze 1 pueblo seems to have been to the south, where it still lies unexcavated below the mass of the great quadrangle; its approximate position may nevertheless be guessed at from the quantities of Glaze 1 rubbish that cumber the eastern mesa slopes below the quadrangle, and which are also heaped along the southern part of the North Terrace itself. The eastern wing of the old pueblo may have been used, however, to some extent, for there are evidences of repair and rehabilitation of many walls. Whether this was done at the very close of Black-on-white times or during the Glaze 1 stage could not be determined, but in either case the east wing lay abandoned, and probably partly covered up, through the whole long stretch of the next periods: Glaze 2, 3, and 4. This is proved by the presence of burials of these epochs in its rooms and actually above some of its broken-down

FIG. 8. Cross-section showing superposition of walls, burials, etc., on the North Terrace at Pecos.

walls, while the courtyard, usually kept free of rubbish in an inhabited pueblo, is choked with Glaze 3 and 4 debris and burials (fig. 8).

We must infer, then, that during these periods the Pecos pueblo was extending itself to the south, and that the great quadrangle, and perhaps also the long, narrow south house, were gradually assuming their final form. Not until this growth was completed, or at least well under way, did the inhabitants turn again to the North Terrace, the neglected site of what we suppose to have been their earliest homes. Here, in the Glaze 5 period, which began apparently some time before the Conquest and lasted until nearly 1680, were presumably built and surely used the rooms of the south wing near the main north wall. Tne floors of these lie well above rubbish of earlier times, and they themselves contained on excavation nothing but Glaze 5 pottery. There seems also to have been at this time some repair of the central apartments of the east series, and a long wall, probably a defensive structure and perhaps the forerunner of the later defense wall, was run out across the long-buried rooms of the north series.

The Glaze 5 period appears to have been the Augustan Age, so to speak, of the town, for the houses then reached their maximum size and the layers of Glaze 5 debris are the heaviest of all. Toward its close the pueblo began to draw in on itself again, the south wing rooms were deliberately filled up with stone and served as the foundation for the last addition to the heavy outside wall of the historic quadrangle. In this drawing in and strengthening we may perhaps see the effects of the ever-increasing menace of the Comanche raids. Even then the old north building was not entirely deserted, for the little group of rooms in the middle of the eastern wing was used well into the historic period, as is shown by the finding in them of crockery of Spanish make, bones of domestic animals, and copper implements. The rooms served as a sort of cookhouse annex and contained many manos and metates for corn grinding, while all about them are the remains of ovens sunk through the Glaze 5 rubbish.

In the final dreary years, when the handful of survivors lived huddled together in the few still habitable rooms of the quadrangle, the old north house was evidently given over to decay, for its mound contains none of the latest pottery at all. On its surface, however, we found lying broken a fine large water jar of the very last period, forgotten perhaps, or perhaps deliberately abandoned, by the last of the Pecos when they set out on their final migration to the homes of their kindred at Jemez.

I have gone into detail in describing the conditions that we encountered on the North Terrace, in order that the reader may appreciate the problems by which we were faced at the close of the 1916 season. We had expected to find on the mesa top the remains of a single large pueblo showing, perhaps, signs of repair and rebuilding, but founded on the rock and permitting the easy examination of its walls from top to bottom. Instead of this it had developed that the historic town was erected on the broken and tumbled walls of earlier houses, and that these again had been built over at least two still more ancient ones.

Such conditions were, of course, exceedingly favorable for the recovery of data on the growth of the pueblo, and might also be expected to disclose many important facts as to changes in architecture, house-grouping, etc., at different periods. But they would undoubtedly render the task of excavation infinitely slower and more expensive; and would necessitate the development of entirely new methods of recording. Furthermore, our original plans for repairing the walls of excavated rooms and leaving the pueblo open for inspection by visitors, had definitely to be abandoned. In the first place, to get at and study the older buried structures it would often be necessary to remove parts of walls which lay above them; and, secondly, the old broken-down early houses formed so irregular and unsteady a foundation that the upper walls were in a most precarious condition. Made of crude and badly laid masonry (pl. 13, a), uncoursed, with unbroken joints and with the corners not tied by binding stones, such walls would be hard to save intact even if built on solid, level rock; founded as they were on disintegrated walls of the same type as themselves, they had become, especially since

a

b

c

PLATE 8. The eastern trenches in the great Pecos rubbish heap. a. The opening cut, June 1915. b. Trench at ten feet deep. c. Trench at nineteen feet deep.

the rotting away of their roof beams, so shaky that, the supporting debris once removed, they fell almost of their own weight.

To sum up the work of the season. The eastern rubbish heap was tested and found to run the entire length of the *mesilla;* the western slope under the north building was shown to be practically barren of archaeological deposits; and the North Terrace was almost completely excavated, disclosing a very old ruin and, overlying it and running off under the main north quadrangle, the remains of several other prehistoric structures. Three large stratigraphic tests were carried out in the deepest rubbish obtainable, and several others were taken in places where it was desired to examine certain strata in detail. In the course of the digging four hundred and seventy-five skeletons were encountered, the most important of these belonging to the Black-on-white period.

Third season (1917)

In this year no excavations were attempted at the main Pecos ruin, but a number of other pieces of work were carried out. I was able, before entering the army, to devote a few weeks to the exploration of the Hopi country in northeastern Arizona, and to locate a site, the ruined pueblo of Awatobi, which resembled Pecos in that its occupancy embraced both the prehistoric and historic periods. Distinct evidences of stratification were noted. Such a site was desirable in order to provide data from a more or less distant region, to use for checking against the Pecos finds.

Dr. Guthe explored the sites along the Pecos River below Pecos, as well as those in the Gallinas drainage to the west. He then investigated many ruins on the upper Rio Grande, and finally ran out the northern limits of Pueblo culture in that direction by following it to its vanishing point in the San Luis Valley of southern Colorado. Returning to Pecos he excavated for six weeks in the ruin at Rowe.

Rowe pueblo lies about four miles south of Pecos. It is a very large ruin which was occupied only during Black-on-white times, a period not extensively represented at Pecos, but a most important one in the history of the Rio Grande. The Black-on-white remains at Pecos are not only relatively scanty, but are also much confused by having been overlaid by, and somewhat mixed with, deposits of later epochs. Hence it was very desirable to collect unmixed data from a pure Black-on-white site. The excavation of Rowe supplied an abundance of such material, clearly illustrating the later phases of the Black-on-white period. The work was far from simple, as there had been several rebuildings accompanied by slight changes in culture. The masonry of Rowe is infinitely superior to that of Pecos.[9]

FOURTH SEASON (1920)[10]

From the autumn of 1917 until July 1919, the Pecos work was at a standstill, and by the time the various loose ends were gathered together, uncatalogued collections arranged, and maps brought up to date, it was too late to take the field. The winter of 1919–20 was spent, accordingly, in studying the specimens already on hand. At this time it was arranged that all skeletal material from Pecos should be turned over to the Peabody Museum of Harvard University, and that Dr. E. A. Hooton, Curator of Physical Anthropology in that institution, should undertake the study of it. The skeletons already recovered numbered nearly seven hundred, future excavations were certain to produce many more, and, as the collection promised to be of great importance, it was desirable to have it in the

9. For a preliminary account of the Rowe excavation, see Guthe, 1917.
10. Dr. Guthe acted as assistant, Dr. Hooton superintended the cemetery work, Mrs. Kidder did the cataloguing and handled the potsherds.

PLATE 9. A stratigraphic test section in the deep rubbish.
a. Working in Cut 3, Test X.

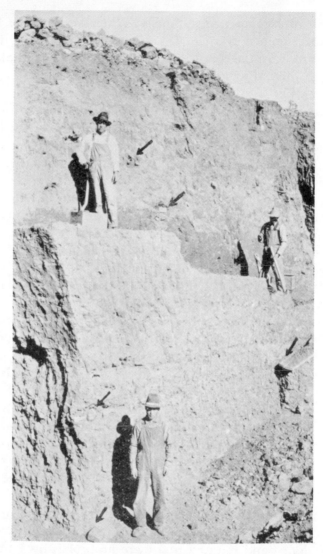

PLATE 9b. Cut 5, Test X, partly removed—the arrows mark the positions of skeletons.

hands of a competent authority. When we took the field
in the summer of 1920, Dr. Hooton accompanied us in
order to learn the conditions under which the material was
found, and also to assist in developing more perfect
methods of caring for it.

Advantage was taken of Dr. Hooton's presence in the
field to run a number of new trenches in the refuse-heap
cemeteries on the east slope. Exploration of the west slope
south of the main quadrangle also disclosed a new cemetery of very large proportions. What we have come to
call the "annual surprise" was, for 1920, the fact that the
upper terrace lying west of the main quadrangle was full
of graves, and that part at least of the plaza of the main
quadrangle itself was crammed with skeletons, which also
ran under the ruins of the later houses.

The greater part of the summer was devoted to excavations in the pueblo itself. Rooms were cleared in both
north and south buildings.

The South House work was undertaken with the idea of
finding out whether or not that structure dated from
prehistoric times. Castañeda, in his description of Pecos,
mentions but one pueblo, a large quadrangle which is
obviously the North House. That so large a building as
the South House should have been overlooked, did not
seem likely if it was inhabited at that time. It was thought
that it might either have been in ruins in 1541, or perhaps
have been built after that date. Excavations proved that
both theories were correct, for when the rooms were
cleared to bedrock, it was found that there had indeed
been an early pueblo on the site, but that it had been
abandoned and reduced to a mere heap of ruins long before the coming of the Spaniards. Some time during the
late 16th or early 17th centuries, however, a new pueblo
was constructed on the same ground. In its rooms were
found many objects of European manufacture, such as bits
of china, iron and copper implements. In the interior of

the mound one ground-floor chamber was uncovered in excellent preservation. Its roof was mostly intact, and from the beams still hung the bark loops that had been used to suspend the goods of the owners; on one smoke-blackened log were a series of handprints, large and small, slapped on in whitewash.

In the North House the excavations were more extensive. The great mound formed by the ruin of this building is quadrangular, and encloses a large level plaza, to which entrance is gained by four gaps in the high-piled ruins. These gaps undoubtedly represent the former presence of passageways giving access to the court.

To explore the mound and the plaza, trenches were started simultaneously at the east entrance and at the west edge of the mesa, so as to cross-cut the entire northern end of the site and meet in the plaza.

The western trench was begun about eighty-five feet from the ruin proper and, like all trenches at Pecos, was run in along bedrock. It was thought that the deposit at this point would be shallow. Rubbish, however, was found at once, quickly deepened to four feet, and contained a number of skeletons of the Glaze 3 period. After passing through this zone of burials, there were encountered the foundation walls of an early building, the presence of which had not been suspected. This was cut through, and the trench continued toward the main mound, only to strike almost immediately a sharp dip in the bedrock. Sinking on the dip we found that we were in a large oval pit filled with rubbishy earth. On complete excavation, which required nearly a week, it proved to be a masonry-lined cistern, fifteen feet deep, ten feet wide, and twenty feet long, built in a natural crevice of the mesa. About its edge was a neatly made coping wall two feet high. The date of the building of the cistern could not then be determined, but it had been abandoned during the Glaze 4 period, and at that time filled full of rubbish. This was

PLATE 10a. Typical extended burial of late period; note shallowness of grave.

PLATE 10b. Partly flexed burial typical of Glaze 4 period; mortuary bowl broken and the pieces scattered over the body at the time of interment.

PLATE 10c. Closely flexed burial on face, typical of Glaze 3 period; mortuary bowl unbroken.

a particularly valuable deposit, as it was very rich in potsherds and cast-off implements, and gave us an unusually full and unmixed collection.

When the cistern was cleared it was bridged over and the trench was continued. Another zone of skeletons was at once encountered, part of a large Black-on-white and Glaze 1 cemetery that seems to run all along the western side of the main ruin. Some very fine pottery was taken from these graves.

About fifteen feet west of the high mound we began to meet low walls built on bedrock and not extending to the surface. Resisting the temptation to follow these north and south, we cut through them, and trenched directly into the main ruin. Here we found a most complex state of affairs; a jumble of early walls, some fallen, others partly incorporated into the bases of later structures (pl. 14). The later houses stood about half way to the tops of their second stories, but they were in exceedingly bad condition in consequence of their poor masonry and of the fact that they had been founded on irregularly broken-down earlier walls.

It had been planned to cut the trench straight across to the plaza, but about half way through the mound we uncovered a room with such a finely preserved roof that we were afraid to excavate close about it and thereby weaken its walls. Accordingly we were forced to change direction to the south in order to pass around it. This proved to be a very fortunate circumstance, as it led us into a series of rooms that were most prolific in specimens.

The majority of rooms in a pueblo which, like Pecos, was abandoned slowly, were left empty, as the people naturally took away all their belongings with them. The rooms, however, that we now came into proved to have been the scene of a bad accident at some time in the historic period subsequent to 1680. The entire outer wall of the pueblo had evidently suddenly given way and fallen inward, crushing the rooms to the east of it and burying them with their entire contents under tons of stone (pl. 13, b). No attempt had been made to clear out and refit this section. That the people had some warning of the catastrophe is probable, as there were no skeletons in the debris.

Our finds here were very rich, including a large series of cooking jars, some modern painted ollas and a vessel from Zuñi; all these, of course, were badly broken; but, queerly enough, we found one nest of small ceremonial pots wedged in among the rocks and quite undamaged. With these were many handsome shell ornaments, two sets of bone flutes, two very large tobacco pipes, one of them elaborately carved, thirty-five buffalo horns, part of a wooden dance headdress, and many other specimens.

At this point the western trench encountered the eastern, which had been slowly worked in across the plaza to meet it. The initial progress of the east trench had been rapid, as it was run into the courtyard through an old entryway. Once in the plaza, however, it was as fruitful of labor-making surprises as was the west trench. Instead of a deposit of two to three feet, as had been expected, there was found an average of five feet of very hard-packed fill. Directly in the path of the cut were encountered the long walls of an old pueblo and just beyond were two large underground ceremonial chambers, or kivas. Both kivas had been built during the early occupancy of the Pecos mesa, but one of them was soon abandoned and afterwards served as a burial place, fifteen skeletons being found between its floor and the surface of the plaza. The other was kept in use until after the conquest, undergoing during the many centuries of its history a number of architectural changes. In a sealed recess in the wall of this kiva was found a small granite idol, the only object of its kind that had so far come to light at Pecos and the fourth ever found in New Mexico.

In addition to the two trenches just described, which cross-cut the North Building, a series of rooms about the east entrance was excavated. By very careful observation of the stratified fillings in the lower parts of these rooms, coordinated with an intensive study of the successive increments of masonry that had gone into their construction, Dr. Guthe was able to work out and record by plans and elevations the exact history of the growth of this section of the pueblo from the foundation of the town down to the time of its final abandonment. The methods of observation and recording developed by Dr. Guthe in this piece of work form a distinct addition to archaeological field technique.

The collection of specimens was large and contained many unique objects, and the result of the summer's work on the history of the pueblo and the development of its arts were highly satisfactory. The year's excavations in the North House, however, confirmed our worst fears as to the condition of the building itself. The ruin is in poorer condition than any other pueblo structure that I have seen. The walls of the late rooms stand to heights varying from ten to fifteen feet, but they are of such wretchedly bad masonry, are laid on such insecure foundations, and have been so thoroughly shattered by the falling of their upper stories, that to remove the filling of earth that holds them upright, means to bring about their almost certain collapse. In the few rooms cleared in 1920, we were obliged to pull down a number of tottering walls to avoid imminent danger to our workmen.

FIFTH SEASON (1921)

During the excavations at Pecos, and particularly from the laboratory work on the material recovered, it had become increasingly evident that the surest archaeological results were to be derived from the study of pottery. We were constantly being called upon to classify wares, make

5

b

PLATE 11. Skeletons in the deep rubbish. The crowded condition of burials in certain areas greatly delays excavation, as each grave requires from one to three hours careful work.

comparisons, and form judgments as to the relations between different ceramic groups. We found that in doing
this we were severely handicapped by a lack of precise
knowledge as to the technology of Pueblo pottery, a lack
which could not be supplied by any printed work. Accordingly, when I found in the spring of 1921, that I
should be unable to excavate at Pecos that summer, Dr.
Guthe went to New Mexico, to make a thorough study
of pottery-making as it is practiced among the Pueblo
Indians of today.

He chose for his investigation the Tewa pueblo of San
Ildefonso, a village on the Rio Grande north of Santa
Fe, whose women have for years been recognized as the
most skillful and versatile potters of that region. During
the weeks that Dr. Guthe spent at San Ildefonso, he
recorded every step in the manufacture of pottery, from
the digging of the clays to the firing of the completed
vessels. His remarkably complete and detailed results will
be published in the near future.

A second investigation bearing closely on the problems
of Pecos, was also inaugurated in the summer of 1921.
This was the study of the ethnology of the pueblo of
Jemez.

The Jemez and Pecos were closely allied linguistically
and their common dialect was not spoken at any other
town. Hence, when Pecos was abandoned, the surviving
members of the tribe naturally went to live with the
Jemez. There they have gradually increased, until today
there is a considerable group of people of more or less
pure Pecos descent.

Since the beginning of the Pecos work it had been
realized that the investigation could not be considered
complete until an attempt had been made to recover from
the descendants of the Pecos at Jemez whatever knowledge
they still had of their former home and of the life which
their ancestors lived there. It was also most desirable to

learn something of the ethnology of one of the modern Rio Grande pueblos, for as to the social and religious organization of those towns we really know very little. Such studies could hardly fail to throw light on many of the problems raised by the Pecos excavations. No member of the expedition staff was qualified to undertake this work, and no opportunity to have it done by anyone else presented itself until Dr. Elsie Clews Parsons decided to include Jemez in the intensive ethnological survey which she had been carrying on at the villages further west. She spent the seasons of 1921 and 1922 at that pueblo, where, in spite of great difficulties due to the conservatism and secretiveness of the people, she has collected a mass of most interesting and important data. Dr. Parsons has generously allowed us to publish the results of her work in the Pecos series.

SIXTH SEASON (1922)[11]

The excavation of the main quadrangle was continued north from the narrow cross-cut trench of 1920, particular attention being devoted to architecture, town growth, and the stratigraphy of the beds of early rubbish adjoining the building on the west side. In the course of the latter work an extensive ruin was developed on the West Terrace where enough of it was cleared to show that it dated from Glaze 1 times, and that its main axis ran north and south; but whether it was a simple structure or whether it was quadrangular like the historic pueblo, has not yet been determined.

As a preliminary to the work on the main quadrangle the inner wall of the building was cleared to its foundations all about the north half of the plaza; this served to remove a great deal of loose stone fallen from the ruined

11. During this summer I was assisted in the field by Miss Ida Sanford and Messrs. G. C. Vaillant and S. P. Moorehead. Mrs. Kidder as usual handled the sorting of potsherds.

a

b

PLATE 12. North terrace excavations. a. From the top of the main ruin mound; the remains of the oldest settlement lie just within the later defense wall; from the trenches here visible there were taken over ninety skeletons. b. The main ruin mound seen from the north.

upper walls of the houses and to define the exact limits of
the courtyard. Such digging was naturally very unproduc-
tive of specimens. The first series of rooms, fronting on
the plaza, was then attacked, and here we at once encountered conditions so typical of the whole summer's
excavations that it seems worth while to describe part of
that work in detail.

Room 39 was the first chamber entered. Under the pile
of fallen rock which covered it was found a well preserved
roof. The main beams, round poles of yellow pine six to
eight inches in diameter, supported a ceiling of split cedar,
twigs, and adobe. Tucked in among the roofing were an
oak digging stick and two wooden arrows, placed there for
safekeeping, and forgotten or abandoned when the owners
left. Below the ceiling the upper part of the room was
choked with earth, finely stratified, entirely barren of
specimens and evidently washed in by rainwater seeping
down the walls. Under this, and extending to the adobe
floor, was a mass of rubbish two to three feet thick which
showed that the room must have been used for a long time
as a dumping place; the debris consisted of cornhusks,
cobs, and stems, chips of wood, broken and discarded
wooden implements and great quantities of animal bones.
Remains of sheep and horses as well as fragments of late
types of pottery proved the deposit to have been made in
post-Spanish times.

In most Rio Grande pueblos when one reaches the floor
of a room one's work is over, but at Pecos it is never safe
to abandon excavations until bedrock is encountered. In
Room 39 a trial pit in one corner showed that there was
soft earth below; so digging was continued and was almost
immediately rewarded by the finding of a large polished
black olla, the mouth covered by a stone slab. This had
been hidden under the floor, and contained a pair of turtle-
shells perforated for suspension, like those worn by the
Santo Domingo corn dancers, and two rattles made of

small gourds. Near this was a second jar, also with a lid, but this one, to our great disappointment, was empty.

While we were clearing away the earth about these vessels we encountered human bones, and after careful brushing found that there were two skeletons buried face down in the deposit of dark soil that directly underlay the cached pots. Work from this point downward was very difficult; the light, which came in from a small hole in the roof, was poor, the space uncomfortably cramped, and the bones of the skeletons so badly decayed that the greatest care had to be exercised in cleaning them. The buried individuals proved to be two females, each one with a Glaze 3 bowl inverted over the head. The particular interest of these two skeletons lay in the fact that the head of one of them extended *under* the foundation of the east wall of the room, whereas the earth in which the burial was made had evidently accumulated *against* the much deeper west wall. This showed that the first, or easternmost, series of rooms along the plaza had been added to the building at some time subsequent to the Glaze 3 period, but that the rear rooms had been built at a date enough earlier to allow the growth of a considerable depth of rubbish against them.

How deep the rubbish ran was not ascertained until we had sunk three feet further, taken out three Glaze 1 skeletons, and eventually reached the solid sandstone of the mesa. Even here the work was not quite finished, for in the cracks of the rock were pockets of very early debris, and tucked away in one of them a much rotted skeleton, identified by its accompanying bowl as belonging to the very first period of occupation, the Black-on-white.

By the time all these remains had been cleared, noted, and removed, and their positions recorded on the plan and the cross-section map of the room, we had reached a depth, under the roof beams, of between eight and nine feet. The wall on the west side was decidedly shaky, that on the east had been undermined in taking out the Glaze 3 skeletons, and we were very glad to be able to get out of the deep, narrow, badly lighted hole.

The room just described was typical of the whole east, or plaza-fronting, series, and from each one we took a number of skeletons, ranging in age from Black-on-white down to Glaze 4 times. The most interesting find in these rooms was made in a chamber a few feet south of Number 39. Here, in a cist or bin built partly of masonry and partly of slabs, was a fine sandstone idol surrounded by a collection of pieces of petrified wood, odd-shaped stones, and concretions.

The next rooms to be excavated were those lying to the west, and here the conditions were somewhat simpler, as these chambers for the most part had been founded directly on the rock in early times, and kept in use, and accordingly clear of debris, until the abandonment of the town. Many specimens were found in them, and much was learned from the remains of roofs, fireplaces, and mealing outfits, as to the height of the original structure and the uses of the different rooms. To summarize, it may be said that Casteñeda's description of the town in 1540 was verified in almost every particular, namely, that the building was terraced up from the plaza to a height at the rear of four stories, that there were balconies at the second and third stories, and that the rooms on the ground floor were without doorways, access to the roofs and balconies having been gained by means of ladders.

During the season's work the entire northwest corner of the building was cleared, and several trenches were run in the rubbish heaps to the west. About two hundred and fifty skeletons were uncovered, most of them of early periods. The most notable specimens found were the idol above mentioned, a fine series of tobacco pipes from a ceremonial room at the north end of the pueblo, and a large stone slab from the plaza, upon which is painted in many colors a representation of a masked head, probably a rain god or kachina. The latter is, as far as the writer knows, the only painting of its kind which has ever been found in the Southwest.

Toward the end of the summer a few days were spent at a large but inconspicuous site at "Bandelier Bend" just across the Arroyo de Pecos from the main ruin. Enough was done to get an idea of the nature of the pottery and to determine that the buildings had been low, rambling structures made of adobe. The study of the pottery showed that "Bandelier Bend" was an ancient settlement founded, apparently, quite early in the Pueblo period, and inhabited for a long time. During its occupancy it seems to have grown by accretion from a small community to a very extensive one. It was abandoned at about the time when Pecos was founded, which makes it seem likely that its people merely moved across the arroyo to the more easily defended site on the Pecos mesa. The most interesting feature of our preliminary excavations was the finding of a round subterranean kiva, the oldest example of such a structure so far reported from the Rio Grande.

SUMMARY OF RESULTS

Let us briefly sum up the results of the field work so far completed. To begin with, we have found that the Pecos site is much more extensive and vastly more complicated than had been expected. The main building mounds, those of the North and South Houses, instead of being the remains of dwellings erected at an early date and kept in use until the abandonment of the pueblo, have been shown to be comparatively late structures which overlie the broken-down walls of several still earlier towns. Where the earth on the mesa-top and along the terraces had been supposed to be a mere skin, it has turned out to be anywhere from five to twenty feet deep, and to cover unsuspected house ruins and cemeteries. The extent of

a

b

PLATE 13. Architectural details. a. Typical Pecos masonry, not coursed and made of untrimmed stones; a sealed doorway appears in the center of the picture. b. Conditions in the rooms of the Great Quadrangle; the badly built lower walls have given way and the upper stones have fallen, crushing the roof timbers.

the rubbish heaps along the east and southwest slopes has hardly yet been gauged. All these facts indicate, of course, a long period of occupancy, a condition which we had suspected from surface signs, but which we had not been able to prove before excavations began. It is now certain, therefore, that the rubbish heaps of Pecos contain the accumulations of several centuries at least; and many of them are so stratified that by careful study of their contents we have been able to trace the development of the arts and industries of the community from beginning to end. Of the various objects found in these stratified heaps, pottery fragments are by far the commonest and most easily classifiable. Hence we have devoted much time, both in the field and in the laboratory, to the study of pottery, and have worked out in considerable detail the changes which have taken place in that art from the unknown date at which Pecos was founded to the early years of the last century.

As originally planned, the work of the Pecos expedition was to be first intensive, then extensive. The intensive phase was to consist of the excavation of the pueblo, and the determination by stratigraphic methods of the sequence of the pottery types found at the site. During the second or extensive phase we were to use our knowledge of the sequence of the pottery types to arrange in their proper chronological order all other ruins which contained those types. This work was to be accomplished by a thorough archaeological reconnaissance of the Rio Grande drainage.

The first phase may, in a sense, be considered complete, since we have determined the sequence of the pottery types; and we should now, if we adhered to the original plan, cease work at Pecos and undertake a general reconnaissance of the Rio Grande. A modification, however, seems advisable. In the first place the Pecos ruin has turned out to be so large that we have as yet succeeded in clearing only about 12 per cent of it. Then, a number of most interesting and important lines of investigation have been suggested by what we have so far done; and none of these can be pursued without continued excavation. But some of these new investigations themselves require the sidelights of reconnaissance. Hence it has been decided to merge the intensive and extensive phases of our work—to continue digging at Pecos and to carry on at the same time as much reconnaissance as possible.

Perhaps the most important of the new lines of investigation just referred to is that of the development of decorative art. Because of the increasing use of pottery, basketry, textiles, etc., as criteria of cultural evolution, the morphology of decoration is receiving more and more attention from anthropologists. But this subject is peculiarly difficult of approach, because to gain a true insight into the development of any decorative complex, one must have not only abundant material but material which is chronologically sequent. Such material for the study of art growth among prehistoric or primitive people has always been exceedingly hard to get. Until now almost all work on the subject has been based on hypothetically arranged series, and conclusions drawn from it are, of course, not to be relied upon. In the Southwest, however, stratigraphic work will eventually provide datable specimens from all districts and of all periods, so that we shall be able to determine with perfect certainty the exact changes which have taken place in the art of that area. The unusually complete pottery series to be had at Pecos will, when carefully studied, make clear the details of the local art growth over a long stretch of time. For this reason alone it seems well worth while to persevere until we have gathered a very large body of data. There enters here, however, the necessity spoken of above for doing concurrent reconnaissance at other sites. The Pecos series, while long, can only be recovered from large, stratified rubbish heaps.

These supply the outline of the development, and also provide abundant material; but, as in all stratified deposits, there has been a certain amount of mixing, so that absolutely pure material from any given period is only to be found under exceptional conditions, as in sealed rooms, quickly filled kivas, cisterns, etc. Hence, to get a perfect series of pure material we must collect pottery from briefly occupied sites of each period, sites which do not contain earlier or later mixtures.

A second investigation which promises much of interest concerns itself with the mechanics of pueblo growth. It was at first supposed that the Pecos ruins were the remains of a single structure, erected *en bloc*, occupied until 1838, and then abandoned. The excavations, however, have shown that we have not only ruin piled on ruin, but that the population kept shifting about from one part of the mesa to another, building and rebuilding. We have uncovered in the course of our limited excavations portions of no less than six distinct towns. While some of these have been nearly obliterated by stone-robbing, all of them can eventually be traced out; and they can all be accurately dated relative to each other by means of the pottery and the burials found in and about them. Furthermore, the later structures, and perhaps some of the earlier ones as well, can undoubtedly be dated absolutely by means of the growth rings of their roof beams.[12] There is also no question but that we shall eventually learn the approximate date for the original founding of Pecos. This will allow us to estimate the number of changes made and the amount of building done during a known number of years, and will give us valuable data on the question of the permanency or impermanency of Pueblo house groups.

The consideration of habitations naturally brings up the matter of population. This, as will be shown in a later chapter, is a question of fundamental importance. We

12. By the Douglass method, see p. 132.

Courtesy National Geographic Society

must learn as much as possible concerning the size of the prehistoric Pueblo tribes, and also as much as possible regarding their racial affinities. On both problems the excavation of Pecos can shed light. We have already taken out some twelve hundred skeletons, and have as yet barely scratched the cemeteries. While some skeletons are too rotted for laboratory measurement, the age and sex of almost all of them can be determined. As there is no evidence that the Pecos ever cremated their dead, or commonly buried them elsewhere than on the mesa, and as cemeteries were not often greatly disturbed by later use, it would seem that if we excavate the entire site we shall find the bodies of practically all the people who ever lived there. Thus we should be able to estimate roughly the total population of Pecos; and when we learn the date of its foundation, we should be able, by correlating this knowledge with what we find out about the size of the town at different periods, to judge of the number of people who lived there at any given time. Such work will also be greatly aided by the fact that we can usually assign any skeleton to its proper period, either certainly by means of mortuary pottery in its grave, or inferentially by taking into consideration the depth of the interment, the nature of the rubbish surrounding and covering it, and its association with other nearby skeletons.

Even if we cannot gauge the size of the population at every period, the skeletons from Pecos will form a very large addition to the material available for somatologists. Being relatively datable they should provide data as to the unity or heterogeneity of the Pecos people at different times; and, if mixtures have occurred, their period and the effect that they had on the resident population should be discernible. Much of value will also be learned as to length of life, infant mortality, and the effects of certain important diseases.

As in the case of the work on art development, so with

the skeletons, outside excavation must be carried on to supplement the data from Pecos, and to acquire material from periods which are not well represented there. The earlier burials at Pecos are generally in bad condition, because of the great amounts of rubbish which have accumulated above them. By going to contemporaneous sites where, because of brief occupation, the interments are not crushed by so great an overburden, we can recover well-preserved skeletons and so complete our series.

The above lines of investigation can only be carried to completion by clearing the whole Pecos mesa and the rubbish slopes that surround it on all sides, a task that seems beyond the present resources of the Trustees. Furthermore, it is not advisable, it appears to me, that so important a ruin be entirely exhausted at one time or by one excavator. Future work will of course serve to introduce better methods of excavation; and the development of the science of archaeology will inevitably result in the raising of new problems which today are not even suspected. Hence it seems best to leave a considerable portion of Pecos untouched, and so available for the improved technique and the broader knowledge of another generation of archaeologists. We do, however, hope to gather much more material, and at least to make a start toward the solution of the important problems of art development, pueblo growth, and the size of the population at different periods.

In the prosecution of such studies as have just been suggested we must be careful to hold ourselves to a proper balance between the detailed and the general. The details of archaeology are in themselves so interesting that it is fatally easy to become completely absorbed in them, and there is always the excuse that without close and accurate work one cannot arrive at trustworthy conclusions. The result is that too often one arrives at no conclusions at all. It is quite as fatally easy to ignore detail (with the plausible excuse that the close worker cannot see the forest for the trees) and strike out blithely on the primrose path of speculation. If archaeology dealt with phenomena less infinitely variable in themselves and less bewilderingly diverse in their interactions, it might be possible to reduce it to rules and formulas, and to decide just how far to delve into detail, and just how much to generalize. But that is not possible, and apparently never can be. Each problem must be attacked in its own way, and every worker must decide for himself how he shall apportion his efforts.

In the case of Pecos, the way seems fairly clear. The nature of the site and the circumstances of its occupancy have resulted in the laying down of deposits important and interesting in themselves, which also epitomize, as it were, a long period in the culture history of the Southwest. Pecos may be made to serve as an index to a considerable part of that culture history, and so, it seems to me, too much effort cannot be spent upon the details of its archaeology. But for the very reason that it is an index, it cannot be treated as an isolated phenomenon, and we must keep constantly in mind the more general problems that it is being used to solve.

To understand the problems of Southwestern archaeology it is necessary to consider the nature of our knowledge of man in America. Historical information in regard to the American Indian runs back at the farthest for only about four hundred years, and in most parts of the New World the record is very much shorter. Furthermore, where the historical record begins, there, as a rule, the history of the Indian abruptly ceases. There are a few exceptions, such as those provided by the datable monuments of the Maya; and certain instances, as in Peru and Mexico, where native traditionists have set down in European characters the more or less legendary histories of their own particular peoples. At best, then, recorded history for the aborigines of the New World is brief, and in the case of most areas it is entirely lacking. The student has before him data as to the distribution of great numbers of tribes, infinitely diverse in language and customs and ranging in culture from the lowest savagery to a relatively high civilization. This state of affairs must of course be the result of a very long sequence of historical events, and our problem, as Sapir has so admirably phrased it, "may be metaphorically defined as the translation of a two-dimensional photographic picture of reality into the three-dimensional picture which lies back of it. Is it possible," he asks, "to read time perspective into the flat surface of American culture, as we read space perspective into the flat surface of a photograph?" [13] Sapir proceeds to answer his question in the affirmative, basing his deductions largely on the inferential evidence provided by ethnology and linguistics; he emphasizes, however, the great potential importance of archaeological studies. Such studies had not, when Sapir wrote, been prosecuted with any great energy, but during the past decade archaeologists have been devoting more and more attention to the chronological aspects of their work. There has been a very general search for definite information bearing on the time relations of the remains of man in America. Nowhere has this search been more diligently prosecuted than in the Southwest, and the results so far obtained are extremely promising.

To make clear the nature of the chronological problems of the Southwest, and to show how the work at Pecos can be brought to bear upon them, it is necessary to lay before the reader an outline of the data which are already at hand, or in other words to undertake a summary of our present knowledge of Southwestern archaeology.

13. Sapir, 1916, p. 2.

The Modern Pueblos

The Southwest, archaeologically speaking, comprises those parts of the southwestern United States and northern Mexico which are, or were formerly, inhabited by Indians of Pueblo culture. This culture will be more fully described in the section devoted to the modern Pueblos; for present purposes it suffices to say that its outstanding characteristics are sedentary agricultural life in permanent villages of stone or adobe, the manufacture of excellent pottery, and the use of the hand loom.

When we come to define the limits of the Pueblo area we find our only serious difficulty in the south. This is partly because little exploration has been carried out in northern Mexico; but to an even greater extent because the peoples of that region were also sedentary agriculturists between whose culture and that of the Pueblos there were few very fundamental differences. Were we to use as a criterion the architecture typical of the Pueblos, we should have to establish our boundary at or slightly north of the Gila River in Arizona, and along the international border of New Mexico. Relying upon the evidence of pottery, however, we can extend our limits to include the Gila and southern Arizona, as well as the great inland basin of northern Chihuahua that lies south of New Mexico. Certain well-marked Mexican traits occur in these areas; but the pottery, as will eventually be shown, is definitely Southwestern in type. Accordingly it seems best to accept, provisionally at least, the more extensive southern boundaries.

To the east, north, and west the problem of delimitation is much simpler, for in those directions the surrounding tribes were all in a much lower state of culture than

were the Pueblos, and wherever regions adjoining the
Southwest show traces of agriculture, permanent stone
houses, and pottery, these may safely be ascribed to Pueblo
influence. Although much exploration remains to be done,
the approximate limits are already apparent. They include, as shown on the accompanying map (fig. 9), most

FIG. 9. Approximate extent of the Southwestern culture area.

of Arizona and New Mexico, a small part of Colorado, and
a large portion of Utah.

This vast area has very distinct topographic and climatic
characteristics; it is essentially a plateau country, high and
arid. Much of it is desert. Where conditions are slightly
better, the land is clothed with cedars and pinyons. Only

the slopes of the eastern mountains and of certain interior ranges are really forested. Grass is everywhere scanty, game is correspondingly scarce; nor are there any wild food-plants of value. Much of the soil, however, is fertile, and where water can be got upon it is surprisingly reproductive. While the country, then, could support only a very limited number of hunting people, it was capable of providing sustenance for a relatively large agricultural population. That this productivity was once fully taken advantage of is proved by the thousands of ruins that are scattered over the length and breadth of the area. In more recent times, however, most of this great territory was abandoned, and when the Spaniards arrived in 1540 they found the Pueblos living in a comparatively restricted region at about the center of their former range.

To trace the history of these people, to discover their origins, to learn how they conquered their harsh environment, how they increased and spread out over the plateau, and how and why they eventually failed to hold their own in the struggle for existence, these are the chief aims of the study of Southwestern archaeology.

A review of the subject matter of Southwestern archaeology must necessarily begin with a consideration of the still inhabited pueblos of New Mexico and Arizona.[1]

1. No attempt has been made to include in the bibliography the enormous literature regarding the modern Pueblos; the following more or less popular works, however, will give the general reader an excellent idea of their life and customs: Bandelier, 1890, 1890b; Donaldson, 1893; Cushing, 1901, 1920; Lummis, 1906, 1910; Hough, 1915; Saunders, 1912; Goddard, 1921. Scientific studies of Pueblo religion, social organization, and material culture are to be found in the writings of Fewkes (*Annual Reports of the Bureau of Ethnology, American Anthropologist, Journal of American Folk-Lore*); J. and M. C. Stevenson (*Annual Reports of the Bureau of Ethnology*); Dorsey and Voth (*Field Columbian Museum Anthropological Series*); E. C. Parsons (*American Anthropologist, Memoirs American Anthropological Association, Journal of American Folk-Lore*); and Kroeber (*Anthropological Papers of the American Museum of Natural History*). See also the articles on the various Pueblo towns and Pueblo linguistic stocks in "Handbook of American Indians" (*Bulletin 30, Bureau of American Ethnology*).

FIG. 10. Map showing the distribution of the Pueblo linguistic stocks and the location of villages inhabited at the present time.

1. Nambe	5. Santa Clara	9. Taos	14. San Felipe	19. Zuñi	23. Shumopovi
2. Tesuque	6. Hano	10. Picuris	15. Sia	20. Sichomovi	24. Shipaulovi
3. San Ildefonso	7. Isleta	11. Jemez	16. Santa Ana	21. Walpi	25. Oraibi
4. San Juan	8. Sandia	12. Cochiti	17. Laguna	22. Mishongnovi	26. Hotavilla
		13. Santo Domingo	18. Acoma		

These fascinating communities preserve the ancient culture of the Southwest in almost its aboriginal purity; even the most sophisticated of them are little more than veneered by European civilization, and we can still, as Lummis has so aptly phrased it, "catch our archaeology alive."

At the time of the Spanish conquest the Pueblo Indians numbered about 20,000, and lived in some seventy towns. These Indians, although very similar to each other in arts, customs, and religion, were divided into several distinct linguistic groups (see map, fig. 10).

In the northwest lived the Hopi, who spoke a Shoshonean language allied to that of the Utes, Paiutes and Comanches. On the western border of New Mexico were the Zuñi, whose tongue has no known affinities. East of Zuñi came the Keres, divided into two groups, one on the middle waters of the Puerco, the other on the Rio Grande north of the present location of Albuquerque. The Keresan language, like the Zuñian, has no known affinities. All the rest of the Pueblos belong to the Tanoan stock, a group which had five well-marked subdivisions: the Tewa, Tigua, Jemez, Tano, and Piro. Tanoan has recently been suspected to be connected in some way with the Kiowan linguistic stock of the Plains. In general the Tanoan peoples were confined to the Rio Grande and its immediate vicinity. The Tewa subdivision occupied a continuous area north of the Keres. The Tigua were partly to the north of the Tewa at Toas and Picuris, partly to the south of the Keres along the Rio Grande below Albuquerque and west toward the Manzanos Mountains. The Jemez were also divided, one group lying west of the Keres in the Jemez Valley, the other at Pecos far to the east on the upper Pecos River. The Tano occupied the eastern tributaries of the Rio Grande south of the Tewa, and between the Keres and the Pecos branch of the Jemez. The Piro villages began below the country of the southern Tigua and extended down the Rio Grande about half

way to El Paso; there were also several towns east of the
river in the Salinas Valley.

All these different Pueblo peoples live today in approximately the same places as they did in 1540, with the
exception of the Tano and Piro, who have become to all
intents and purposes extinct, and the Pecos, who, as we
have seen, moved in 1838 to join their kindred at Jemez.
There are at the present time only twenty-six villages, and
their inhabitants number not over 9,000 souls.

Although reduced in numbers, and to a greater or less
extent affected by European contact, the life of the Pueblos
of today is surprisingly like that of their ancestors of the
sixteenth century, as described by Castañeda and the other
early Spanish chroniclers.

The most characteristic feature of Pueblo life is the
pueblo itself, that peculiar type of village which has given
the culture its name. A pueblo is a closely built agglom-
eration of rectangular living rooms, a sort of exaggerated
beehive, or great apartment house, which shelters an entire community (pl. 15, a). The individual rooms may be
grouped in various ways, as in a long row, about a court,
or in a solid mass; but close adherence of room to room
is always the rule, and for even greater compactness the
villages are usually terraced, sometimes to a height of
several stories (pl. 43). The people live, cook, and sleep
in the outer and upper chambers, and use the inner and
lower ones for the storage of their belongings and particularly for their hoards of harvested corn.

The system of architecture is simple. The unit of construction is a rectangular room with walls of heavy masonry
set in adobe mud or laid up of pure adobe. Each room is
spanned across its short axis by four or five large peeled
logs; over these in the opposite direction are placed
smaller poles, then twigs or bark for chinking, and finally
a layer of adobe. If a second room is to be built above the
first, the walls are simply continued upward and the roof

PLATE 15. Modern Pueblo villages. a. Taos, a terraced village of the old type in northern New Mexico. b. Two-story house in Tesuque pueblo, New Mexico; harvest time, corn heaped at the right, strings of chile drying in the sun, and jerked meat hanging under the balcony.

of the lower serves as the floor of the upper. Lateral rooms are added by merely constructing walls against those already erected. Doorways are small and in old times seldom opened on the ground level, first-story apartments having been entered by trap doors in their roofs. Windows did not exist; little ventilating holes near the fireplaces and smoke vents in the roof kept the air breathable. Although modern frame doors and glazed windows have now appeared at the more progressive towns (pl. 15, b), and the rooms of such pueblos are larger and more comfortable than of old, the people still live largely out-of-doors, in the courtyards, under the balconies, and on the housetops; so much so that even today a person's housetop is still considered a public thoroughfare and no Pueblo ever takes umbrage at its being used as such.

In addition to the rooms of the houses proper, each pueblo of the early historic period possessed several kivas, round or rectangular chambers, usually sunk into the earth so that their roofs were flush with the ground, and entered from above by means of a hatchway and ladder. The kiva is found in practically all the modern towns, and plays a most important role in Pueblo life; it is a social and work room for the men, a council chamber, and (its most important function) the scene of the secret portions of the religious observances; all modern kivas, except those at Taos and the Hopi towns, are above ground (pl. 16, b).

In spite of the solid construction of their towns, and the great labor involved in building them, the Pueblo Indians are (or rather were in the recent past) less firmly anchored to them than might be supposed. As evidence of this we have the fact that none of the modern pueblos, except Acoma and Zuñi, occupy exactly the same sites as they did in 1540. Every other town has moved at least once, and many of them several times. Much of this shifting about was due, of course, to the wars of the re-

a

b

PLATE 16. Modern Pueblos. a. Harvest dance at San Ildefonso, New Mexico. b. The kiva at San Ildefonso.

volt and reconquest between 1680 and 1700; but the
Pueblos were always ready to abandon their dwellings
on what seem to us the slightèst pretexts, and were usually
little disposed to return to them again, even under Spanish
coercion. Many freshly abandoned villages were seen by
the earliest explorers; and in more recent times many
shifts have been made for apparently the most trivial
reasons. The influence of the priests and the establishment
of land grants have served to render the towns of the last
two centuries more or less permanent, but it is clear that
the Pueblos have little feeling for mere localities and small
compunction in abandoning old homes.

This relative impermanency of towns whose construction
seems so very permanent is a highly important phenomenon; it helps to explain many otherwise puzzling features
of Southwestern archaeology, and will be more fully discussed when we come to consider the subject of the prehistoric ruins.

The Pueblos are primarily agriculturists. They have
always hunted to a certain extent, and at present possess
more or less livestock, but their main reliance is now,
as it was in the past, upon corn. Corn, with beans and
squashes, forms the bulk of their sustenance. The Pueblos
are expert farmers. They grow crops in places, and under
conditions, that at first sight appear to be absolutely hopeless. Irrigation is practiced where possible, but their success depends mostly upon the intelligent choice of ground,
deep planting, and the most careful cultivation and
weeding. Centuries of selection have resulted in the development of hardy, deep-rooted varieties of corn which
will germinate with little moisture and mature quickly
after the brief midsummer rains.

After harvest the corn is dried, husked, and stored away
on the ear. For use it is ground tò meal on a flat stone
slab, the metate, and made into various dishes, the most

characteristic of which is a thin paper-like bread cooked on a stone griddle.[2]

The governmental, social, and religious organizations of the Pueblos are highly complex and at present are imperfectly understood. The reason for this is that among the Pueblos the secular and the religious are inextricably intertwined, and the people are so exceedingly reticent in regard to their religion that investigators have had the greatest difficulty in finding out the true meaning of what would appear to be the simplest phenomena. To make the most general sort of statement, one can say that each pueblo is a strictly self-contained, closely knit, and autonomous unit, essentially democratic so far as wealth and living conditions are concerned. It is governed by elective officers, whose functions are both religious and civil. Marriage is monogamous, descent is, or was, usually through the mother, and the social unit is the clan, or group of blood relatives in the female line.

The religious system concerns itself principally with the growing of crops; its ceremonies have to do, therefore, with the fertilization of corn and particularly with the production of the ever-needed rain. Minor but still important features are the propagation of game, success in the chase, and the cure of sickness. The ritual is elaborate, involving the use of a great mass of paraphernalia. The public ceremonies are often highly spectacular. During the ceremonies many "prayer sticks" are made and deposited in shrines; much cornmeal is used, both symbolically, and in the form of actual offerings to the gods.

The house building, the agriculture, the religious practices, and the social system of the Pueblos have been relatively little affected by their three hundred years of intercourse with the whites. But their native minor arts, with

---

2. See *Zuñi Breadstuff* (Cushing, 1920). This is a work remarkable for its completeness of detail, its keen insight into pueblo life, and its literary charm.

the single exception of pottery-making, have disappeared, particularly since the American occupation with its influx of good tools and serviceable textile fabrics. For information as to the old arts we must therefore turn to the narratives of the early Spanish explorers, and to such objects as have been preserved by the people and have found their way into museum collections.

One of the most important industries was weaving. In the sixteenth century cotton was grown at all the pueblos where the local climate was not too rigorous, was spun into yarn, and woven on primitive but efficient hand looms. The cultivation of cotton has now been given up everywhere except in the Hopi country, where a few plants are still raised to provide the native fiber which is considered indispensable for certain ceremonial usages.

Weaving was, and still is, considered man's work, the looms usually being set up in the kivas. Few of the old cotton fabrics survive in everyday use, but ceremonial kilts are still made; the yarn, however, is of American manufacture. After the introduction of sheep, wool largely took the place of cotton; the Hopi were particularly adept in the making of woolen textiles, and even now produce some blankets and a large number of women's dresses, the latter being one of their principal articles of trade.

The clothing of all the Pueblos, except those of the extreme northwest, where contact with the Plains tribes served to make popular the use of fitted skin garments, was essentially alike. Although native clothes are no longer much worn, the ceremonial dress probably reflects older conditions quite accurately (pls. 16, a; 17, b). In dances the men wear a breechcloth and a short kilt fastened about the waist and falling to a little above the knees. The man's short-sleeved cotton shirt, not tailored, but made by simply sewing two square pieces of fabric together and attaching small sleeves, was apparently once in common use; a few such shirts are still in existence as treasured heirlooms,

PLATE 17. Pueblo costumes. a. Woman of San Ildefonso in everyday dress.

PLATE 17b.   Corn dancers at Santo Domingo.

and are sometimes worn by the musicians during religious dances. The footgear is a hard-soled moccasin; it is uncertain whether or not the sandal of ancient times survived in the early historic period.

The women are somewhat more conservative in dress than the men. Their principal garment is a sleeveless dress of native (usually Hopi) weave, made in a single piece. When put on, the dress reaches to just below the knees, and is so fastened as to leave the left shoulder and sometimes the left breast exposed (pl. 17, b). During ceremonies the women of some villages go barefoot, but for everyday wear most Pueblo women have moccasins with long attached uppers which are wrapped about the calf of the leg (pl. 17, a). Both sexes complete their costume with a robe thrown over the shoulders; in old times this was of rabbitskin or turkey feathers, now it is either a Navaho blanket or an American shawl.

Basketry is a lost art at most of the pueblos, the requirements of the people being supplied by trade with the Apache, Pima, and Paiute. It is probable that this was to some extent also the case in the early historic period. At the present time heavy coiled basketry is made at the Hopi towns of the Second Mesa, wickerwork trays at Oraibi, and a plaited yucca basket with a wooden ring about the rim is produced at several towns, notably at San Felipe, whose people make a specialty of this particular type.

Pottery, in spite of the growing use of tin oilcans for carrying water, and of cheap American china for serving food, still plays an important part in the domestic economy of the Pueblos. Even today, cooking is largely done in native pots, and earthen ollas serve almost exclusively for the storing and cooling of drinking water. The art of pottery-making, too, has been kept alive by the constant demand for decorated vessels by the traders, who ship them in large quantities to curio dealers. While this commercial demand has naturally resulted in careless work and a certain degeneration in technique and ornamentation, its effects have been less pernicious than might be expected. There are still many expert potters, who turn out fine vessels, even with the knowledge that they are to be sold to white men.

Pottery is now regularly made at some of the Hopi towns, at Zuñi, Acoma, Laguna, Sia, Santo Domingo, Cochiti, San Ildefonso, Tesuque, Santa Clara, and San Juan (pl. 18). Elsewhere it is only manufactured in limited quantities in the form of undecorated cooking jars, or is turned out by women from the pottery-making pueblos who happen to have married away from home. Pottery was formerly, of course, a common product at every village. A detailed report on the subject of pottery-making will be published in an early number of the present series.

To sum up, the Pueblos live in closely knit autonomous groups, a single large building, made up of many small rectangular rooms, often sheltering an entire community. The people are primarily agriculturists, raise corn and grind it on the metate; are excellent and prolific potters; and understand the use of the hand loom.

No description of the Pueblos can be complete without mention of their hereditary enemies, the nomadic tribes of the Southwest. These Indians gained their livelihood principally by hunting, and were not bound down by the possession of permanent towns or cultivated fields. What little agriculture they practiced was of a haphazard sort, and they were always free to shift their range at will. Between the village-dweller and the nomad there has always, and in every part of the world, been bitter enmity; never more bitter, perhaps, than in the Southwest.

Apparently the roaming tribes seldom waged definite wars against the Pueblos, nor did they often carry out organized attacks on their towns. They hung about in the mountains ready at any time to pounce upon outlying

PLATE 18. Modern Pueblo pottery. a. Hopi. b. Cochiti. c. Santo Domingo. d. Acoma. e. Zuñi. f. Santa Clara. g. Tesuque. h. Sia. i. San Ildefonso.

farm settlements, cut off hunting parties, steal women, plunder cornfields, burn crops, and in general make life as miserable as possible for their more sedentary neighbors. Their raids were intermittent, there were often periods of quiet, and even times of actual peace with open trading between the Pueblos and the nomads. But such armistices never lasted long.

Against these tactics the Pueblos were singularly helpless. Good fighters they were, but tied to their villages and fields they could seldom bring their whole force to bear upon enemies so bafflingly elusive. They maintained themselves, however, by constant watchfulness, prompt defensive measures, and the strength of their fortress-like dwellings.

Nomads were present in the Southwest in 1540, for Castañeda records depredations in the Rio Grande country by the Teyas, apparently a Shoshonean Plains tribe, and states that villages had recently been abandoned because of their raids.[3] Since the middle of the seventeenth century the Navaho and Apache have been terrible scourges, the latter having forced the desertion of many Piro and Tigua towns to the west of the Rio Grande. About 1700 the Comanche began to press in from the northeast and east, with disastrous results for Pecos. The Utes and the northern Apache were always troublesome to the Taos and northern Tewa. It is, indeed, only since the American occupation of Arizona and New Mexico that any effective protection has been furnished to the Pueblos, and only in very recent years has the ancient menace of the nomad been entirely removed.

3. Winship, 1896, pp. 323, 324.

The Prehistoric Pueblos

The Spanish explorers of the Southwest were indefatigable travellers, acute observers and, best of all, accurate recorders of the places they visited and of the things they saw. Their accounts enable us to locate the sites, and in most cases the actual ruins, of practically every pueblo that was inhabited in the sixteenth and seventeenth centuries. That any large or important towns could have escaped their thorough search and careful recording is almost impossible. Hence, any ruin which is not identifiable as a village mentioned in one or another of the documentary sources must, unless it holds internal evidence to the contrary, be considered to have been abandoned prior to the year 1540.

Internal evidence of historic occupancy is usually easy to find, for very soon after the conquest the Spanish introduced horses, sheep, goats, and cattle, whose bones come to light in every refuse heap of historic times; they also traded to the Indians glass beads, iron tools, china, and other objects of European make that turn up in considerable quantities in the rooms of the ruins and in the graves of the dead. While the presence of these things proves white contact, their absence does not certainly prove the contrary; nevertheless any given site containing no object of European provenience may be pretty safely considered prehistoric, particularly if extensive excavations have been carried out in it.

Applying the above two tests to all the known ruins, we find that for every village of the historic period there are literally hundreds which must have been abandoned before 1540. These lie not only in the districts inhabited by the present-day Pueblos and their sixteenth-century an-

cestors, but are scattered far and wide over the entire
Southwest. The ruined dwellings and the specimens found
in them show so close a similarity to the houses and artifacts of the modern tribes that there has never been any
serious doubt that they are relics of the direct cultural ancestors of the Pueblos. The immense number of the ruins,
however, and the vast territory which they occupy make
it certain that one of three conditions, or some combination of two or more of them, must have obtained:
either the population was formerly very much larger than
it was in 1540; or the country was inhabited for a tre-
mendously long time; or the ancient Pueblos occupied
their villages for very brief periods. It will be noticed that
the time element is the unknown quantity which prevents
our choosing between these three possibilities. If we knew
the relative date of the founding and abandonment of
every ruin in the Southwest, it would be a comparatively
simple matter, by estimating the approximate population
of each, and plotting the results on a series of maps, to
visualize the entire history of the Pueblo peoples. Our
task, therefore, is: first, to locate all the ruins and record
their size; second, to determine the length of their
occupancy, and their age relative to each other; and, third,
to establish their age, not only in relative terms, but according to the years of our own calendar. This is a heavy
program and one which naturally can never be completely
carried out, but it is best to face the situation as it is, and
to realize that if our researches are to be worth anything
they must be undertaken not only with a clear idea of
the end to be attained, but also with a full realization of
the difficulties to be encountered.

The location, description, and measurement of ruins
can be accomplished by industrious exploration; an arbitrary rule for estimating population according to size of
settlements should, if consistently applied, yield more or
less valid results; both these things are merely matters of

persistent work. The all-important questions of chronology, however, are less obvious in nature and less easy of solution; to settle them we must rank the ruins in the order of their building and determine if possible the length of their occupancy. The following methods of attack have been tried:

Legendary evidence. Great dependence has been placed by certain students upon the migration legends of the modern Pueblos, and many prehistoric ruins have been classified as to age and as to cultural affinities by this means alone. Recent ethnological studies, however, seem to show that the Pueblo as an historian is at best unreliable; while archaeological evidence seldom confirms, and often directly refutes, the statements of the native traditionist.

Preservation. The state of preservation of ruins is seldom a good criterion of age. The nature of the site, the exposure of walls to the elements and of foundations to surface drainage, conflagrations, the removal of roof beams, all these more or less fortuitous and generally indeterminable factors cause deductions based upon preservation to have very doubtful value.

Comparison of types. Crude and primitive-looking remains, when compared with relics of an obviously more advanced type are usually, and doubtless often correctly, assumed to belong to an earlier period. This method of chronological evaluation must, however, be very cautiously applied and should always have the support of corroborative evidence, since in the history of the Southwest many cases of degeneration in culture and of irregularity in culture growth have occurred.[1] Care must also be exercised not to mistake the survival of archaic traits in peripheral regions for evidence of antiquity.

1. For example, the excellent masonry and fine ceramics of the Chaco might easily be considered later than the slipshod building and poor pottery of many actually younger ruins on the upper Rio Grande not far to the east.

Stratigraphic evidence. The ideal form of chronological evidence is provided by stratigraphy, i.e., when remains of one type are found lying below those of another. Such evidence is of course conclusive, and has provided us with sure data as to the relative age of several phases of Southwestern culture. If we could find in each district sites containing material running from the very earliest times down to the period of abandonment, our task would be a comparatively simple one; but no such site has ever been discovered. Pecos presents the longest complete series so far known, but Pecos does not carry us back to really remote times. Even short series, covering two or three periods, are rare enough; but they do occur and can be made, by the principle of overlapping, to yield excellent results.

To take full advantage of stratigraphic evidence, whether it be presented in a comparatively long series or by an overlapping of several short ones, the investigator must select for study those phenomena which most accurately reflect changes in culture or, what amounts to the same thing, chronological periods. Pottery has so far provided the most useful material for such studies, as it is abundant at all sites except the very earliest, is readily classifiable, and is a highly sensitive register of cultural change.[2]

Apparently the first application of the principle of stratigraphy to Southwestern problems was made by Richard Wetherill, when in the nineties he defined the Basket Maker culture, and then determined, by discovering its remains below those of cliff houses, that it represented an earlier chronological period rather than a mere local development.[3] Fewkes at Casa Grande[4] and

2. Valuable but much less easily acquired evidence is provided by architecture, physical type, skull deformation, mortuary customs, sandals, etc.; these should all be taken into account and used to check the results obtained from consideration of the pottery.

3. Prudden, 1897, p. 61.

4. Fewkes, 1912, p. 102.

Cummings in the Kayenta district[5] used the evidence of superposition for the relative dating of archaeological material; and in 1914 Guernsey and the writer established the stratigraphic position of the pre-Pueblo.[6] It remained for Nelson, however, to recognize that the most reliable results could be obtained by passing downwards, so to speak, from the known to the unknown. He attacked the problem, accordingly, at the early historic ruins of central New Mexico and worked backwards, basing his conclusions on stratigraphic evidence, and using pottery as the criterion for classification. In this way he was able to arrange in their proper sequence the principal pottery types, and hence the principal chronological periods, of the Rio Grande.[7] Nelson also conducted the first well-thought-out attack on the chronological problems of the Southwest in their broader aspects[8]; and, although his work in this field has unfortunately been interrupted, he has blazed a trail which will be more and more followed as time goes on.

A fifth method for obtaining chronological data has been devised by Prof. A. E. Douglass of the University of Arizona. It depends upon the study of the annual growth rings of coniferous trees. The Douglass system, which holds out the most brilliant prospects for accurate dating, has not yet been extensively employed. For this reason, and also because its application can be more clearly understood when the reader is better acquainted with the nature and distribution of the ruins, discussion of it will be de-

5. Cummings, 1910, p. 10.

6. Kidder-Guernsey, 1919, p. 42.

7. Nelson, 1916. An attempt to do the same thing on the basis of comparative studies of the pottery had been made by the writer (Kidder, 1915); the fact that the sequence of types there suggested was proved by Nelson to be correct is encouraging because it shows that such comparative studies may be of value in regions where no stratigraphic evidence can be discovered. The latter, however, must always be diligently searched for, as it forms the only certain basis for deduction.

8. Nelson, 1919.

ferred until after we have presented such data as we have
in regard to the prehistoric remains.

In the following chapters we take up the description of
the antiquities of the Southwest by river drainages (fig.

Fig. 11. The culture areas of the Southwest: 1. San Juan; 2. Northern
Peripheral; 3. Rio Grande; 4. Eastern Peripheral; 5. Little Colorado; 6.
Upper Gila; 7. Mimbres; 8. Lower Gila 9. Chihuahua Basin.

11). This is not only a convenient method for arranging
the material but, as will be seen, the river drainages form
in most cases definite areas of specialization. At the end
of each chapter is given a selected bibliography of the
archaeology of the region; the titles included are in most

cases modern scientific papers embodying original material; notices of ruins by early travellers, brief references in popular articles, and secondhand descriptions are only listed where better sources are lacking. The most valuable contributions are marked with asterisks.

The San Juan

The San Juan is considered first because it is in many ways the best known archaeologically of the major territorial divisions of the Southwest. Furthermore, it has yielded a great amount of material in regard to the oldest phases of human development in our area. More important still is the fact that the San Juan appears to have been the breeding ground for many of the basic traits of Southwestern culture and center of dissemination.

The San Juan rises in the mountains of southwestern Colorado, and flows in a generally westerly direction through northern New Mexico and southern Utah to empty at last into the Colorado River. Its watershed, if such a term can be applied to country which normally sheds no water, covers an area of some 30,000 square miles.[1] It is for the most part a high, barren, and arid plateau cut by a multitude of dry, sandy washes and equally dry, gorgelike canyons. The San Juan itself carries water throughout its entire length, but its tributaries, except those upper ones which find their source in the parent mountains, contain no living streams, and only run during the early spring or after the violent downpours of the midsummer rainy season. In spite of this great general aridity, the San Juan country, from its peculiar geological formation, possesses a large number of fine springs of clear, pure water. They usually appear at the heads of gorges or at the bases of cliffs, are seldom large, and their overflow sinks at once into the sand, to seep off thus hidden along the rocky beds of the canyons. But these springs

1. For an excellent description of the topography and climate of the San Juan, see Prudden, 1906. Much useful information, and a very complete bibliography, are also to be found in Gregory, 1916.

redeem a land which would otherwise be hopeless for human occupancy, they furnish abundant drinking water for those who know how and where to find them, and their trickling underflow moistens the earth of the valley bottoms just enough to permit the growing of drought-resisting varieties of corn. Many parts of the mesa tops, also, can in favorable years be cultivated. Hard as these conditions would appear to be for an agricultural people, they did not prevent the ancient Pueblos from occupying the country for a long period of time, or from developing there the greatest achievements of their civilization. No one has attempted to compute the number of ruins in the San Juan drainage, but it must run well into the thousands.

To bring some order into so vast an amount of material, it is necessary to make at least a preliminary classification. For this purpose we have depended primarily upon the evidence of pottery; there are:

1. Sites with well-developed pottery (Pueblo ruins).
2. Sites with less-developed pottery (pre-Pueblo ruins).
3. Sites with crude pottery (post-Basket Maker ruins).
4. Sites with no pottery (Basket Maker sites).

Of the first class there are certain ruins which show evidences of high specialization; these may conveniently be considered under the following heads: Chaco Canyon, Mesa Verde, and Kayenta. Each of the groups is named for the district in which the culture producing the characteristic pottery reached its highest development, but it must be understood that the names are by no means geographically descriptive, for the cultures in question all extended beyond the limits of the type localities and, indeed, in some cases even beyond the confines of the San Juan drainage (fig. 12).

Fig. 12. The San Juan area. The different shadings indicate the three principal subcultures; the districts of highest specialization are shown in black. 1. Chaco Canyon. 2. Mesa Verde. 3. Kayenta.

PUEBLO RUINS
(Sites with well-developed pottery)

CHACO CANYON

The enormous ruins that represent the greatest achievement of this culture lie in and near the Chaco Canyon, a southern tributary of the San Juan in northwestern New Mexico. There are in this locality ten or twelve major sites and a considerable number of smaller ones; some of the latter seem to belong to the Chaco Canyon group, while

a

After Jackson

After Judd

Courtesy Nat. Geog. Soc.

LARGE STONE

SCALE OF FEET

b

PLATE 19. Pueblo Bonito. a. Restoration showing interior terracing and high, blank outer wall. b. Ground plan; the circular chambers are kivas, the rectangular structures living rooms.

others are obviously of other types. Of the major ruins the best known are Pueblo Bonito, Chettro Kettle, Pueblo Alto, Peñasca Blanca, and Hungo Pavie. Each of these great buildings contained one hundred or more ground-floor rooms and was terraced from front to back to a height of three, four, or possibly even five stories, thus considerably more than doubling the number of ground-floor chambers. Although they vary considerably in detail, all the Chaco pueblos are alike in general plan. The building normally surrounds three sides of a court, being terraced back from an initial height of one story at the court to three or more stories at the rear, which is always a high blank wall. The third side of the court is enclosed by a tier of one-story rooms, usually bowed outward and connecting the two ends or wings of the main building. Within the court are the kivas, and usually just outside the tier of low rooms lie the rubbish heaps. The frontage is always southerly. The accompanying ground plan and restored elevation (pl. 19) are of Pueblo Bonito, the greatest single structure in the valley; Bonito is in most respects a typical example of Chaco architecture, but differs from the majority of the ruins in being D-shaped rather than rectangular.

Aside from their large size, the Chaco ruins are noteworthy for massive architecture and particularly for excellence of masonry. The walls of the best period are generally made with a hearting of adobe-laid stonework, or rubble, and are finished on the two surfaces with what might be called a veneering of carefully selected tabular stones, evenly arranged in courses that often vary in thickness and thus give the work a very pleasing texture (pl. 20, a). The details of construction, such as the roofs of rooms, the jambs of doorways, and the corners of walls are notable for excellence of finish and accuracy of line. The living rooms are of unusually large size and height.

Our knowledge of the kivas is still incomplete, but they

appear to be of much interest and importance. As we shall often have occasion to refer to the kivas in the various groups of ruins, it may be well to give here a brief description of the principal features of such rooms. The prehistoric kiva was normally a round subterranean chamber, the roof being flush with the ground. Entrance was ordinarily gained by a ladder leading down through a combined hatchway and smoke vent in the roof. In the floor there was always a firepit. Ventilation was supplied by a flue running downwards outside the kiva wall and opening at the floor level. The hot air and smoke from the fireplace passed up and out through the entrance hatchway; fresh, cool air being sucked down the flue and into the room. Such were the essentials of kiva construction; the details of interior arrangement vary greatly from one region to another, but are usually quite uniform for any given culture, thus providing a most useful criterion for classification.

The Chaco Canyon ruins contain kivas of two sorts: great kivas, of which there seems to be but one, or at most two, at each village; and small kivas, of which every village has several. The great kiva is very large, measuring from forty to sixty feet in diameter (pl. 21). The lower part of its wall is encircled by a bench of masonry; near the middle of the floor is a raised fireplace, on either side of which is a rectangular, vaultlike structure of masonry. The central part of the roof was supported by four large pillars. At the north side of each kiva is a sort of antechamber, lying at a higher level, and reached by a ladderlike stairway. In most cases the kiva is surrounded by small rooms, also at a higher level, formed by partitions running out spokelike from the kiva proper to an outer wall surrounding it concentrically.[2]

2. Only three great kivas have so far been excavated, viz. at the Aztec ruin (see Morris, 1921a, for a full description, with discussion of function and relations); at Pueblo Bonito (see Judd, 1922, p. 322, photograph and plan); and at Chettro Kettle (see Hewett, 1922, pp. 121–28).

The small kivas have not as yet been adequately described. Their diameter appears seldom to exceed twenty-
five feet. Like the large structures they have a low bench
about the base of the wall. On the bench are several (six
to ten) small blocks of masonry a foot or so in height, set
at equal distances apart, each one enclosing a short heavy
beam which runs back into the main wall of the kiva.[3] In
the floor there is a central firepit, and under the south side
of the wall runs the intake of the ventilator to open
through the floor near the firepit. To the west of the
firepit is a single rectangular masonry-lined vault (see
pl. 19, b, small kivas). The exact system of roofing is
problematical, but appears to have been by means of a
cribwork of logs, as in Mesa Verde kivas (see p. 196 below,
and pl. 28).[4]

One of the many mysteries of the Chaco is the fact that
in spite of persistent search the cemeteries of the large
ruins have never been found. The burial mounds of the
smaller and apparently earlier sites are obvious, and can
easily be located; but the rubbish heaps of Bonito, Chettro
Kettle, and the other great communities contain no graves
whatever. Although a few bodies have been taken from
rooms,[5] these do not represent a hundredth part of the
number of individuals that must have died during the
occupancy of the towns. There is no hint of cremation,
and so one can only suppose that the Chacones differed
from all other Pueblos of whom we have knowledge in
that they buried their dead at a distance from their houses.
When the cemeteries are eventually discovered, they should
yield a marvellously rich harvest of pottery, ornaments,
and utensils.

3. Pepper, 1920, p. 251, and fig. 104.
4. As to the details of Chaco Canyon kiva construction little has so far
been published, but these and other now puzzling features will soon be
thoroughly understood, when the results of the excavations now being
carried on by the National Geographic Society are published.
5. Moorehead, 1906, p. 34; Pepper, 1909.

In the minor arts the ancient people of the Chaco were no less skilled than in architecture. Their work in wood, in stone, and in the weaving of cotton textiles is very superior. They were remarkably expert in the making of turquoise beads and ornaments, and particularly in the production of inlay work on stone, bone, or wood with small bits of turquoise, jet, and shell.[6] The grooved stone axe is rare and, as elsewhere in the San Juan, is always poorly made. Although several types of sandals were produced, the finest and most characteristic were woven of *apocynum* string. These sandals have pointed toes, and each one bears a small jog or offset on the outer edge (pl. 36, a).[7] This is also the case with Mesa Verde, Kayenta, and other San Juan Pueblo period sandals, and provides a ready means of distinguishing them from the footgear of earlier periods.

Chaco Canyon pottery, as found at the large ruins, forms a typical and easily identifiable group.[8] The two principal wares are corrugated and black-on-white; redware appears, but in such small quantities that it may be disregarded in so general a summary as this.

Most Southwestern pottery was made by laying up on each other rings or spirals of clay, each added ring or turn of the spiral carrying the vessel wall a little higher. All trace of this process was usually obliterated before firing by working over the surfaces of the vessels with the fingers or with a smoothing tool. At certain periods, however, the coiled spiral of clay was allowed to remain unobliterated on the exterior of pots, producing a horizontally ridged or corrugated effect. The coils were furthermore often

6. For illustrations of many Chaco Canyon specimens, see Pepper, 1920. Pl. 1, and figs. 50, 71–74 show examples of turquoise and inlay work.

7. The specimen figured illustrates the characteristic shape. It is of yucca, no example of the fine *apocynum* sandal being available for reproduction.

8. Illustrations of Chaco Canyon pottery are to be found in Pepper, 1906, 1909, 1920; Moorehead, 1906; Chapman, 1921; Goddard, 1921, p. 43.

c

PLATE 20. Masonry of San Juan ruins. a. Chaco Canyon (Pueblo Bonito). b. Mesa Verde (Cliff Palace). c. Kayenta.

pinched and indented as they were applied, giving a still more elaborate texture to the surface. This technique was normally used for the making of cooking pots.[9] Chaco Canyon corrugated ware is well made, the corrugations are unusually sharp and clear-edged, the indentations vary in depth and arrangement to produce a variety of pleasing textures. As to vessel shapes we have as yet few data, but the prevailing form appears to have been a large jar with very wide mouth (fig. 13, a).

Black-on-white ware, which in the Southwest is almost invariably associated with corrugated, occurs in many well-

FIG. 13. Chaco Canyon vessel shapes.

defined local varieties. Qualities common to all black-on-white groups are hardness, clear "ring" when struck, surface slips running from light gray to pure white, and prevailingly geometric decoration in sharp black lines.

The most marked characteristics of the Chaco Canyon variety of black-on-white ware are its very white, almost paper-white, slip and the unusually fine lines of its black decoration. The commonest vessels are bowls, pitchers, and ladles; rare but typical forms are human effigy pots and cylindrical vases.

The bowl (fig. 13, d; pl. 22, e-h) approaches the hemi-

9. For an excellent description of the manufacture of corrugated ware, see Holmes, 1886, p. 273.

spherical in shape, with rounded bottom and curving sides. Examples over twelve inches in diameter are uncommon. The rim is "direct," i.e., not bent inward or flared outward; the actual lip is never flat-topped, but is rounded or even brought to a sharpish edge. The exteriors of bowls are undecorated and, indeed, are often left unslipped; or the slip is run down for an inch or two below the rim. The edge of the rim is painted black (this is a useful diagnostic trait for Chaco Canyon pottery); the black of the edge is often interrupted by a tiny space purposely left unpainted, and this space is sometimes emphasized by the turning down of the ends of the encircling line into little dashes or scrolls on the exterior.

Pitchers occur in two varieties, the large bodied and the small bodied. Although intermediate forms appear, the small-bodied type (fig. 13, b; pl. 22, b–d) is the commoner and more characteristic. Examples run from five to eight inches in height. The neck is tall, either cylindrical or in the form of a truncated cone; the body is low (usually about one-third of the total height), with a rather sharply angled shoulder; the handle is a flat strip of clay running from just below the rim to just above the junction between neck and body; the rim is flatter than in bowls and is generally painted black. The large-bodied type (pl. 22, a; fig. 13, c) is a rounder, usually more capacious, vessel with a small handle.

Ladles are either of the "bowl-and-handle" (fig. 13, e) or the "half-gourd" type (fig. 13, f).

Rarer forms, which appear to be confined to the Chaco Canyon culture, are the cylindrical vase (fig. 13, g)[10] and the effigy pot.[11] The large decorated olla or water jar seems to be much less common than in other black-on-white areas; I have never seen a specimen complete enough to give a good idea as to its shape.

10. Pepper, 1920, pls. 2–6.
11. Pepper, 1906.

The decoration of all the black-on-white pottery of the Southwest is preponderatingly geometric and rectilinear. Although the actual number of design elements employed is not great, they are handled in such a great variety of ways, and used in so many different combinations that a thoroughgoing analysis is necessary before one can really understand the system of ornamentation in any single group. Most groups, however, possess certain characteristic features, certain earmarks, so to speak, which enable one after a little practice to recognize them at once. The earmarks of Chaco Canyon decoration are best shown by a few illustrations and explanatory notes.

In plate 23 is presented a selection of typical Chaco Canyon black-on-white designs. The majority of them are band decorations that encircle the interiors of bowls. The bands may be made up of a repetition of identical units (pl. 23, f, g, h, i), or of an alternation of two different units (pl. 23, e). Most bands are framed above and below by a single black line. Very characteristic of Chaco Canyon work is the use of lines dotted along one side (pl. 23, e, h). The interlocking spiral in one form or another (pl. 23, g, h) is also abundant, as is the sharp-pointed "bat wing" figure (pls. 22, a, b; 23, f, j). Large terraced elements are often outlined with a series of two to four or five thin black lines, which follow accurately the angles of the basic figure (pls. 2, g; 23, a, b). Hatching is perhaps the best earmark of Chaco art; the individual lines used are narrow and often slightly wavy, and they are always framed in or enclosed by outer lines much heavier than themselves (pls. 22, a, d, e, h; 23, c, d). All these qualities are much more clearly brought out by the illustrations than by any verbal description. The drawings also show that there are several quite distinct types of decoration: those based on the outlined terrace figure; those making use of interlocking scrolls; hatched ornaments, etc. Whether these were all contemporaneous parts of a single design system or whether they represent successive phases of a changing system cannot be decided at present. Chapman's studies of the sherds from a rubbish-filled kiva at Chettro Kettle, and Nelson's stratigraphic work in the Pueblo Bonito middens, while not extensive enough for definite results, indicate that the ceramic art, even during the occupancy of the great pueblos, was not at a standstill.[12] The intensive excavations now being carried out by the National Geographic Society and the School of American Research will undoubtedly serve to answer this and many other perplexing questions in regard to the Chaco Canyon ruins.

The archaeology of Chaco Canyon presents many baffling problems. To begin with, the district is little better than a desert; many parts of it, indeed, are absolutely barren wastes of sand and rock which do not even support the usual dry-country flora of the Southwest. It is almost devoid of springs, has no permanent streams, is subject to severe sandstorms, is blistering hot in summer and bitterly cold in winter. It is hard to see how life in the Chaco could have been anything but a continual struggle for bare existence. Yet in this harsh and difficult environment Pueblo culture reached its highest development. The towns are large, excellently constructed, and lie in close proximity to each other. If all of them had been inhabited at the same time, they might well have housed more than 10,000 people. But how so large a population could have supplied itself with the mere necessaries of life, and still had time and energy left for the development of so remarkable a civilization, has puzzled every observer who has visited the Chaco country.

The explanation of course suggests itself that the climate of ancient times was moister than that of today. If such an hypothesis could be accepted, all our difficulties would be removed. The truth is, however, that no convincing evidence has yet been presented to warrant a belief in

12. Chapman, 1921; Nelson in Pepper, 1920, p. 383.

After Morris

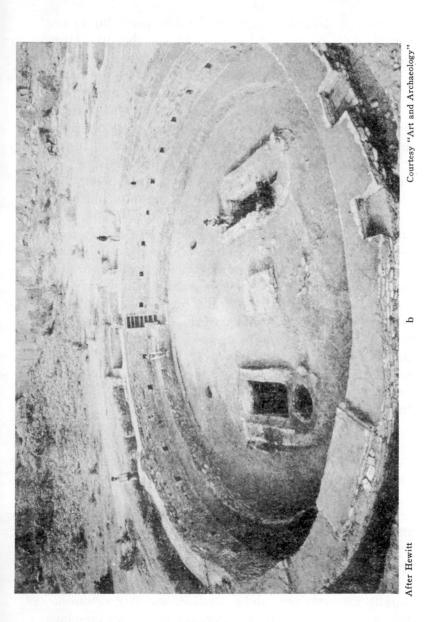

After Hewitt

b

Courtesy "Art and Archaeology"

PLATE 21. The great kiva of the Chaco Canyon culture. a. Plan of the great kiva at Aztec. b. The great kiva at Chettro Kettle.

any marked climatic change in the Southwest during the period of its occupancy by man. Those who, like Huntington,[13] have based their conclusions in large part upon the testimony of the ruins, have failed to realize the ability of the Pueblo Indian to support himself quite comfortably in the face of conditions of dryness which would stagger the white farmer. Such investigators have not taken into consideration how little water the Pueblo Indian actually uses, how carefully he conserves his supply, or how little he thinks of climbing up and down steep, precipitous paths to get it. Furthermore, the modern Pueblo often lives many miles from his cornfields; and numbers of ancient ruins are situated at considerable distances from the nearest land which could ever have been cultivated even under the most favorable climatic conditions. One more point which is often not recognized is that the Indian farms only for himself and his family, while every modern cultivator helps to feed an enormous industrial population which produces no foodstuffs whatever; hence the acreage the white farmer must plant is vastly greater, and no comparison between the amount of cultivable land necessary for his support with that necessary for a Pueblo Indian can have any bearing on the subject.

I think there is no ruin in the entire Southwest that one hundred years ago could not have been successfully reinhabited by Hopi Indians in numbers equal to its ancient population. I say one hundred years ago, because during the past century sheep and cattle have been extensively introduced, and have in many places so denuded the country of grass, and so stripped the soil of the binding protection of the grass roots, that the formation of deep, water-cut gullies has everywhere resulted. The destructive action of such gullies is enormous; not only do they rapidly eat away the adobe earth of the valley bottoms, but they carry off the flood water, and also lower the plane

13. Huntington, 1912, 1914.

PLATE 22. Chaco Canyon black-on-white ware.

of underground seepage to such an extent that the remaining land on either side of them becomes permanently parched.

This very thing has happened in Chaco Canyon. In former times the spring rains and summer showers spread out evenly over the flat floor of the valley, depositing year by year layers of enriching silt, and penetrating and moistening the earth from top to bottom. Now, however, every drop of water is immediately diverted into a deep, steep-sided arroyo, which after every heavy rain becomes a raging torrent, undermining, cutting down, and carrying away more and more of the cultivable soil of the valley.

Thus, the Chaco has recently become less favorable for agriculture than it was in former times, but even so it could never have furnished what one might call an ideal environment. My feeling is that the population of the valley was never over 5,000 or 6,000 souls and that not more than four or five of the large towns were inhabited at any one time. This impression is due to the fact that each of the great ruins was obviously laid out and completed in a relatively short time and according to a preconceived plan. Some of them have been more or less extensively altered, and Bonito shows signs of much remodelling, but few appear to have grown slowly by the accretions of generation after generation of inhabitants. The small extent of the rubbish heaps, as well as the paucity of burials, tends to confirm the belief that not more than one or two of these ruins was continuously occupied for more than, say, one hundred years.

Definite answers to many of these questions will doubtless be provided by the new methods of research now being applied by Judd and his associates. I should not present speculations on matters so soon to be cleared up, were it not for the fact that the remains of Chaco Valley are so important for the study of other manifestations of Southwestern culture that a proper appreciation of the problems of the Chaco is necessary for a true understanding of the archaeology of the rest of the area.

The groups of great ruins that stand as the type of this culture are strung along the Chaco wash for a distance of some thirty miles. The easternmost of them, Pueblo Pintado, situated on the divide between the San Juan and Rio Grande drainages, marks the eastern limit, so far as is known, of the culture. To the south are no large ruins of Chaco type, but the characteristic pottery appears in collections made in the vicinity of Gallup, N. M.[14] The Kintiel ruin on Leroux Wash in northeastern Arizona has been regarded as allied to the Chaco group;[15] but although it shows distinct Chaco influence in architecture, the pottery found there by Fewkes and that observed by me on the surface are by no means typical of the Chaco culture. Not far from Kintiel, however, in the so-called Red Rock country on Black Creek, sixteen miles south of Fort Defiance, Arizona, are sites which produce absolutely typical Chaco pottery;[16] as to the ruins we know nothing, but they are apparently not large. North from the Red Rocks is the Canyon de Chelley, a district notable for its abundance of cliff houses. These dwellings have not been examined by archaeologists for many years, so that our knowledge of their pottery is confined to collections made by "pothunters." In such collections are a few pieces of Chaco-like pottery, though that type is not the prevailing one.

When we turn to the north we find clearer evidence for extensions of the culture. In many of the lots of pottery, excavated and sold to museums by the commercial diggers

14. Specimens in the Peabody Museum of Harvard University. Chaco influence is also to be seen in certain early kivas in the Zuñi country (Hodge, 1923).

15. Fewkes, 1904, p. 127.

16. Collection in Brooklyn Institute of Arts and Sciences. This district should not be confounded with the Red Rock country of the Verde River, described in Fewkes, 1896.

of the nineties, are pieces from Montezuma Valley, Mc-
Elmo Canyon and the mesas of southeastern Utah; among
these are almost always to be found examples which more
or less resemble Chaco vessels. These pots are seldom of
the most pronounced Chaco types; they give one the impression of being either the product of a peripheral
development affected by Chaco influence, or of an earlier
and less specialized stage of the Chaco culture. Morris has
recently demonstrated that the great kiva with radiating
rooms about it is an integral part of the Chaco Canyon
system of architecture, and has called attention to the apparent extension of this kiva form across the Mesa Verde
and west into the Montezuma Valley.[17] Although we do
not know the exact provenience of the Chaco-like vessels
in the pothunters' collections from this district, it is probable that both they and the great kivas may indicate a
northwestern spread or a northwestern origin of the Chaco
culture.

In the northeast there is definite evidence of Chaco influence, shown by the architecture and ceramics of a ruin
discovered by Jeancon in the Pagosa Springs region of
Archuleta County, Colorado.[18] The actual building is not
large, yet its masonry is distinctly Chacoan, and its kivas
are of the same low-benched type as the small kivas of the
Chaco; although not built in a radiating manner, there
is a hint of great-kiva arrangement in the small rooms
surrounding one of them.[19]

The clearest and most interesting occurrence of Chaco
culture outside the limits of the actual Chaco Canyon district is furnished by the great Aztec ruin. This site lies
about sixty-five miles north of Pueblo Bonito on the lower
waters of the Animas River, a northern tributary of the
San Juan. The Aztec ruin is architecturally a perfect ex-

17. Morris, 1921a, p. 138.
18. Jeancon, 1922, pp. 14 ff.
19. Roberts, 1922, pl. 3.

PLATE 23. Designs of Chaco Canyon black-on-white ware.

ample of a Chaco pueblo, not only in ground plan but in
the most minute details of construction. The pottery, however, from the surface of the mounds is equally typical
of the Mesa Verde culture. I formerly believed, as did
Morris,[20] that this indicated a hybrid settlement, but
Morris's thorough excavations have resulted in the important discovery that Aztec was built and occupied by Chaco
people, whose characteristic pottery he found in the lower
strata of the rubbish; and was later reinhabited, apparently after a period of abandonment, by Mesa Verde col-
onists.[21] Thus we can be certain that the Mesa Verde
culture outlived the Chaco in the north at least, and it
seems probable that it survived it generally, for in certain of the rooms excavated by Pepper at Pueblo Bonito
there were found Mesa Verde potsherds, and these were
in sufficient abundance to indicate that those rooms had
actually been occupied for some time by Mesa Verde people at a time subsequent to the abandonment of the
pueblo by its original builders. The reoccupation could
not have been extensive or prolonged, as Mesa Verde
sherds are not found about Bonito or any of the other
Chaco ruins to the extent to which they occur at Aztec.[22]

While the above evidence shows that the Mesa Verde
culture held on in the San Juan somewhat longer than
did the Chaco Canyon civilization, it is equally certain
that the former was not an outgrowth of the latter, but

20. Kidder-Guernsey, 1919, p. 201; Morris, 1919a, p. 106.
21. Morris, 1921a, p. 136.
22. The rooms in question are nos. 59, 88, 109 (see Pepper, map, fig.
155); the fact that they contained almost exclusively Mesa Verde sherds
was noted during an examination of the Bonito collection in the American
Museum of Natural History, New York. I did not go over the entire
collection, so that it is possible that the same conditions obtained in other
rooms. I have inferred, on the analogy of the Aztec finds, that the Mesa
Verde sherds are of late date; but it is of course conceivable that the
reverse may have been the case; Judd's excavations will undoubtedly clear
up this important question of relative chronology.

that the two more or less overlapped in time. This is proved by the finding by Nelson of Mesa Verde sherds in the middle strata of the Bonito rubbish heap.[23]

We have so far concerned ourselves principally with the larger ruins which architecturally or ceramically seem to belong to the Chaco Canyon culture. In the Chaco Canyon itself, however, and out from it in all directions to a distance not yet established by exploration, are other ruins, smaller in size, less elaborate architecturally, and containing less highly specialized pottery. A few of the larger of these may well be of the true Chaco culture; but the majority are small, are very badly ruined, and as regards pottery are obviously different from the great dwellings. Their wares are corrugated and black-on-white. The corrugated is often very elaborately decorated with wavings and indentations of the coil; it is, in fact, in many ways the finest corrugated pottery of the entire Southwest. The black-on-white is hard to characterize, partly because so few well located whole pieces are available, partly because it seems to be of a generalized type vaguely resembling Chaco ware, but without any readily grasped peculiarities. As to the structure of these small ruins in and near the Chaco region, nothing is known, as none of them have yet been excavated. Morris,[24] however, has demonstrated the presence of an early black-on-white Pueblo period in the San Juan, a period antedating that of the large ruins; and from his description of its characteristics (small houses, excellent coiled ware, etc.) it would seem that these little sites must belong to it, and must therefore represent a stage in culture antecedent to that of the great Chaco pueblos, which would thus appear to have been the latest inhabited dwellings in the district. The studies of San Juan archaeology now being carried on by Morris can con-

23. Pepper, 1920, p. 384.
24. Morris, 1921.

fidently be expected to settle the age and affinities of these inconspicuous but most important sites.

MESA VERDE

The type locality for this culture is the Mesa Verde, a large plateau in the drainage of the Mancos River in southwestern Colorado. This country is a much better one than the Chaco Canyon. It is higher, nearer the mountains, and so receives considerably more rainfall in summer and more snow in winter. The top of the mesa supports a heavy growth of cedar and pinyon, in certain favorable spots there are good stands of spruce; springs are relatively abundant. The mesa is cut by a series of deep canyons, in the upper walls of which are many very large caves. Although a number of ruins are found on the level uplands of the plateau, the largest and most characteristic settlements are the great cliff houses that are built in the shelter of the caves. Cliff Palace and Sprucetree House are excellent examples, which may well serve as types.

The ground plan of a cliff house is naturally dependent upon the shape of the cave which contains it. Most caves, not only in the Mesa Verde, but also throughout the sandstone formations of the Southwest in general, lie at the top of rocky talus. The floor slopes upward more or less steeply, and at the rear often flattens out to a semicircular platform hugging the back wall of the cave. The roof arches high overhead.

When such caves were used as village sites the first houses were naturally built along the flatter portions of the rear platform, then the irregular places were levelled up and utilized, and finally terraces were constructed upon the sloping front floor to provide still further space for foundations. Because of the cramped conditions room was often piled on room, sometimes clear to the roof of the caves, the buildings reaching a height of several stories. So strongly does the structure of such caves influence the

FIG. 14.

shapes of the buildings that it has been thought that the peculiar crowded room grouping and terraced arrangement typical of pueblo architecture must have originated in the cliff houses.[25]

The accompanying ground plan (fig. 14) is that of Cliff

25. Cushing, 1886, p. 479. The arguments advanced are very convincing. This is, however, a question which involves the entire history of pueblo architecture. It cannot be discussed in the present paper, but it may be pointed out that there surely was no such thing as a true cliff-dwelling period, when all houses were built in caves. The cave, as a house site, has always been the exception rather than the rule; and while cave occupation may have had some influence on the form of pueblo dwellings, their basic peculiarities will, I feel sure, eventually be traced to other sources.

Palace, one of the largest known cliff dwellings. It contains about ninety-five ground-floor rooms and twenty-three kivas, the former clustering about the rear of the cave, the latter lying in general to the front (pl. 24). This is the normal arrangement in cliff houses both on the Mesa Verde and elsewhere.

The masonry of Cliff Palace is typical of the other Mesa Verde ruins. It is much less massive than Chaco stonework, but is composed of larger individual stones (pl. 20, b), often hewn to shape, carefully coursed, and brought to an even surface on the face of the wall by a pecking process that results in a characteristic dimpled texture. Rooms are more irregular in shape and smaller in size than those of the Chaco ruins; they appear to have been added on as needed. Mesa Verde villages seem always to have started in a modest way and grown by accretion; I do not know of a single large secular building of this culture that gives evidence of having been erected at one time and according to a preconceived plan.

The Mesa Verde kivas are fairly uniform in size, and in the details of interior arrangement. They average about thirteen feet in diameter. All of them are either actually subterranean or, if the exigencies of the site will not permit that, are surrounded by retaining walls, packed about with earth and so put technically at least underground (pl. 28; reference should be had to this plate and to fig. 17 to make clear the details of the following description). It was evidently a strict requirement that kivas should be below the surface, and in essence all of them are merely holes in the ground lined with masonry. Orthodoxy no less stringent is seen in construction. The typical kiva is as nearly round as its builders could make it. At about three feet from the floor the wall is set back a foot or more, thus leaving a narrow bench encircling the room. On this bench are built six masonry pilasters two to three feet high. Their tops come to within two or three feet of the

PLATE 24a. Cliff Palace, Mesa Verde, Colorado. The many round and square towers incorporated in the building are typical of the larger Mesa Verde cliff houses.

PLATE 24b. Cliff Palace, Mesa Verde, Colorado.

PLATE 24c. Cliff Palace, Mesa Verde, Colorado.

surface. The pilasters produce in the upper wall of the chamber six broad recesses. All the recesses are of equal width, but the southernmost is very much deeper than the others. The roof is made by laying short beams from pilaster to pilaster all around the kiva; a second set of beams is then laid across the angles made by the first set. By such cribwork the structure is gradually extended upward, and drawn together into a domed roof, which is completed by horizontal beams laid across the remaining opening, but leaving space for a combined ladder hole and smoke vent.[26]

Just outside the back wall of the deep south recess a small flue leads vertically down. When it reaches the level of the kiva floor it turns inward, runs under the floor of the recess, and opens into the chamber itself. An imaginary line drawn straight across the floor from the mouth of the ventilator bisects the other standard kiva appurtenances. First, and lying two to three feet from the ventilator opening, comes a wall-like erection of masonry or wattlework, two or three feet wide and of about the same height. This evidently acted as a screen or deflector to prevent the draught which is sucked down the flue from blowing too directly upon the fire, as well as to distribute the air more generally through the room. Behind the deflector is the firepit, a round depression, with a coping of adobe which rises a little above the floor level. Lastly, still in the same line, and usually situated about halfway between the firepit and the north wall of the kiva is a carefully made little hole, round, three or four inches in diameter and five or six inches deep. This has been identified with the *sipapu* or symbolical entrance to the underworld found in Hopi kivas.[27] Such is the normal kiva of

26. Fewkes, 1920, figs. 54, 55, gives photographs of models that illustrate very clearly the roofing of Mesa Verde kivas. See also Fewkes, 1908.
27. By Fewkes, who was the first to study intensively the kivas of prehistoric ruins, work out their roofing system and explain the true sig-

the Mesa Verde culture. Minor variations are found, but in general the type is very strictly adhered to even in the smallest details.

Besides living rooms and kivas most large dwellings of the Mesa Verde culture contain one or more towerlike structures (pl. 24). These may be round, oval, D-shaped, or rectangular in ground plan. Their exact function is not understood; many of them were doubtless ceremonial in nature; but from the fact that they are often loopholed in such a way as to command by archery the approaches to the villages, they are usually referred to as watchtowers. Not only do towers occur in the cliff houses and pueblos, but very commonly they are found at a distance from the larger settlements, occupying points easily defended and having a wide outlook over the surrounding country.[28]

As was the case at the Chaco ruins, the cemeteries of the large Mesa Verde dwellings have never been located. Although a few burials have turned up in rubbish heaps, in sealed rooms, and under floors, as well as a few among the rocks of the talus slopes below the houses, not enough have been discovered to account for a hundredth part of the bodies which must have been disposed of. Dr. Fewkes found in Cliff Palace some evidence of cremation,[29] but in view of the rarity of this practice in the San Juan drainage, it does not seem to me conclusive enough to discourage further efforts to locate cemeteries.

The minor arts of the Mesa Verde culture have been well described by Nordenskiold, Fewkes, and Morris.[30] In most ways they do not appear to differ greatly from

nificance of the ventilator and deflector (see Fewkes, 1908 and 1920). Richard Wetherill, however, evidently recognized the purpose of the ventilating apparatus, as he calls the deflector a "wind-wall" (1894, p. 288).

28. For a discussion of the functions of towers, see Fewkes, 1919. Certain isolated ceremonial buildings, of which "Sun Temple" and "Fire Temple" are examples, are described by Fewkes (1916 and 1921).

29. Fewkes, 1910; and 1911, pp. 39 and 77.

30. Nordenskiold, 1893; Fewkes, 1909, 1911a; 1916a; Morris, 1919.

the minor arts of Chaco Canyon, although in general there
is less richness of materials, and less perfection of workmanship. The decorated pottery, however, is entirely distinct, even small sherds being easily distinguishable.[31]

The wares are corrugated, black-on-white, and a very
small percentage red.

Corrugated vessels are of two sorts: large jars with wide
mouths and egg-shaped bodies (fig. 15, b), and small
pitcherlike jugs with single handles. The workmanship of

FIG. 15. Mesa Verde vessel shapes.

the large jars is very fine; the walls are thin, the corrugations regular, the indentations evenly spaced, and the
proportions remarkably symmetrical.

Mesa Verde black-on-white ware may be recognized by
its clear, pearly, grayish-white slip, which seems to have a
certain softness and "depth" not found in other groups.
The surface of the vessels is carefully polished, so highly

31. Good illustrations of Mesa Verde type pottery are to be found in:
Nordenskiold, 1893; Morley, 1908; Fewkes, 1909, 1911a, 1922; Prudden,
1914; Morris, 1915, 1919.

in some cases as to produce a distinct gloss. There are four standard shapes: ollas, bowls, mugs, ladles; less common vessels are kiva-jars, pitchers, seed jars, and canteens.

The Mesa Verde olla (fig. 15, g) is generally twelve to fourteen inches high; it has a full, globular body and short cylindrical neck; at or slightly below the point of greatest diameter is set a pair of horizontally placed loop handles, which almost always tend to rake slightly downwards.

Bowls run from three to four inches up to fourteen or even fifteen inches in diameter. The smaller examples usually have rather flat bottoms and steeply rising sides; the larger pieces, those ten inches or more in diameter, show no distinct change in angle between sides and bottom, there being a very even curve from rim to rim (fig. 15, a; pl. 25). The ware is usually a full quarter of an inch thick, and this thickness of the vessel wall is carried clear to the edge without any thinning or bevelling. Thus a very square, flat rim is produced, which is one of the most characteristic features of Mesa Verde bowls.

Mugs (fig. 15, d) are in shape much like small German beer "steins." They are three to six or seven inches high, have flat bottoms and straight or slightly bulging sides that converge somewhat toward the orifice. The single flat handle with which these mugs are always provided, runs from just above the base to a point a trifle below the rim. The rim is usually square, as in the case of the larger bowls. Mugs range from three and one-half to six inches in height.

Ladles are apparently exclusively of the "bowl-and-handle" variety (fig. 15, c); each one has a small, complete bowl three to four and one-half inches in diameter, to the outside of which is luted a handle six to eight inches long. The handle is usually round and almost always hollow; sometimes it contains tiny pebbles or balls of clay, which act as rattles. I know of no case of the "half-

a

c

e

After Morris

Courtesy Am. Mus. Nat. Hist.

b

d

f

PLATE 25. Black-on-white bowls of the Mesa Verde culture.

gourd" ladle having been found in association with true
Mesa Verde ware.

Of the less common forms, the vessel for which I suggest
the name kiva-jar is interesting because it seems to occur
only in Mesa Verde sites or in sites obviously related to
the Mesa Verde culture. Kiva-jars vary greatly in size,
running from six to eighteen inches in diameter, but in
shape they are very uniform (fig. 15, f). The body is of
flattened spherical form, with a round orifice three to
three and one-half inches in diameter on the top. The
distinguishing feature is a ridge one-fourth to three-fourths
of an inch high, which so encircles the orifice as to leave
between it and the ridge a narrow ledge for the reception
of a cover or lid. Much the same practice is followed in
making our modern teapots and sugar bowls. With each
jar is usually found its lid, a neatly made pottery disc
with a small knob or loop for a handle. The name kiva-
jar is applied to these vessels because the great majority of
them have been found in ceremonial rooms.

Seed jars are called "heart-shaped bowls" by Holmes,[32]
a misleading term, as the objects are not bowls at all.
"Seed jar" is, perhaps, little better, but the vessels have
often been found containing seeds, and it is possible that
this may have been their primary purpose. They average
about seven inches in height by eleven inches in diameter,
and are characterized by a rounded bottom; they grow
gradually larger toward the top, and the greatest diameter
is usually near the greatest height. The top is flattish, but
not truly flat, and the orifice small. The walls are sometimes depressed to the mouth, sometimes slightly raised,
but there is in no case any trace of neck or lip. Some
examples show a set of four, six, or eight small holes about
the mouth, which seem to have served for suspending the
vessels.

The canteen is a small spherical vessel seven or eight

32. Holmes, 1886, p. 306. See pl. 34, c, for an illustration of a seed jar.

inches high, with short, raised neck and very small orifice. Two small loop handles, one on either side of the neck, served for the attachment of a carrying string. In the National Museum there is a specimen from Sprucetree House with a yucca cord still in place.[33]

The decoration of Mesa Verde black-on-white ware is, with the exception of certain zoomorphic figures on bowl exteriors (fig. 16), pretty strictly geometric. It is neverthe-

FIG. 16. Exterior decorations of Mesa Verde bowls.

less bold and free. Large, striking elements are used, and the contrast between them and the clear, pearly-white slip is very pleasing. The earmarks of Mesa Verde design are: the use of balanced sets of framing lines above and below band decorations (pl. 26), the prevalence of patterns, either continuous (pl. 25, c, f) or of repeated units (fig. 16; pl. 25, b), on bowl exteriors, and the common occurrence of large designs in solid black and hatching which cover the entire interiors of bowls (pl. 25, c, e). Mesa

33. Fewkes, 1909, pl. 20, b.

PLATE 26. Designs of Mesa Verde black-on-white ware.

Verde hatching may be distinguished from that of Chaco
Canyon by the coarser quality of the component lines, and
by the fact that the lines which edge the hatched areas are
of approximately the same weight as the hatching lines;
whereas in Chaco Canyon work the bordering lines are
much heavier than the hatching itself (compare pls. 25, e,
and 22, e, h). The normal pattern, however, is the band
(pl. 26); it is seldom if ever panelled, but is occupied by
a repetition of a single unit or pair of opposed units, these
elements being almost always some form of triangle or key
figure.

The foregoing description of the Mesa Verde culture is
based on the study of the architecture and pottery of the
cliff houses and pueblos of the Mesa Verde proper. Similar
ruins are found in abundance along the Mancos River and
in its eastern tributaries. The Aztec pueblo and the Bloom-
field ruin were occupied by Mesa Verde people subsequent to their abandonment by their original Chaco
tenants; and Mesa Verde pottery appears in certain rooms
of Pueblo Bonito. These seem to mark the eastern and
southern limits of the culture, nor was there any extension
of it to the north. When we turn to the west, however,
we find many Mesa Verde remains.

West of the Mesa Verde and extending as far as the
Colorado River, there is a great stretch of upland covered
by cedar and pinyon, drained by the following northern
tributaries of the San Juan: the McElmo, Montezuma
Creek, Recapture, and Cottonwood Canyons, and Grand
Gulch. These tributaries and the mesas lying between
them are literally crowded with ruins of all sorts; there
are probably more archaeological sites to the square mile
in this district than in any other equal area in the entire
Southwest. Unfortunately the study of the antiquities of
the district is still very incomplete; and were it not for
the work of Prudden and Fewkes we should know next to
nothing about it. A certain number of ruins, however,

may safely be classed as of Mesa Verde type, and many others are of a type somewhat less well marked but which may nevertheless be considered as bearing a close relationship to the Mesa Verde culture.

Of the definitely Mesa Verde settlements a good example is the Cannonball pueblo, near the junction of the McElmo and the Yellow Jacket. It occupies a site of a kind very frequently chosen for habitations of late period in the northern San Juan country, namely the rimrock about the head of a steep-walled canyon. The ruins consist of two houses, one on either side of the canyon head, and a square tower perched on the top of a large rock in the canyon itself. One of the two main houses was excavated by Morley, and proved to consist of some thirty ground-floor rooms, a round tower, and seven kivas. In its masonry, its kiva construction, and its pottery the Cannonball pueblo closely resembles the type ruins of the Mesa Verde.[34]

Of the many other sites in the neighborhood of the junction of the McElmo, the Yellow Jacket, and the Hovenweep, very little is actually known. They have often been described, but no investigator has so far paid any attention to their pottery, the best criterion for the classification of unexcavated ruins. Lacking such evidence we must turn to architecture. The most characteristic features of pure Mesa Verde construction are, it seems to me, the block-stone masonry and the use of round, rectangular, or D-shaped towers. I exclude the six-pilastered kiva, for that structure, as will be shown presently, is also found in ruins of slightly different type; kivas, too, can seldom be examined without excavation.

Using block-stone masonry and the presence of towers as criteria, we are led to believe that a number of sites in this district should be classed as of Mesa Verde culture. Among them are the Yellow Jacket spring ruin, ruins in

34. See Morley, 1908.

Hovenweep, Bridge, Holly, and Square Tower Canyons (pl. 27, b), and a large site just below the confluence of the McElmo and the Yellow Jacket. The westernmost example of the type, far as I know, is a pueblo at the head of an unnamed canyon which runs into Montezuma Creek from Alkali Ridge.

Proto-Mesa Verde ruins. This term is tentatively used to designate a large and very important class of ruins which are in many ways similar to typical Mesa Verde structures, yet differ from them in being in most respects less highly developed.

These dwellings were first recognized and described by Prudden.[35] The house (fig. 17 and pl. 28) consists of a single or double row of one-story rooms. Sometimes there are also short right-angled wings extending outward from either end. Directly south of the house lies a kiva; and south of the kiva is a rubbish-heap burial mound. Prudden observed that groups of this nature were very abundant in the northern San Juan country between the Mesa Verde in Colorado and Comb Wash in Utah; and that they were normally built in unencumbered situations in open country, as on mesa tops or in broad valleys. He further noticed that the characteristic unit, consisting of a series of living rooms, a kiva, and a burial mound, was employed in the construction of certain very much larger settlements, each of which appeared to be merely a consolidation or grouping together of a number of the villages; and, finally, that the latest and most highly developed structures of the San Juan, such as Cliff Palace and Pueblo Bonito were also laid out on the same general plan as the little mesa-top hamlets. He accordingly called the small houses "unit-type" dwellings, and advanced the theory that they represented the unit or germ of the characteristic pueblo method of house building.

It was natural to suppose that if the unit-type ruins

35. Prudden, 1903, p. 234.

a

b

PLATE 27a. Proto-Mesa Verde pottery. b. Towers in Ruin Canyon, Utah.

N

Scale
4 Feet

FIG. 17. Ground plan of unit-type dwelling. (After Prudden.)

were at the bottom, so to speak, of the ladder, they would prove to be at least fairly primitive in such important features as kiva construction and pottery. Prudden excavated several unit-type ruins, and from the published results[36] the surprising fact appears that far from being primitive the kivas are as uniform in plan, and as highly specialized in details, as any kivas known; while the pottery bears strong resemblance to that of the great ruins of the Mesa Verde.

This "maturity" of the unit type was to me at first very perplexing, but further consideration leads to the belief that Prudden's original thesis, that the unit-type holds the germ of true Pueblo architecture, is correct. It really serves to explain many hitherto puzzling phenomena and to emphasize the extreme importance of the role that the San Juan has played in the cultural history of the Southwest. We must, however, be ready for the discovery of still more primitive, yet typically Puebloan, villages in the San Juan area. Discussion of this question must be deferred until the rest of the evidence has been presented.

The unit-type ruins excavated by Prudden proved to be built of masonry much less perfect than that seen in the large pueblos and cliff houses of the Mesa Verde and in the canyon-head settlements of the McElmo. The kivas were uniformly six-pilastered, with deep southern recess, ventilator, deflector, firepit, and sipapu (fig. 17 and pl. 28). One feature which is rare in the kivas of the Mesa Verde culture[37] is present in all the unit-type examples excavated by Prudden, namely an underground passageway running back from the north recess and opening upwards through a manhole into one of the adjacent rooms of the dwelling.

The pottery is corrugated and black-on-white, with a

36. Prudden, 1914 and 1918.
37. Seen only in Kiva A of Cliff Palace and Kiva D of Sprucetree House, Fewkes, 1919, p. 42, note 2; absent from Cannonball ruin.

PLATE 28. Section of a kiva and dwelling house. Photograph of Dr. Prudden's model of an early unit-type settlement. The cribbed log roof supported by masonry pilasters is found in the Pueblo kivas of the northern San Juan. This particular variety of kiva is typical of the Mesa Verde and proto-Mesa Verde ruins.

very small percentage of red. The black-on-white vessels resemble in shape those of the Mesa Verde; there is the olla with down-raking handles, the bowl-and-handle ladle, and the mug (pl. 27, a). The kiva-jar also occurs. The bowls,. however, tend to have steeper sides, less pronouncedly squared rims, and much less of exterior decoration. The designs are not so involved, and certain typical Mesa Verde elements, such as the split and toothed triangle (pl. 26, f), are rare or absent.

Unit-type sites complying with these general specifications are found, as Prudden says, most commonly from the Mesa Verde to Comb Wash. It is possible that they are present on the Mesa Verde itself, and I have record of a similar ruin on the mesa between White Canyon and Grand Gulch. South of the San Juan the type appears to change, ceramically at least; but the architecture of the small dwellings in the open of that region is very little known, no excavations in them having as yet been published.

Of larger aggregations, formed of several unit-type houses gathered together, there seem to be numbers north of the San Juan. Such settlements are easily distinguishable from the compact Mesa Verde type pueblos that occur in the same range, by the fact that they are usually built in the open country rather than about canyon heads, by their straggling arrangement, mediocre masonry, lack of towers, and particularly by their somewhat less specialized pottery. Excavations have only been carried out in a single instance, at a large ruin on Alkali Ridge, Montezuma Creek, Utah. Here the grouping together of a number of unit types is very clear, the pueblo being made up of sets of living rooms, each set having its own kivas and burial mounds.[38] The kivas are identical with Prudden's, even to the passage running back from the north recess.[39]

38. Kidder, 1910, fig. 2.
39. This feature was not recognized as such during the original excava-

To sum up, in country occupied by typical Mesa Verde sites there occur many small unit-type settlements, and a number of larger ones composed of several unit-types loosely amalgamated. The kivas are very uniform in construction, more so, indeed, than in true Mesa Verde dwellings; the masonry is inferior to that of the Mesa Verde houses and the pottery is somewhat less specialized. It is difficult to escape the conclusion that the three classes: unit type, multiple unit type, Mesa Verde type, are all parts of a single cultural sequence of which the Mesa Verde remains are the culmination. Hence the term proto-Mesa Verde, used to describe the first two stages, is perhaps justifiable; the truth, however, can only be ascertained by more detailed comparative studies, supported if possible by stratigraphic evidence.

There are other ruins in the area which we have been considering that appear to belong to a still earlier period. They are low, inconspicuous mounds, sprinkled with fragments of archaic looking pottery. No excavation has been done in any of them, but in general appearance their wares seem to be allied to those of the small, old sites of the Chaco country.[40]

KAYENTA

South of the San Juan and west of the Chinlee there is a broad stretch of sandy desert. Still further to the west the land rises in a succession of high mesas, finally culminating in the round-topped mass of Navajo Mountain. The country is remarkably rugged, gashed with numberless rock-walled gorges, cut across by great jagged black dykes, and dotted over with buttes carved by erosion into

tion, and is therefore not mentioned in the report; in my field notes I find reference to a "hole in the earth" which is surely such a passage.

40. A preliminary account of such a site, "Pipe Shrine House" on the Mesa Verde, has just appeared (Fewkes, 1923).

the most fantastic forms. These uplands, though comparatively dry, receive more rainfall and contain more springs
than do the lower flats along the San Juan.

Near the edge of the mesas lies the trading post of
Kayenta, Arizona, and within a distance of fifteen or
twenty miles from it are found the large ruins which
mark the culmination of the Kayenta culture. The type
locality is Sagi Canyon, a tributary of Laguna Creek,
which in turn empties, when it has water to empty, into
the Chinlee.

The sites are both cliff houses and pueblos, but, as was
the case on the Mesa Verde, the cliff houses have been
more thoroughly worked, and are better known than the
pueblos. The largest are Kietsiel (fig. 18 and pl. 29, b)
and Betatakin (pl. 29, a), the former containing about one
hundred and fifty, the latter about one hundred ground-
floor rooms.

The architectural differences between these dwellings
and the ones previously considered are numerous and
important. The masonry is inferior in finish, being composed of irregularly shaped stones not very accurately
coursed, and laid up with a great deal of adobe mortar (pl.
20, c); wattlework walls, rarely seen on the Mesa Verde
and in the Chaco, are relatively common. The round
towers, which add so much picturesqueness to the Mesa
Verde cliff houses, do not appear.

The greatest difference is seen in the kivas. Those of
Kietsiel have not been excavated, but from surface indications seem to be round, semisubterranean rooms without pilasters, and to have a single deep recess with a
ventilating shaft opening behind it (see fig. 18). A second
type of ceremonial chamber is a square aboveground apartment, entered by a door in one of the short walls, and
containing a deflector (to cut off the draft from the door,
there being no ventilating apparatus), and a firepit. Fewkes

a

PLATE 29. Kayenta cliff houses. a. A corner of Betatakin.

b

PLATE 29 b. Eastern end of Kietsiel, Sagi Canyon, northern Arizona.

Fig. 18. Ground plan of Kietsiel cliff house, Sagi Canyon, Arizona.

suggests calling such structures "kihus." [41] Kietsiel contains both kivas and kihus; Betatakin, on the other hand,
has only kihus, while Bat Woman House has nothing but
round kivas. The ceremonial room situation, in the larger
Kayenta sites at least, is a difficult one to understand, particularly as the pottery from all these ruins appears to be
of exactly the same type.[42]

There also exist large surface sites with pottery that
seems to be of normal Kayenta types. Those in Marsh
Pass alone have so far been investigated.[43] They are loose
aggregations of houses, each house consisting of a block
fifty to one hundred feet long, made up of a single or
double row of two-story rooms. The masonry, which is
superior to that of the cliff houses just described, is composed of large stones, fairly well coursed. The kivas of
these surface pueblos are round and subterranean, with
firepit, ventilator, and deflector, but without pilasters.
They lie near the houses, but unlike the Mesa Verde and
Chaco Canyon kivas, are not incorporated in the house
clusters.

No burials have been discovered in the large Kayenta
cliff houses, but a number of interments of the same
period came to light during the writer's excavations at
the surface pueblos of Marsh Pass. The bodies were placed
in oval grave pits dug in the rubbish deposits near the
houses; they were closely flexed, and were usually accompanied by mortuary pottery.[44]

In view of the apparent complexity of the archaeological conditions in these large ruins, and the present dif-

41. Fewkes, 1911, p. 15, note a. No plans or drawings of kihus have been
published; the only descriptions are in Fewkes, 1911, pp. 14, 15, 17, and
pl. 14; see also Cummings, 1915, p. 277.

42. Professor Cummings has done a great amount of work in this district; the publication of his notes will throw much light on many now
obscure problems.

43. Cummings, 1910, p. 28; Fewkes, 1911, p. 10; Kidder-Guernsey, 1919,
p. 61.

44. Kidder-Guernsey, 1919, pp. 66–70.

ficulty of recognizing characteristic architectural traits, it is a relief to turn to the pottery, where the types are well-marked, and easily distinguishable from those of any other region in the entire San Juan drainage. The following brief description is based on specimens from Kietsiel, Betatakin, and the surface pueblos of Marsh Pass.[45]

The wares are corrugated, polychrome, and black-on-white.

The corrugated ware is somewhat inferior in execution to that of Mesa Verde and Chaco Canyon. The coils are

FIG. 19. Kayenta vessel shapes.

less regular in width, and are sometimes not carefully indented. Only one or two whole jars have been recovered; they are fat, round-bodied pots with large apertures (fig. 19, b), quite different in shape from the graceful corrugated vessels of Mesa Verde (fig. 15, b) and of the proto-Kayenta sites.[46]

Black-on-white is characterized by fine, hard paste, clear, white slip, and excellence of decoration. The common

45. So little material from the large Kayenta ruins has found its way into museums that the classification here given is necessarily tentative.

46. Cf. Kidder-Guernsey, 1919, pl. 58, g, h.

PLATE 30. Kayenta black-on-white pottery.

Courtesy Peabody Museum

vessels are ollas, bowls, ladles, and colanders. Much less common forms are small handled jugs similar to those of polychrome ware, and seed-jars. Cylindrical mugs, tall pitchers, and kiva-jars do not, apparently, occur at all except as trade pieces.

The large Kayental olla is exceedingly rare in collections, but from an examination of the sherds at Kietsiel and Betatakin, it is obvious that many such vessels were in use. Our outline (fig. 19, g) is from Holmes.[47] The flattish upper-body appears to be typical. A second variety with more sloping shoulders was also made (pl. 30, g). There are no handles, nor do ever appear, as far as I can discover, on any Kayenta olla. A small flat-topped olla (fig. 19, c) appears to be fairly common.

Bowls are approximately hemispherical, run four or five up to twelve or thirteen inches in diameter, and have either straight (fig. 19, f) or slightly out-curved rims (fig. 19, a). The larger examples tend to be deeper in proportion to width and to lack the outcurved rim. A single horizontally placed loop handle is a common feature of Kayenta bowls (fig. 19, f; pl. 30, d, f), and is never, or almost never, seen on bowls of any other black-on-white group. Decoration is confined to the interior.

Ladles are all of the "bowl-and-handle" variety (fig. 19, d). They average nine inches long. The handle may be either a solid bar, a hollow tube, or, less commonly, an elongated loop of clay.

The colander is a little seed jar-shaped vessel three to six inches in diameter with a fairly large orifice (fig. 19, e; pl. 30, a). Each one has a number of small holes in the bottom (pl. 30, b), evidently fitting it for use as a sifter or strainer. The colander is confined, so far as I know, to the Kayenta culture.

The decoration of Kayenta black-on-white pottery is

47. 1886, fig. 327. The exact provenience of this specimen is unknown, but it is of sound Kayenta type.

a

b

c

d

PLATE 31. Designs of Kayenta black-on-white ware.

very elaborate. As the illustrations (pls. 30, 31) show, the most marked characteristic is the close-set arrangement of the elements. Little of the white background is allowed to appear, and the drawing of the interlocking frets, keys and spirals is often extraordinarily accurate. The use of an underframework, so to speak, of parallel or cross-hatched lines is the best earmark of this ware. In the finest examples the cross-hatching gives a sort of mosquito-bar effect.

Polychrome pottery is abundant at Kietsiel, Betatakin, and the surface pueblos of March Pass. It occurs in the form of bowls and small, handled jars; polychrome ollas, ladles, or seed jars seem not to have been made. The base color of this ware is yellow or orange, and the decoration is applied in black, red, and white.

Polychrome bowls average about ten inches in diameter, but examples as large as fourteen inches across are occasionally met with. Most bowls have outcurving rims and bear a single horizontal handle on the upper part of the exterior. Exterior ornament is confined to one or two heavy, carelessly drawn lines that encircle the bowls just below the rim. The interior designs (pl. 32) are almost without exception of the "all-over" type; that is to say, they cover, more or less completely, the entire inner surface of the pieces. The framework of all the designs is made up of broad red bands outlined in black, often having a second outlining of chalky white pigment. The simplest figures consist of the bands alone (pl. 32, a, b). In somewhat more elaborate examples the bands bear angular projections or terminal key figures (pl. 32, d). The most ornate and perhaps the most typical specimens have supplementary decoration painted in black over the yellow background between the red bands (pl. 32, c, e, f). This supplementary decoration is characteristic of the group and is generally carried out in the following manner: the spaces to be ornamented are filled with a

PLATE 32. Designs of Kayenta polychrome ware (the shading indicates red).

coarse hachure of parallel lines; while this may completely fill the field, the lines are usually divided into
groups of from three to eight or ten, and the small inter-
spaces thus produced are occupied by elements of a different nature, of which by far the most common are
stepped lines (pl. 32, c, f).

The range of the Kayenta culture as indicated by the
distribution of the above characteristic wares includes, of
course, the type localities near Kayenta: Marsh Pass and
Sagi Canyon. How far it may have extended to the north
and west we do not know, though it is not probable that
in these directions it ever overstepped to any great extent
the formidable barrier of the Colorado River. There appears to have been little or no eastward spread. To the
south a few pieces of Kayenta pottery appear in collections
from Canyon de Chelley.[48] To the southwest, however, in
the neighborhood of the Hopi towns, there are ruins which
produce typical Kayenta black-on-white ware.[49] The same
sort of material crops up in the neighborhood of San
Francisco Mountain, and on the Little Colorado at Black
Falls and above.[50]

Proto-Kayenta sites. In the same region which contains
the great Kayenta ruins, such as Kietsiel and Betatakin, and
also spreading out over a much more extensive sweep of
territory, are many sites, mostly small pueblos and cliff
houses, obviously allied in some way to the great ruins,
but lacking certain of the traits which are most characteristic of them. The strongest likenesses are seen in the
mediocre masonry with its copious use of adobe, in the
variability and characterlessness of the kivas, and in the
prevalence of colored pottery. The differences, aside from
the smaller size of the dwellings, lie in the absence of the

48. Peabody Museum, Brooklyn Institute of Arts and Sciences.

49. Ruins along the eastern side of the East Mesa at Polacca and
vicinity; a small ruin near Payupki, Middle Mesa (exploration of the
author).

50. Colton, 1920; and see Fewkes, 1904, pl. 20.

rectangular ceremonial room, or kihu, and in the less specialized nature of the pottery.

What may be called proto-Kayenta pottery appears in four varieties: corrugated, red, polychrome, and black-on-white. The corrugated vessels are distinctly better made than those of the typically Kayenta sites, the ollas are taller, more gracefully shaped, and the corrugations themselves much sharper, more evenly spaced, and more carefully indented.[51] The redware, which is possibly lacking and certainly less common in the true Kayenta sites, is of a rich dark color. The ornamentation is very uniform, consisting almost entirely of running hachured designs (fig. 20, a). The shapes are small, round-bodied pitchers or

FIG. 20. Proto-Kayenta pottery designs.

jugs, with a few bowls. The polychrome, practically limited to bowls, has a yellowish base color, the decoration being mostly in black hachuring, and the elements filled with red. Bowl exteriors bear broad, carelessly drawn horizontal lines in red. It thus closely resembles the typical Kayenta polychrome, but lacks almost entirely the latter's characteristic white design edgings. The black-on-white vessels are principally ollas and bowls. The ollas are round-bodied and have no handles,[52] the bowls are usually simple in form, with less tendency to outcurving rim and with fewer cases of exterior handles. Colanders and flat-topped ollas

51. See Kidder-Guernsey, 1919, pl. 58, g, h.
52. See Kidder-Guernsey, 1919, pl. 53.

seem to be absent. In decoration, "mosquito barring" and close-set black designs are rare or lacking; the commonest and most characteristic element is shown in Figure 20, c; it is worked into an almost endless number of different patterns.

Sites containing proto-Kayenta pottery of the sorts just described occur in the Kayenta country of Arizona in considerable abundance.[53] The same wares appear, to some extent at least, in the ruins of Grand Gulch and White Canyon; in the Chinlee and Canyon de Chelley; and in sites along the San Juan from Bluff, Utah, nearly to the mouth of the McElmo[54]; I have not seen them in the Hopi country. I have, however, picked up sherds of proto-Kayenta polychrome ware (without white edgings) at Pueblo Bonito and Hungo Pavie in Chaco Canyon, in Cliff Palace on the Mesa Verde, and on Alkali Ridge in the Montezuma Creek drainage.

From the fact that the so-called proto-Kayenta ruins are obviously allied to the Kayenta ruins, but are more abundant, smaller, more widely distributed, and less specialized, it is to be inferred that they are older. As in the case of the proto-Mesa Verde remains, however, definite proof can only be supplied by further studies; but it seems likely from the finds of their typical pottery at Bonito and Cliff Palace that the proto-Kayenta villages were inhabited at the same time as the great dwellings of the Mesa Verde and Chaco Canyon; and that the late Kayenta sites were erected after the Mesa Verde and Chaco Canyon had been abandoned. Thus Kietsiel and Betatakin may well have been the last large communities that existed in the San Juan drainage.

53. Ruins 2, 3, 4, 5, 7, of the Peabody Museum survey of 1914 (see Kidder-Guernsey, 1919).
54. Explorations of the author.

PRE-PUEBLO
(Sites with less developed pottery)

Hitherto we have had to deal with dwellings definitely puebloan in structure and room arrangement, and in the possession of one form or another of the kiva. The pottery of each group has been made up largely of two types, the corrugated and the black-on-white. We must now consider a class of remains from which the characteristically puebloan grouping of rectangular rooms built of horizontally coursed masonry is absent; which has no kivas, properly so-called; and whose pottery complex does not contain true corrugated ware.

These remains have been called "slab-house," "early," "pre-Pueblo," etc. The latter term is now the generally accepted one, and properly so, for, as will be shown presently, it is certain that the pre-Pueblo dwellings are earlier, in the San Juan at least, than the mesa villages and cliff houses which we have so far been describing.

There is considerable variety in the pre-Pueblo ruins that have come to light. To summarize, we may say that the houses were constructions with more or less fragile walls, round, oval, or rectangular, built in such a way that the lower parts of the rooms were sunk well into the ground. Each chamber had a semi-subterranean lower third, made by scooping a hole of the requisite size in the earth. If the earth was sufficiently solid to stand alone, it was merely smoothed down, coated with plaster, and made to serve as the lower wall of the room. If it was loose or crumbly it was reinforced with stone slabs set edgeways against it, and often protruding well above the level of the ground. The wall was sometimes carried even higher by building it up with successive courses of large, hand-molded lumps of adobe. In other cases the above-ground or free-standing wall was constructed of upright poles, wattled together with withes and coated inside and out with mud. Nothing definite is known of roof construction, other than that the coverings of the rooms were made of light poles, twigs, bark, and adobe. In some cases at least they were conical or pitched.

Such rooms seldom exceeded ten or twelve feet in diameter. They were normally round, or rectangular with rounded corners, and so could not conveniently be built in the close juxtaposition typical of pueblo room arrangement. Accordingly they are found in loose aggregations of from two or three to several scores, each one-room house being an independent unit in the settlement. The settlements sometimes also contain entirely subterranean round chambers, perhaps prototypes of the Pueblo kivas; they do not, so far as is known, possess any of the specialized features of kivas, such as pilasters, recesses, or deflectors, but were sometimes provided with a ventilating shaft.

Pre-Pueblo house groups are found in caves, in valley bottoms, and on the tops of mesas. The commonest sort of situation appears to be the crest of a slight rise of ground, such as a low ridge between two canyon systems or a swell in the contour of a valley. Considerations of surface drainage rather than of defense evidently led to the selection of these elevated sites, for the small size and scattered nature of the settlements show plainly enough that their inhabitants can not have had much cause to fear the attacks of enemies.

The pre-Pueblo people were agriculturists, growing corn, beans, squashes, and cotton; they also domesticated the turkey. They buried their dead with offerings of mortuary pottery in graves close to the houses. The heads of the babies, like those of most prehistoric Pueblo children, were flattened posteriorly by the pressure of a hard cradleboard, this flattening of course persisting in the adult skull (pl. 33). As to their artifacts in stone, bone, and wood we know very little beyond the fact that they used the bow and arrow. A single well-made basket has

PLATE 33. Deformed and underformed skulls. The lefthand specimen (top and side views) shows the typical posterior flattening of the Pueblo and pre-Pueblo periods; it was produced by the use during infancy of a hard cradleboard. The righthand specimen (top and side views) illustrates the natural or undeformed skull typical of the post-Basket Maker and Basket Maker periods.

been recovered, and a few pieces of cotton and turkey-feather cloth.[55] No sandals have so far been found. Of pottery, however, both mortuary and in the form of sherds from in and about the houses, we have a fairly large amount.

Three wares are represented: black, black-on-white, and red. The black ware corresponds to the corrugated of the pueblos and cliff houses in that it served largely for cooking vessels; but the pots are to be distinguished from true corrugated pieces by the fact that all traces of the structural coils have been obliterated except at the necks of the jars, where they are left in the form of a half-dozen or so broad flat rings of clay entirely without indentations (pl. 34, g, h). Black-on-white ware occurs in the form of bowls, ollas, and small jars. We have as yet few whole pieces, but it is certain that large ollas were made. Bowls (pl. 34, d, e, f) are small, thin rimmed, and decorated only within; pitchers (pl. 34, b), seed jars (pl. 34, c), and small pots with lugs (pl. 34, a) also commonly occur.

The decoration is fairly elaborate, but shows a marked crudity of brushwork; the designs are characterized by dotting of lines and edges, by projections from the angles of key figures, and in particular by sets of widely spaced lines drawn about the edges of triangular or stepped elements (pls. 34, 35). A peculiar and still unexplained resemblance exists between these line edgings and similar work on certain Chaco Canyon vessels (compare pls. 35, d, and 23, a, b). Although red ware is uncommon, a small percentage of sherds seems to turn up at each site. Little can be made out as to shapes, but the prevailing forms are evidently bowls and gourd-shaped vessels; the decoration is in a slightly lustrous but not vitrified blue-black paint.

While all the above wares are well made, they are in-

55. Collected by Guernsey, in Sagi Canyon, Arizona. To be published in the Peabody Museum Papers.

a

b

c

d

e

f

g

h

Courtesy Peabody Museum

PLATE 34. Pre-Pueblo pottery.

ferior to the run of Pueblo pottery in finish and in variety of decoration. The crudeness of the coiled technique, as shown by the cooking vessels, is, however, the best indication of lack of development.

Because of their inconspicuousness pre-Pueblo ruins for many years escaped notice and recording. Of late, however, the type has been recognized, and investigators are now on the lookout for it. The result has been that sites are reported in increasing numbers. They are known to occur abundantly in the Kayenta region, as well as in the Chinlee, Canyon de Chelley, Chaco Canyon, the Pagosa country,,on the mesas between the Animas and the Mancos, in the McElmo, and on Recapture Creek.[56] It is probable that further explorations will reveal the presence of many hundreds of pre-Pueblo sites in all parts of the San Juan.

The statement made above, that the pre-Pueblo people antedated the inhabitants of the pueblos and cliff houses, rests on definite stratigraphic evidence. In 1914 Guernsey and I found in a cave in northeastern Arizona a pre-Pueblo ruin overlaid by proto-Kayenta puebloan rubbish.[57] Guernsey's subsequent explorations have resulted in the discovery of several other similar cases.

POST-BASKET MAKER
(Sites with crude pottery)

During the early years of my acquaintance with the Southwest it was always puzzling to me that a district which produced so great an amount of fine pottery did not seem to contain any traces of the first crude stages of pottery-making. The fact that the oldest wares then known, the corrugated and the black-on-white, were in many ways the finest of all, made it seem as if the potter's art must

56. The Pagosa ruins have been reported by Jeancon (1922); those of the Animas-Mancos, by Morris (1919); those of Chaco Canyon by Judd (1923); the others were located by Guernsey and the writer.

57. Kidder-Guernsey, 1919, p. 42; in that publication we called the pre-Pueblo remains "Slab-House."

PLATE 35. Designs of pre-Pueblo black-on-white-pottery.

have been developed in some other region, and been brought into the Southwest in an already perfected form. Then came the recognition of the pre-Pueblo wares, which indicated a certain amount of local growth; but even these were obviously by no means the product of a nascent industry. It is only within the last few years that material has come to light which appears to show that pottery-making is actually an indigenous growth in the Southwest.

The finds which justify this belief were made by Guernsey in Sagi Canyon.[58] There in 1920 he found a cave containing Pueblo and pre-Pueblo remains. At one end of the place he also uncovered a series of rounded rooms of apparently normal pre-Pueblo slab-and-adobe workmanship; but the pottery in them proved, to his great surprise, to be a crude gray ware quite different from anything that had hitherto been reported. Further excavation showed that the people who built and lived in these rooms practiced, in addition to pottery-making, certain arts which had until then been considered typical of the Basket Makers, a non-pottery making race of very early times; Guernsey also found that they lacked certain objects which are equally lacking from the Basket Maker culture. A search for burials disclosed in a low mound in front of the cave several skeletons resembling Basket Maker skeletons in the fact that the skulls were undeformed (see pl. 33). The interments were accompanied by mortuary vessels of the same sort as those found in the rooms of the cave.

Following up this lead, Guernsey has since succeeded in collecting a large body of data in regard to these people. He has called them post-Basket Makers. Their houses, he finds, are similar to those of the pre-Pueblo, but there the likeness ceases. The post-Basket Makers resemble the Basket Makers in that their skulls are always undeformed; in the possession of twined-woven bags and furcloth blankets; and in the fact that they had no cotton and no

58. See Kidder-Guernsey, 1921.

a

PLATE 36. Chronological series of sandals. a.
Pueblo type; pointed toe with offset on outer
edge.

b

PLATE 36b. Pre-Pueblo type sandal: toe broadly scalloped.

c

PLATE 36c. Basket Maker type sandal: square toe with buckskin or fiber fringe.

domesticated turkeys. At least, no cotton cloth and no
turkey-feather blankets have so far turned up. The typical
sandal has a single broad scallop at the toe end (pl. 36, b).
The pottery is mostly dark gray, but a primitive form of
black-on-white ware appears, as well as a few undecorated
red pieces. Although Guernsey's material has not yet been
published, I have his permission to state that the run of
the pottery is inferior to that of the pre-Pueblo and that
certain post-Basket Maker sites contain wares of exceeding
crudeness.

The present known range of this interesting type of
remains is restricted to the Kayenta district, the Hopi
country, and the Chinlee Valley of northeastern Arizona;
I believe, however, that certain graves opened by Morris
on the La Plata will ultimately prove to belong to a late
phase of the same culture.[59] It is also possible that the
"earth lodges" of the Mesa Verde are of post-Basket Maker
origin; the published description of them is, however, not
full enough to justify any definite conclusions.[60] Another
reason for strongly suspecting the former presence of the
post-Basket Makers on the Mesa Verde is furnished by the
crude pottery and the scalloped-toed sandal discovered by
Nordenskiold in Step House.[61]

It is of course to be inferred that the post-Basket Makers
were intermediate in time between the Basket Makers and
the pre-Pueblos. This was practically proved during the
past two summers, when Guernsey in the Chinlee and the
writer in Sagi Canyon found typical post-Basket Maker
pottery underlying pre-Pueblo deposits. To date no superposition of post-Basket Maker on Basket Maker remains

59. Morris, 1919, p. 194; Kidder-Guernsey, 1920.
60. Fewkes, 1920, p. 58.
61. Nordenskiold, 1893, pls. 23, 1; 24, 2, 10; 46, 6. Since the above was
written, the author has visited the Mesa Verde and found that Step
House Cave contained a large post-Basket Maker settlement. Many other
sites of this culture were observed on the Mesa.

has come to light; but there can be little doubt that Guernsey's relative dating is correct.

BASKET MAKER (Sites without pottery)

Although Basket Maker specimens have been known for many years, they have only recently been brought to prominence, and their position at the bottom of the Southwestern cultural sequence firmly established. They were discovered by Richard Wetherill in Grand Gulch, Utah, during the late eighties or early nineties. He recognized the peculiarities of his finds, named them Basket Maker, and also determined, by the first use of stratigraphic evidence ever made in the Southwest, that they belonged to an older period than the cliff houses. Montgomery soon after published notes on certain Basket Maker graves and specimens, but did not believe that they represented a distinct culture.[62] Prudden was the first to give an adequate account of the finds,[63] but it was a matter of ten years after the original discovery before a description of the specimens themselves was published.[64] Students of the Southwest even then paid little or no attention to the chronological position of the Basket Makers, believing that the Grand Gulch remains represented merely a specialized local phase of the general pueblo cliff-house civilization. In 1914, however, Guernsey and the writer hit upon Basket Maker graves in northeastern Arizona, and since that time Guernsey has fully established their antiquity and has gathered a great quantity of data in regard to their culture.

The houses of the Basket Makers have never been identified, which makes it seem probable that they lived in more or less temporary structures, built of perishable materials, and located in the open. Although they did not live in caves, except perhaps during periods of unusually

62. Montgomery, 1894.
63. Prudden, 1897.
64. Pepper, 1902.

severe weather, they habitually availed themselves of the sandy floors of large dry caverns for the storage of their crops and for the burial of their dead. The storage places were slab-walled cists (pl. 37); or, where the earth was firmer, jar-shaped excavations. These were often put to a secondary use as graves. Because of the dryness of the sites picked out for cist-building the contents of the graves are usually excellently preserved, and where subsequent disturbance has not taken place, everything is found in almost perfect condition, the bodies of the dead desiccated to "mummies," the baskets, textiles, and wooden implements as sound and as perfect as if they had been buried yesterday (pl. 38).

The normal Basket Maker grave contains two or three individuals, each tightly flexed, wrapped in blankets, and accompanied by numerous mortuary offerings of foods, tools, weapons, ornaments, and particularly baskets. From a study of the graves we can get an unusually detailed picture of the life and arts of the people. The Basket Makers were long-headed and of medium stature; they did not practice skull deformation (see pl. 33). They were, to a certain extent at least, agricultural, for their caches and graves often contain large amounts of corn. This corn is of special interest because it is of a single and apparently fairly primitive variety, rather than of several distinct varieties as in the case of pueblo and cliff-house corn. Squashes were grown, but no beans or cotton have yet been found among Basket Maker remains. The turkey was evidently not domesticated.

Although they had no cotton and apparently did not use the loom, the Basket Makers were very expert in the making of large and elaborately ornamented twined-woven bags (pl. 38, d, g). Their sandals, too, are twined-woven and are easily distinguishable from later sandals by their square, fringed toes (pl. 36, c). Coiled basketry was made in large quantities in the form of trays (pl. 38, c), bowls, jars (pl. 28, b), and large panniers (pl. 38, f); twilled work in the form of mats and baskets, such as occur commonly in the prehistoric pueblos, is very rare. Fur cloth (pl. 38, a) instead of turkey-feather cloth was used for blankets.

No trace of the use of the bow and arrow has ever been found. The projectiles of the Basket Makers were light darts four or five feet long hurled by means of the spear thrower or atlatl, a device intended to add greater length and therefore greater propulsive force to the arm. The most striking difference between the Basket Maker culture and that of the other people whom we have so far been considering, is seen in the total absence of true pottery. A few unbaked clay dishes of the crudest sort have been found, but no vessel or even sherd of fired pottery assignable to the Basket Makers has ever turned up in the many cists and graves examined.

One might catalogue a dozen more traits in which the Basket Makers differ from the Pueblos, but enough has been said to show the wide cleavage that exists between the two cultures. It was at one time difficult to see any direct connection whatever between them, but the discovery of the post-Basket Maker and pre-Pueblo remains have served in large measure to bridge the gap.

The position of the Basket Makers as the oldest people of whom we have knowledge in the Southwest so far is clearly indicated. Stratigraphic finds have proved that they antedated the Pueblos; and while no Basket Maker remains have yet been found underlying those of the post-Basket Makers or of the pre-Pueblos, the inferential evidence for greater antiquity is so strong as practically to amount to proof.

The known range of the Basket Makers has been considerably enlarged since the first discoveries in Grand Gulch, Utah. It now includes all the northern tributaries of the San Juan from Comb Wash to the Colorado; it covers the Chinlee Valley, and the entire drainage of its largest affluent, Laguna Creek; recently it has been extended to the Kanab district north of the Colorado River (fig. 28, p. 327).[65] Outside these limits no surely Basket Maker remains have yet come to light, but certain specimens taken by Hough from caves in the Tularosa country of southern New Mexico have a Basket Maker look.[66]

Thus the known range of the Basket Maker culture is a fairly restricted one; but I feel sure that it, or cultures closely allied to it, will ultimately be found to have covered a vastly more extensive territory, embracing, perhaps, all the arid lands drained by the Colorado River and running south along the central plateau well into Mexico.

NORTHERN PERIPHERAL DISTRICT

Although they are not in the San Juan drainage, it is convenient to mention here the ruins that occur in the country to the north and northwest of the San Juan. To the northeast the high Rockies contain no traces of Pueblo occupation; but in the lower arid and semi-arid regions of Utah, from the Colorado line westward to the Great American Desert and northward to Salt Lake, are the remains of numerous settlements. The archaeological data for most of this vast territory are unsatisfactorily vague, and were it not for the recent work of Judd in western Utah we should have little idea as to the nature of the sites.

The accompanying map (fig. 21) shows the general location of such remains as have been reported. In the drainages of the Green and Grand Rivers are a few sites briefly described by Newberry, Montgomery, and Fewkes.[67] All these are small groups of rooms and towers, built of rough masonry on pinnacles, juts of mesas, and other places easy of defense and commanding wide outlooks.

65. Nussbaum, 1922.
66. Hough, 1914, p. 21, and pl. 20, fig. 2, a spear thrower.
67. Newberry, 1876; Montgomery, 1894; Fewkes, 1917a.

FIG. 21. Distribution of the several types of remains in the Northern Peripheral district.

The ruins visited by Fewkes contained no pottery, but both Newberry and Montgomery state that painted wares are to be found at the sites they examined. They give no information, however, which allows us to judge of the type of vessels encountered.

The ruins of central and southwestern Utah are better known. As the map shows, they extend in an almost continuous line from the northern shore of Great Salt Lake to the extreme southwestern corner of the state. Throughout this whole region there are, or rather there were before repeated plowings resulted in their destruction, great numbers of low adobe mounds. Excavations have been made by many investigators, mostly treasure seekers, but the only adequate published accounts are those of Montgomery and Judd.

The mounds consist of adobe from the disintegrated walls of houses, and of rubbish deposits that grew up about the dwellings while they were still in use. The sites would seem to have been occupied for relatively long periods, as each one shows evidence of the erection and decay of many successive structures. No differences, either in architecture or in artifacts, is, according to Judd, to be observed between the oldest levels and those above. The villages were more or less loosely grouped assemblages of rectangular one-story rooms, built singly or placed end-to-end in sets of three or four, and all arranged about an open central space or plaza.[68] The walls of the rooms were of adobe laid up in lumps or "gobs" and worked to an even surface with the hands. Entrance must normally have been through the pole-and-adobe roofs, as lateral doorways are exceedingly rare.

In the courtyards of the villages are found remains of round chambers so sunk into older rubbish deposits as to be wholly subterranean. Each one has a central firepit, and although no ventilating device has been recorded, there can be little doubt that Judd is correct in considering them closely allied to the kivas of more southerly ruins.

Of the mortuary customs practically nothing is known, but Montgomery notes the finding of a few burials in a mound at Paragonah. They lay deep in the deposit, well below house floors; but from the fact that there was always so much rebuilding at these sites it is not certain that the original interments were made under floors. One skull was strongly flattened posteriorly, the others all undeformed.

Among the minor antiquities recovered from the Utah mounds are fragments of coiled basketry, great numbers

68. See Judd, 1919, pl. 1.

PLATE 37. A Basket Maker storage and burial cave. The Basket Makers dug shallow holes in the sandy floors of caves, lined them with stone slabs, and roofed them with poles and bark. Such cists were used primarily for the storage of crops, but burials were often made in them. The round, slab-walled rooms of the post-Basket Maker and pre-Pueblo periods doubtless developed from the Basket Maker cist.

of bone implements, as well as manos and metates for grinding corn. Charred corn, also, has been found in considerable quantities. The grooved stone axe is not represented in any collection. The pottery is of particular interest. There is much crude undecorated gray ware, but with it there always occur a number of pieces of very well-made corrugated vessels, and a certain percentage of black-on-white sherds. The latter are usually from bowls, decorated only on the inside, and bearing geometric ornamentation. Judd's pottery has not yet been illustrated, but a number of decorated pieces from St. George, Utah, are figured by Holmes.[69] They bear a rather generalized type of ornament, not definitely to be associated with any of the specialized design systems of the San Juan. One peculiarity is mentioned by Judd, the interlineal use of red paint, superficially applied after the bowls had been fired.[70]

Such are the common mound ruins of central and southwestern Utah. There is also a different kind of site. Near Willard, on the northeastern shore of Great Salt Lake, Judd opened a mound which covered the remains

> of a structure which must have resembled, more or less closely, the well-known winter hogan of the Navaho Indians. The central and most prominent feature was a fireplace, two feet seven inches in diameter and three and one-half inches deep. Surrounding this, and nearly four feet from each other, were four post holes, marking the former position of as many upright supports. Since the floor of this dwelling could not be traced beyond a diameter of fifteen feet, and as the ease with which it could be traced decreased with the distance from the firepit, it may be assumed that the hut had been circular in

69. Holmes, 1886, figs. 258–71.
70. Judd, 1919, p. 19.

form, and that its roof and walls were of heavy timbers which rested upon the ground and leaned against crosspieces supported by the four posts surrounding the fireplace. Fragments of charred wood, and large quantities of baked clay bearing impressions of logs, willows, and grass, furnished material evidence respecting the nature of the roof construction.[71]

The potsherds in this mound were of coarse plain ware, and corrugated ware. Black-on-white had been reported from the vicinity but Judd was unable to find any specimens.

At Beaver City, about forty-five miles southeast of Sevier Lake, Judd found further examples of the hogan-like houses, and in these were the same sorts of pottery, besides many fragments of black-on-white. The Beaver City round houses lay *above* the disintegrated walls of a typical rectangular-roomed adobe village. Special emphasis should be laid on this find, for although we cannot yet decide what its exact significance may be, it illustrates very clearly how vitally important it is to excavate carefully and to be constantly on the lookout for any case of superposition. Had Judd been less keenly observant, he might easily have missed this particular bit of evidence, and might well have considered the primitive-looking Willard houses as belonging to a stage of development earlier than that represented by the adobe ruins, and so have gained an entirely wrong impression of the archaeological problems of the area.

We have not as yet enough data to allow us to draw final conclusions as to the place of the Utah ruins in the general scheme of Southwestern archaeology. They are, however, surely Puebloan, as is proved by the evident permanence of the settlements, the pottery, the corn and the use of the metate. Their age, relative to that of more

71. Judd, 1917b, p. 119.

PLATE 38. Basket Maker specimens. a. Blanket of fur-cloth. b, c, f. Baskets. d, g. Bags of fiber-string with colored designs. e. Cradle originally covered with mountain-sheep hide.

southern ruins, is hard to estimate. The simple nature of the houses, and the primitive appearance of the kiva-like structures, might seem to indicate that they were actually pre-Puebloan; but the black-on-white and corrugated pottery is certainly of Pueblo types. This would appear to show that they were built during the first part of the Pueblo period, when the vigorous early culture of the San Juan was spreading out and exerting its influence far and wide, but before the highly specialized subcultures of that region (the Chaco Canyon, Mesa Verde, and Kayenta) had yet come into being. How long the inhabitants of these Utah settlements managed to hold their country we have as yet no means of knowing, but eventually they disappeared entirely. Their end, it is to be supposed, came suddenly, because nowhere in this district do we find that they gathered together into large communities, as Pueblos normally did when in difficulties. That the end came early is indicated by the fact that pottery of early types was made to the very last, and that no sherd of late southern wares, Little Colorado, Gila, or Tularosa, has turned up in any of the mounds excavated.

No pre-Pueblo remains have yet been found in Utah outside the San Juan drainage, although one small neck-coiled jar from St. George has a suspiciously pre-Pueblo look.[72] A very interesting Basket Maker cave, however, was recently discovered in the southern part of the state by Nussbaum.[73] This greatly enlarges the previously known range of the Basket Maker culture, but whether it penetrated still farther to the north and northwest is not known.

72. Holmes, 1886, fig. 242.
73. Nussbaum, 1922.

BIBLIOGRAPHY OF THE SAN JUAN

GENERAL

Prudden, 1903.*
Hewett, 1908, chap. 6.
Cummings, 1910.
Kidder, 1917.
Morris, 1921.*

Pueblo Remains
by Districts

PAGOSA DISTRICT
Jeancon, 1922.*
Roberts, 1922.

LA PLATA—ANIMAS DISTRICT
Newberry, 1876, pp. 79–80.
Holmes, 1878, pp. 387–88.
Birnie, 1875.
Morgan, 1880; 1881, pp. 172–88.
Moorehead and Gunckel, 1892
Moorehead, 1902, chaps. 13–16; 1908.
Morris, 1915*; 1917a; 1917b; 1918; 1919, pt. II; 1919a*; 1921a.*
Nelson, 1917a.

MESA VERDE—MANCOS CANYON DISTRICT
Jackson, 1876, pp. 369–77.
Holmes, 1878, pp. 388–98.*
Chapin, 1890; 1892.
Nordenskiold, 1893.*
Fewkes, 1908; 1909*; 1910; 1910a; 1911a*; 1916*;

1916a; 1916b; 1916d; 1916e; 1917; 1917a; 1917b*; 1920; 1922; 1923.
Morris, 1919, pt. 1.*

MONTEZUMA VALLEY— McELMO DISTRICT
Jackson, 1876, pp. 377–81; 1878, pp. 411–15.
Holmes, 1878, pp. 398–400.
Morgan, 1881, pp. 188–93.
Wetherill, 1894.
Gunckel, 1897.
Crotensburg, 1900.
Prudden, 1903, pp. 257–67*; 1914.*
Morley, 1908.
Morley and Kidder, 1917.
Fewkes, 1918*; 1919*; 1923b.

MONTEZUMA CREEK—GRAND GULCH DISTRICT
Jackson, 1878, pp. 425–30.
Moorehead and Gunckel, 1892.
Montgomery, 1894, pp. 227–34.
"H," 1894.
Prudden, 1903, pp. 267–76*; 1918.*
Kidder, 1910.

KAYENTA DISTRICT
Prudden, 1903, pp. 282–85.
Cummings, 1910*; 1915.
Fewkes, 1911.*

* Major contribution.

Judd, 1918.
Kidder and Guernsey,
1919*; 1921.

CANYON DE CHELLEY—
CHINLEE DISTRICT
Simpson, 1850, pp. 102–05.
Jackson, 1878, pp. 415–25.
Putnam, 1879, pp. 372–73.
Stevenson, 1886.
Bickford, 1890.
Mindeleff, C., 1895; 1897.*
Fewkes, 1906.
Prudden, 1903, pp. 279–82.
Kidder and Guernsey, 1919,
pp. 71–74.

CHACO CANYON DISTRICT
Simpson, 1850, pp. 75–86.
Jackson, 1878, chap. 2.*
Morrison in Putnam, 1879,
pp. 366–69.
Loew, 1875.
Hoffman, 1878.
Morgan, 1881, chap. 7.
Bickford, 1890.
Pepper, 1899; 1905; 1906;
1909; 1920.*
Hewett, 1905a; 1921a; 1922.
Huntington, 1914, pp. 75–
82.*
Chapman, 1921.
Bradfield, 1921.
Judd, 1922*; 1922a; 1923.
Wetherill and Cummings,
1922.
Wissler, 1922.

* Major contribution.

NORTHERN PERIPHERAL
DISTRICT
Newberry, 1876.
Palmer, 1876; 1880.
Holmes, 1886, pp. 287–88.
Montgomery, 1894.*
Duffield, 1904.
Judd, 1917; 1917a; 1917b*;
1918; 1919*; 1920.

PRE-PUEBLO REMAINS
Morris, 1917b, p. 462; 1919,
pp. 182–94.*
Kidder and Guernsey, 1919,
pp. 41–45, 152–54.*
Jeancon, 1922, pp. 5–11.*

POST-BASKET MAKER REMAINS
Nordenskiold, 1893, pp. 37–
43.
Morris, 1919, pp. 194–95.
Kidder and Guernsey, 1920;
1921.

BASKET MAKER REMAINS
Montgomery, 1894, pp. 227–
34.
"H," 1894.
Prudden, 1897.
Pepper, 1902*; 1905a.
Kidder and Guernsey, 1919,
pp. 74–90, 154–92; 1921.
Guernsey and Kidder,
1921.*
Nussbaum, 1922.*

The Rio Grande

The sources of the Rio Grande are in the same high mountains of southern Colorado which give birth to the San Juan. Thence the river turns eastward, enters New Mexico, and flows practically due south through the entire length of that state (fig. 22). Its western tributaries head against the continental divide, on the other side of which lie the upper tributaries of the Little Colorado and the Gila. The Rio Grande drainage in New Mexico comprises every sort of land, from lofty mountain ranges to bleak, sandy desert; a large part of it, however, is typical Southwestern country, arid, yet not hopelessly dry; its mesas covered with cedars and pinyons, its lower stretches overgrown with sagebrush, cactus, and other semidesert vegetation. Such parts of this great area as are between 3,000 and 7,000 feet in elevation, and as are not absolute desert, usually contain the relics of former sedentary inhabitants in the form of house ruins great and small. Below the Texas line there seem to be no ruins.

Archaeologically, the Rio Grande is like all other parts of the Southwest in that certain sections of it have been carefully explored and their antiquities more or less fully studied; while other areas, much larger in extent and equally prolific in ruins, still await adequate investigation. It differs, however, from all other parts of the Southwest, with the exception of the Little Colorado drainage, in that it is still occupied by living tribes of Pueblo Indians, who to this day carry on most of the arts and customs of their prehistoric ancestors. Thus we have an invaluable starting point for our researches, and can work back from the known to the unknown without meeting any very serious obstacles.

The most carefully studied part of the Rio Grande country is what may be called Santa Fe region, viz., the Rio Grande Valley from San Juan to Santo Domingo, with the Pajarito plateau on the west and the Galisteo basin and the upper Pecos Valley on the east. In this area prior to 1912 much exploration had been done by Bandelier, Hewett, and others, a great number of ruins had been mapped, and several had been excavated.[1] Little progress, however, had been made toward the relative dating of the numerous prehistoric remains; and few convincing results of a correlative nature were attained until N. C. Nelson began his studies in the Galisteo basin. Here, as has been said in a previous section, he dug in the hitherto neglected early historic ruins and made himself familiar with the styles of pottery in vogue in the sixteenth and seventeenth centuries. Then, by working in the rubbish heaps of sites whose occupancy had lasted back into prehistoric times, he was able by stratigraphic methods to recognize the pottery types of the late prehistoric period. By an extension of the same stratigraphic methods, and by using pottery as a criterion, he succeeded in determining the outline of culture growth in his area from a very early period down to the time of the Pueblo revolt of 1680. The writer's excavations at Pecos have served to amplify these data and to extend our knowledge well past the beginning of the last century; from which point studies at the still-inhabited pueblos carry it to the present day.

To summarize the knowledge gained from these investigations, we may say that the earliest remains of which we so far have knowledge are certain small settlements, apparently of pre-Pueblo type, observed by Nelson but as yet undescribed.[2] Such settlements seem to be rare in the Pajarito plateau and in the Galisteo basin and have so far entirely eluded search in the Pecos Valley. The next stage

1. See bibliography of the Rio Grande at the end of this section.
2. Nelson, 1916, p. 171, footnote, and table, p. 179.

that we can recognize is marked by small houses scattered in considerable abundance over the whole region; they consist of from three or four to twenty or thirty rooms, were probably not over one story high, and may or may not have contained kivas. Their small size and the nature of

FIG. 22. The Rio Grande area (outlined), the Santa Fe region (shaded), and Pecos (star).

the sites upon which they were built show plainly enough that their inhabitants were in little fear of attack by enemies. The pottery of these ruins is black-on-white and corrugated, with a very small percentage of black-on-red. The black-on-white is of a generalized style not closely identifiable with any of the specialized types of the San

Juan or other regions. The corrugated ware is distinctly poor, the coiling uneven and the indentation work slipshod.

Following these small ruins in time are much larger structures, definitely puebloan in form, the rooms being built about courtyards and terraced to a height of at least two stories.[3] They contain round subterranean kivas with a central firepit, and a ventilator opening to the east, but have no recesses or pilasters.[4] The pottery (pls. 39, a; 40, a) is similar to that of the small ruins, but a number of the black-on-white bowls have flaring rims. A few red bowl-sherds appear bearing interior decoration in dull black and exterior designs in white.

The next step in ceramic evolution was the introduction of glaze paints (pls. 39, b; 40, b). These first occur on red, shortly afterward on light-colored vessels; black-on-white ware dies out and is replaced by a thick gray pottery called biscuitware. The ruins at which this first glaze (Glaze 1 of the Pecos series) occurs are large; indeed, from Glaze 1 times onward, the settlements become greater in size, more compact in ground plan, and fewer in number.

The continued development in pottery-making brought in the use of dull red paints to add to the beauty of the glazed designs (Nelson's "three-color glazed and painted wares"; Glazes 2, 3, 4, 5, of the Pecos series; see pls. 39, c-f; 40, c-f); biscuitware gradually declined, and corrugated gave place to plain black for cooking pottery. The ruins of this general period are well exemplified by the large pueblos of the Pajarito such as Puyé and Tyuonyi, great quadrangular or circular villages surrounding courts

3. Examples in the Pecos Valley are at Rowe and on the Pecos mesa (North Terrace and underlying main plaza); for an account of the Rowe ruin see Guthe, 1917. The same type evidently occurs in the Galisteo basin; as Nelson says: "the large quadrangular village was fully developed before the black-on-white pottery went out of style" (1916, p. 171).

4. This description is of the only kiva of the period so far excavated. It lies in the plaza of the north quadrangle at Pecos (see p. 118).

a

b

c

d

e

f

g

h

PLATE 39. Pecos pottery. Chronological series arranged to illustrate the sequence of types from the Black-on-white ware of early prehistoric times (a), to Modern ware made during the first part of the nineteenth century (h).

PLATE 40. Pecos pottery. Chronological series of bowl designs: a. Black-on-white; b. Glaze 1; c. Glaze 2; d. Glaze 3; e. Glaze 4; f. Glaze 5; g. Glaze 6; h. Modern.

(pl. 41, a). Their kivas are round subterranean rooms with plain unrecessed walls, central firepits, and ventilators opening to the east.

Toward the close of the glazed-ware period, and after many of its most flourishing sites had already been abandoned, came the discovery of the Southwest by the Spaniards. Glazing held on for a hundred years or so, becoming more and more degenerate (Nelson's "historic two-color glazes"; Pecos Glaze 6; pls. 39, g; 40, g); until at or about the time of the revolt of 1680 it was finally abandoned and the Rio Grande potters began to produce light-colored wares ornamented with dull black and red paints (Nelson's "modern painted"; Pecos "Modern"; pls. 39, h; 40, h), closely resembling the present-day pottery of San Ildefonso, Cochiti, and Santo Domingo.

The above sketch of the archaeology of the Santa Fe region has been made very brief because papers on the general problems of this area, as well as detailed studies of the different periods, will appear in the later reports of the present series.

We have, as has just been shown, a fairly good knowledge of the Santa Fe district, but there are many other parts of the Rio Grande drainage as to which we have so far very little information. Of these the Jemez area, the country about Acoma, the region of the Salines, and the lower valley of the river itself are the most notable examples. What little we do know, however, indicates that throughout the whole central Rio Grande drainage in New Mexico the course of development was analogous to that in the Santa Fe district; i.e., there was an early period in which the people lived in small communities and made black-on-white and corrugated pottery, a later time when they gathered together into larger villages, and a still later time when they became concentrated in a few great pueblos, discontinued the more archaic types of pottery, and turned to the use of colored wares decorated with

glaze paint. With the increase in concentration ensued a
tendency to draw in toward the centre of the area and
toward the valley of the river, and when the Spaniards arrived, the country held by the Pueblos was far less extensive than it had been in the Black-on-white and earlier
Glaze periods.

When we come to consider the archaeology of the Rio
Grande as a whole, we are struck by the paucity of pre-
Pueblo remains and by the entire absence, so far as we
know, of any sign of the post-Basket Maker and Basket
Maker. As to the pre-Pueblo, I feel certain that further
reconnaissance will result in the finding of many more
sites, but I should expect them to occur in the northern
and western parts of the Rio Grande rather than in the
eastern and southern. If evidence of the post-Basket
Maker and Basket Maker cultures ever turns up, it will be
found, I think, in the same districts. In other words, it is
my opinion that the eastern and southern parts of the
Rio Grande drainage in New Mexico were not occupied
by agricultural people prior to the early Pueblo period.
This feeling is based on the general lateness of development in the Rio Grande as compared to that in the San
Juan.

There are not many data to correlate chronologically
the Rio Grande with the San Juan, for the latter country
had been deserted for an unknown length of time before
the arrival of the Spanish in 1540. We do have, however,
a few scraps of evidence. At Bandelier Bend, a late archaic
Black-on-white site in the Pecos Valley, there have turned
up several undoubted Mesa Verde bowl sherds; thus, the
late archaic Black-on-white period in the Pecos Valley
appears to have corresponded in time to the epoch of
greatest development in the San Juan. Furthermore, the
entire life of the glaze-paint stages seems surely to have
been later than the abandonment of the San Juan, for no
scrap of glazed ware or of the contemporary biscuitware

a

b

PLATE 41. Rio Grande habitations. a. Large circular pueblo, Tyuonyi. b. Artificial caves used as dwellings near Tyuonyi.

has ever been found in any San Juan ruin. It would seem, therefore, that all the more sizeable villages of the Rio Grande were built subsequent to the abandonment of the San Juan; and that at the time of the great towns of the Chaco and the Mesa Verde, which represented the culmination of San Juan civilization, the Rio Grande people, although they were already definitely puebloan in culture, were only just beginning to gather together into large communities.

The chronological correlation between the Rio Grande ruins and those of the Little Colorado will be taken up after the discussion of that area.

EASTERN PERIPHERAL DISTRICT

The country lying east of the Rio Grande drainage in New Mexico has not been explored by archaeologists. It is not known, therefore, just how far in that direction ruins of pueblo type extend. I have been told by ranchers that there are sites almost to the Texas border. From the descriptions and from the few potsherds I have seen, the villages would all appear to have been small and to have belonged to the early part of the Black-on-white period. The limits indicated on the map (fig. 9, p. 141) show the extent, so far as we can determine it at present, of such sites in eastern and southeastern New Mexico. The ruin in Scott County, Kansas, described by Williston and Martin[5] was undoubtedly built during the historic period by Pueblos seeking to escape from Spanish rule.

BIBLIOGRAPHY OF THE RIO GRANDE

CHAMA-TAOS DISTRICT
   Cope, 1875.
   Holmes, 1878, p. 401.

Yarrow in Putnam, 1879,
   pp. 362–65.
Bandelier, 1892, chap. 1.

5. Williston, 1899; Martin, 1909.

Hewett, 1906, pp. 33–44.*
Jeancon, 1911; 1912; 1919;
    1921; 1923.*
Harrington, 1916, pp. 107–
    205.

PAJARITO PLATEAU DISTRICT
Stevenson, 1883a, pp. 430–
    32.
Bandelier, 1892, chaps. 1
    and 4.*
Starr, 1900.
Hewett, 1904a; 1906, pp.
    16–32*; 1908, chap. 9;
    1909*; 1909a*; 1909b;
    1920.
Bierbower, 1905.
Beam, 1909.
Morley, 1910.
Hewett, Henderson, and
    Robbins, 1913.*
Huntington, 1914, pp. 82–
    85.
Kidder, 1915.
Harrington, 1916, pp. 205–
    390.
Wilson, 1916; 1916a; 1918.

JEMEZ DISTRICT
Loew, 1875, pp. 176–77.
Bandelier, 1892, chap. 5.

* Major contribution.

Holmes, 1905.
Hewett, 1906, pp. 44–51.
Reagan, 1917; 1922.
Bloom, 1922; 1923.

PECOS DISTRICT
Bandelier, 1881*; 1892,
    chap. 3.
Hewett, 1904.*
Kidder, 1916a; 1916b;
    1917a; 1917b.
Kidder, M. A. and A. V.,
    1917.*
Guthe, 1917.

GALISTEO DISTRICT
Bandelier, 1892, chap. 2.
Nelson, 1913; 1914*; 1916*;
    1917.

RIO PUERCO DISTRICT
Lummis, 1889.
Bandelier, 1892, pp. 305–26.
Hodge, 1897; 1897a; 1914.

LOWER RIO GRANDE—MAN-
    ZANO DISTRICT
Bandelier, 1892, chap. 6.
Huntington, 1914, pp. 72–
    74.
Walter, 1916.

The Little Colorado

The Little Colorado River rises in the highlands of western New Mexico and flows a little north of west to empty into the Colorado (fig. 23). Its course roughly parallels that of the San Juan, but unlike the San Juan its sources are not in high, snow-covered mountains, so that the actual amount of water it carries is not great. It often runs dry in midsummer, and much of the country along its lower reaches is practically uninhabitable desert. The upper tributaries, however, particularly those of the east and southeast, traverse some of the most beautiful hill and mesa land of the Southwest, well watered and often heavily forested.

The ruins of the Little Colorado drainage are for the most part reduced to low, inconspicuous mounds. This is evidently due to poor construction, and perhaps in some degree to climatic conditions, rather than to great antiquity. The result of it, however, is that a classification based on architectural features is impossible without house excavation, very little of which has ever been done, almost all investigators having contented themselves with digging in the easily found and extremely prolific burial grounds. Hence we know almost nothing of the details of room arrangement, masonry, or kiva construction; in most cases, indeed, we are even ignorant as to whether or not kivas are present. Accordingly, in attempting a classification, one is forced to rely upon the evidence of pottery to an even greater degree than elsewhere. Here again difficulties are encountered, for the pottery situation in the Little Colorado is evidently a very complex one and no comprehensive classification of the wares has yet been made. The trouble is that most work in the Little Colorado, particularly in the very important central regions along the river itself, has been carried on by explorers who have placed more reliance upon the clan-migration legends of the Hopi and Zuñi, than upon the empirical evidence offered by the ruins and their contents. Hence

FIG. 23. The Little Colorado area.

the strictly archaeological aspects of the problem have been to a large extent disregarded.

To make a start, therefore, we are forced to turn to the Zuñi district at the extreme eastern end of the drainage, where recent studies by Kroeber, Nelson, and Spier of the Archer M. Huntington Survey of the American Museum of Natural History, have achieved clear-cut and satisfactory results.

This region contains a single inhabited town, the pueblo of Zuñi, and the ruins of a great number of other villages, large and small. Certain of the sites had been identified by previous students as the "Seven Cities of Cibola," which were visited and described by the Spanish explorers of the sixteenth and seventeenth centuries; most of them, however, are obviously prehistoric. Spier, who carried on most of the investigation, paid particular attention to the pottery, and was able, by a combination of stratigraphic, comparative, and statistical methods, to work back from the wares of the historic ruins, and eventually to arrange many sites in a chronological sequence which is without much doubt correct.[1] By relying upon empirical evidence rather than upon native legendary testimony Spier proved that one ruin, Hallonawa, hitherto considered historic, is in reality prehistoric; and that Zuñi, long thought to have been founded since the conquest, was actually settled prior to 1540.

The process of development, as determined by Spier, may be summarized as follows. The earliest sites were little buildings with pottery identical with that of the pre-Pueblo ruins in the San Juan. Then came somewhat larger houses whose pottery is preponderantly corrugated and black-on-white (pl. 42, c); then began a decline in black-on-white ware, accompanied by a rise of redware with decoration first in black paint (pl. 42, a), later in both black and white paint (pl. 42, b). During the earlier phases of this period the structures were still small, and lacked the compact grouping and terraced arrangement of the later pueblo. After the introduction of three-color (i.e., black-and-white-on-red) painted decoration, there came into use the true pueblo form of architecture. Painted

1. For the details of this important contribution to archaeological method, see Spier, 1917, and review by the writer (Kidder, 1919).

PLATE 42. Little Colorado pottery.

decoration soon gave way to decoration in black glaze, the three-color scheme still obtaining (i.e., black glaze and white paint on red, pl. 42, d, f). After a considerable time glaze painting and red backgrounds declined more or less together, and were replaced by light backgrounds (buff or white). Glaze paint, although it lingered upon the white backgrounds for a while, was steadily losing ground. This period saw the arrival of the Spaniards. During historic times dull paint finally triumphed over glaze, and the wares gradually changed, and grew into the styles which are made at Zuñi today.[2] From the time of the introduction of the pueblo form of architecture the tendency was always toward a reduction in the number of towns and an increase in their size.

Spier's sequence of pottery types is undoubtedly correct in its main outlines. Its correctness, however, will be thoroughly tested, and much valuable information will surely be added, by the excavations now being carried on by Hodge for the Museum of the American Indian, Heye Foundation, at the large Zuñi ruin of Hawikuh, an historic pueblo founded in prehistoric times, whose rubbish heaps contain a splendid stratification of several of the more important wares in Spier's chronological series.

Hodge has, indeed, just published the following preliminary chronological classification of Hawikuh pottery, which in general confirms Spier's results:

A. Black-on-gray; black-on-red; finely corrugated. Pre-Hawikuh period.

B. Black or green glaze on red or orange-red. Corrugated much cruder. Earliest Hawikuh (prehistoric).

C. Black, green, or purplish glaze on white or creamy slip. Early Hawikuh (prehistoric).

2. Whole vessels of some of these wares are not at present available for illustration, but Spier (1917, 1918, 1919) figures a representative series of sherds; and Fewkes (1909b) gives some excellent color plates of early glazed ware from Zuñi sites.

D. Black or green glaze on white or cream, with non-glaze colors introduced. This was the first step toward a pure mat polychrome. Prehistoric.

E. Polychrome. Various colors were used and life forms became much more common. The glaze decoration has disappeared. The range of decorative designs indicates two periods, one merging into the other, the first prehistoric, the second prehistoric but extending into the historic period.

F. Recent glaze. The glaze, especially black, and green of varying shades, was revived, but the glaze was crudely applied. This style of ornamentation seems to have been gradually superseding the polychrome when Hawikuh was abandoned.[3]

Of the kivas of the Zuñi area we have so far little information. Hodge states that the ceremonial rooms of Hawikuh, both prehistoric and historic, are rectangular.[4] At a pre-Hawikuh site in the vicinity, which was built during Hodge's period A, there were found by the Museum of the American Indian expedition two circular kivas. The excavation of these was so carefully done and the publication of the results is so full and clear that they may well serve as models for future work of the sort.[5] The two kivas lay side by side with remains of a house structure to the north of them. They were round and subterranean, the larger seventeen feet, the smaller a trifle over fifteen feet in diameter. Each one was encircled by a low inner wall without roof-support pilasters; and each one contained a ventilating shaft opening in the floor, a deflector, and a rectangular firepit. In both kivas there was sunk into the floor west of the firepit a rectangular, stone-lined vault. No traces of roofing were discovered.

These two kivas show strong Chaco Canyon influence,

3. Hodge, 1923, p. 29.
4. Hodge, 1923, p. 10.
5. Hodge, 1923.

but they appear to represent a sort of cross between the
great kiva and the small kiva types. They resemble the
great kivas in possessing an unpilastered encircling bench,
and a rectangular firepit; the small kivas in having a sub-
floor ventilating shaft, a deflector, and a single rectangular
vault west of the firepit.

The pottery found by Hodge in the undisturbed lower
portions of the kivas was black-on-white, black-and-white-
on-red, and corrugated. The black-on-white is not, to my
mind, of the typical Chaco style, but belongs to what I
believe we shall eventually be able to recognize as a distinctive Little Colorado group influenced by Chaco ware
and by the black-on-white of the Upper Gila (see p. 284
below). Contemporaneousness of these kivas with the upper Gila culture is indicated by Hodge's discovery in the
original undisturbed fill in one of them of an Upper Gila
type corrugated bowl.[6] In view of finds made in the upper
layers of the kivas this becomes a fact of great importance.
The finds just mentioned consisted of the remains of two
rudely made chambers built in the kivas, but well above
their floors. They were obviously constructed after the
kivas had been abandoned and had fallen into decay. They
were identified by Hodge as of the Hawikuh period, for
they contained pottery of several definitely Hawikuh types.
Associated with these later rooms were several skeletons
accompanied by mortuary pottery, also of Hawikuh types.
With skeleton no. 1, was a bowl of Lower Gila polychrome
ware, and a Hawikuh Type C or D canteen with purplish
glaze on a white slip.[7] The significance of the Upper Gila
corrugated bowl from the kiva proper and the Lower Gila
bowl in a later grave and associated with a Hawikuh Type
C or D vessel, will be reverted to in a subsequent section.
Here I wish merely to call the facts to the reader's attention, and to emphasize, as I did in the case of Judd's ob-

6. Hodge, 1923, pl. 22, a; and see p. 283 below.
7. Hodge, 1923, p 31 and pls. 28, c; 29, c.

servations on the Beaver City mounds (see p. 252), the great importance of careful observation and recording, particularly where there is the least suspicion of a superposition of the remains of different periods. Had Hodge merely dug out his kivas and burials, allowed the sherds from different levels to become mixed, and failed to note the small details of depth and position which allowed him to state positively that the burials belonged with the later rooms rather than with the earlier kivas, all these most valuable data would have been lost. Consideration of this particular case makes it seem likely that the strange mixtures of pottery types recorded by other students from some of the ruins of the Little Colorado valley were due to like reoccupations of sites, and that the evidence of such reoccupations was not recognized by the excavators.

We must now turn to the Hopi district in the extreme northern part of the Little Colorado drainage. Here no stratigraphic work such as that of Hodge has been done; nor have any comparative and statistical studies of the pottery been made comparable to those of Spier in the Zuñi country. We have, however, thanks to Fewkes, an intimate knowledge of one very characteristic ware, and the writer has made brief reconnaissances at a number of sites at and near the East Mesa.

The general conditions duplicate those in the Zuñi country; that is to say, there are inhabited pueblos (pl. 43), a few early historic towns, and many prehistoric ruins. The recent wares of the Hopi[8] are light colored, with decorations in brownish blacks and reds (see pl. 18, a); the light backgrounds are a dirty white, the slip being thickly seamed with fine cracks. A surface examination of the rubbish heaps below Walpi and Sichomovi seems to show

8. Pottery making is now extensively carried on only at Walpi and Hano. By recent wares I mean those produced prior to 1897; at that time the Hopi potters began to copy the fine old vessels unearthed by Fewkes at Sikyatki, and this archaistic style has now practically superseded the nineteenth-century pottery.

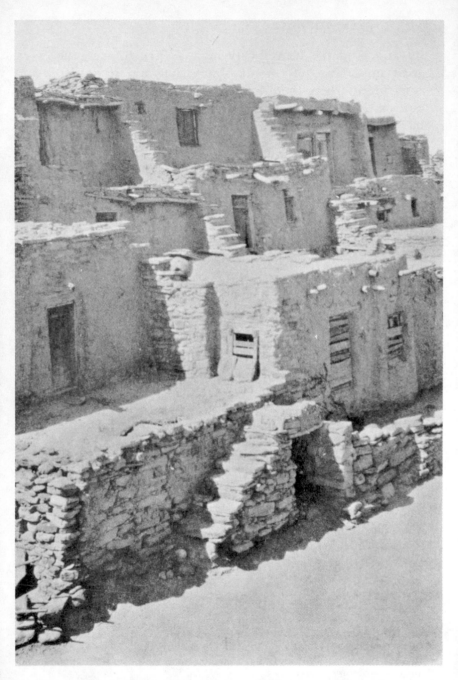

PLATE 43. Typical terraced pueblo. Hopi town of Oraibi.

that this ware has been made for a long time. It must, however, have come into use after 1700, for the surface pottery at the nearby ruin of Awatobi, which was destroyed at about that date, is dissimilar to it. The latest Awatobi ware is much yellower in tone, its slip lacks the characteristic modern Hopi crackling, and the decoration in browns and reds is more skillfully applied. This ware, although better than modern Hopi, is much less fine than a third style which is also found at Awatobi and at various other sites, but which is best known as Sikyatki ware. The beautiful plates in Fewkes' monograph on Sikyatki[9] have made this pottery well known. Its surface color ranges from creamy white through the yellows to shades of flushed orange; the elaborate designs are executed with marvellous sureness and accuracy in brown-blacks and reds (pl. 42, g, h). The best pieces of the Sikyatki type are technically and artistically the finest ceramic products of the Southwest, ancient or modern.

Sikyatki, the type site for this ware, is believed by Fewkes to be prehistoric.[10] Finds of Sikyatki pottery at Pecos seem to show that it was contemporaneous with Rio Grande late Glaze 4 and early Glaze 5, which would place it in the late prehistoric period; this supposition is further borne out by its obvious family resemblance to the seventeenth-century wares at Awatobi.

Sikyatki pottery is found well under the surface at Awatobi, and also occurs at a site below the mesa near Walpi, at Old Shumopovi, and at several other ruins. What preceded the Sikyatki wares in the Hopi district has only just been determined. During the past summer I made a series of stratigraphic tests in the deep rubbish heaps of Old Shumopovi and the Jeddito Valley ruins of Awatobi, Neshepatanga, and Kokopnyama.[11] At each of

9. Fewkes, 1898.
10. Fewkes, 1898, p. 636.
11. For the location of these sites, see Hough, 1903, pl. 82.

these sites I found underlying the Sikyatki wares similar but easily distinguishable pottery which I have tentatively called Jeddito yellow (pl. 42, e). It is decorated with brown-black paint alone, rather than with brown-black and red, and the vessel shapes and the ornamentation show plainly enough that it is directly ancestral to Sikyatki ware. Beneath the Jeddito yellow there occurred still older pottery of an orange-red shade, the ancestry of which is still unknown, but which may prove to be allied both to the Kayenta polychrome and to the early dull-black-and-white-on-red of the Zuñi series. These data show that the latest prehistoric Hopi pottery, the Sikyatki, is a local growth from local prototypes, and not, as had formerly been supposed, an importation by clans from the Rio Grande. These local prototypes, first the orange-red and then the Jeddito yellow, were evidently contemporaneous with the early glazed wares of the Zuñi district.

The still older steps in the Hopi series are to be found at many almost obliterated ruins which contain only black-on-white and corrugated ware; some of this is a sort of amorphous stuff like generalized San Juan, some is quite distinctly proto-Kayenta and Kayenta. There are also in the Jeddito Valley and at the East Mesa a number of unmistakable pre-Pueblo ruins, little slab-walled structures with characteristic black-on-white and neck-coiled black pottery. Finally, at two places on the East Mesa are small sites marked by a few scattered stones and containing sherds of typical rough, gray, unornamented post-Basket Maker vessels.

To sum up, we have in the Hopi country the post-Basket Maker, pre-Pueblo, prehistoric Pueblo, and modern Pueblo cultures. The prehistoric Pueblo culture probably passed through, first a generalized, and later a more specialized, black-on-white stage. Then came a period when both degenerate black-on-white and a new orange-red style were in vogue. Black-on-white eventually disappeared and the Jeddito yellow ware became the predominating type. Toward the close of prehistoric times there developed from it the beautiful black-paint-on-yellow Sikyatki wares, whose influence certainly extended down into the Little Colorado. The early modern ware surely, and the late modern ware probably, grew from this.

From the foregoing it will be seen that the general course of development in the Hopi and Zuñi countries was virtually the same, particularly during the earlier phases. In the later prehistoric periods, however, specializations set in which became more and more pronounced, until at the time of the discovery in 1540 the two regions were marked by cultures which, ceramically at least, were quite distinct.

I am not able to throw much light on the problems presented by the numerous and important ruins in the river valley of the Little Colorado and in its southern tributaries. An examination of the plates in the works of Fewkes and Hough[12] shows that the situation is by no means simple; there are vessels of all sorts, black-on-white, black-and-white-on-red, glazed, Jeddito yellow, and Sikyatki, as well as pieces of Kayenta, Tularosa, and Lower Gila types. This very complexity, however, is encouraging, for it shows that the Little Colorado has been a meeting and mixing ground of several cultures. The discovery of stratified sites or, if such cannot be located, further work along the lines developed by Spier, will not only surely result in the solution of local problems, but will also give us invaluable data as to the time-relations of many other Southwestern groups.

As to time correlations between the Little Colorado and the Rio Grande, we are provided with a good starting point by the fact that the upper ends of both series run into historic times and are therefore contemporaneous. Dropping to the bottom, we find each series beginning

12. Fewkes, 1904; Hough, 1903.

with more or less similar types of generalized black-on-white ware; this would also seem to imply approximately equal age for the beginnings of puebloan development in the two areas. The Black-on-white period, however, appears to have lasted somewhat longer in the Rio Grande than in the Little Colorado, for fragments of the dull paint redware with white exterior decoration which succeeded the black-on-white in the latter region, have been found in otherwise pure black-on-white sites in the Rio Grande. The next stage, that of glaze painting, began at about the same time in both areas, though it may perhaps have started a trifle earlier in the Little Colorado.[13] Evidence for these statements is provided by the finding of sherds of Little Colorado glaze-paint wares of Hodge's Type B (see p. 270) in Glaze 1 strata at Pecos, and, indeed, in some very late black-on-white deposits at Pecos and at Rowe.

The above correlation between these two regions, while by no means detailed or complete, is reasonably convincing. It depends in large measure upon the evidence of cross-finds of fragments of non-local pottery. Such fragments of vessels belonging to types not standard in a region, but which *are* characteristic of another region, are of the greatest importance for determining chronological relationships. It is immaterial whether the vessels were actually traded from one district to another, whether they were made by women married or captured into a tribe, or whether they were produced locally in imitation of foreign styles; their significance in showing contemporaneity is the same. I wish to lay particular stress upon this method of correlation as it is one which has proved very useful in the past, and may be depended upon to help us greatly in the future. To take full advantage of it, however, the field archaeologist must be a close student of ceramic types, and must be constantly on the lookout for

13. See Kidder, M. A. and A. V., 1917, p. 354.

fragments, no matter how small, which differ in any way from the run of material in the site that he is excavating.

BIBLIOGRAPHY OF THE
LITTLE COLORADO

ZuÑi District

Simpson, 1850, pp. 117–33.
Cushing, 1886.
Mindeleff, 1891, chap. 3.*
Fewkes, 1891*; 1909b.
Bandelier, 1892, pp. 326–45; 1892a.
Hodge, 1895; 1918; 1920; 1921; 1922; 1923.*
Kroeber, 1916; 1916a.
Spier, 1917.*
Anonymous, 1918.
Wissler, 1919.

Hopi District

Mooney, 1893.
Mindeleff, 1891, chaps. 1, 2.*
Bandelier, 1892, chap. 9.
Fewkes, 1893; 1896a; 1896c; 1896d; 1898, pp. 577–

742,* 1898a; 1904, pp. 111–34; 1919a.
Hodge, 1904.
Hough, 1903, pp. 326–52.*

River Valley and Southern Tributaries

Nelson, E. W., 1884.
Hough, 1902; 1903, pp. 289–325; 1920.
Fewkes, 1896b; 1898b; 1900; 1904, pp. 20–111, 134–68.*
Palmer, F. M., 1905.
Spier, 1918; 1919.
Colton, M. R. F. and H. S., 1918.
Colton, 1920.

* Major contribution.

The Upper Gila

This district comprises the headwaters of the Gila in southeastern Arizona and southwestern New Mexico (fig. 24). The Gila River forks near the interstate border, one branch (still called the Gila) draining the high land north of Silver City, New Mexico, the other, the San Francisco, swinging northward to head in the mountains of northern Socorro county, New Mexico, just west of the barren San Augustin plains. Both these main tributaries run through rough, broken country, abundantly watered and for the most part heavily forested.

Of the archaeology of the southern branch, the Gila proper, nothing, or next to nothing, is known. Bandelier states that there are numerous ruins, both surface sites and cliff houses, and that the former are similar to the ruins of the Upper Mimbres. He also describes a small cliff house on Diamond Creek.[1] As to the pottery of the district we are entirely ignorant.

The northern fork, the Rio San Francisco, and its tributaries, the Blue and the Tularosa, are, thanks to the explorations of Hough,[2] much better known. This river system drains a high, broken, and in general well-forested region, with abundant water supply but with rather limited amounts of land easily available for primitive agriculture. Because of this the ruins are confined, apparently, to the immediate vicinity of the watercourses, where there are stretches of alluvial bottoms suitable for growing corn. It would seem, from Hough's accounts, that nearly every locality of this sort contains vestiges of former occupation.

1. Bandelier, 1892, pp. 359–62.
2. Hough, 1907, 1914.

The dwellings are situated on the crests of low ridges over-
looking the flats, and although most of them have been
reduced to more or less inconspicuous mounds, enough
remains to show that they were fairly compact aggregations of living rooms enclosing courts or plazas. The rooms

FIG. 24. The Upper Gila area (1) and the Mimbres area (2).

are built of horizontally coursed masonry, but not enough
excavation has been done to allow of any generalizations
as to the details of arrangement or of architecture; nor do
we know whether or not the buildings were more than
one story high. Hough believes that there are kivas in
these ruins, as, indeed, seems probable from the occurrence

in them of round and square depressions. None, however, have been cleared for examination.

The cemeteries usually adjoin the buildings, but burials are also encountered below the floors of rooms.[3] Interments were both at length and flexed; cremation was apparently not practiced except in the lower reaches of the San Francisco near its junction with the Gila.[4]

One very striking feature of the culture under consideration is the abundance of offertory shrines. These occur on mountain tops, in caves, and at springs. Hough describes a large number of such shrines, the most important being the Bear Creek and Tularosa Caves, in each of which were found large deposits of offerings such as miniature pottery vessels and effigies, miniature bows and arrows, cane cigarettes, carved wooden sticks, and many other objects plainly ceremonial in nature. In cleaning out springs great numbers of small pots, chipped implements, and stone beads have been discovered.

So little digging has been done in the San Francisco-Tularosa region that we cannot further characterize the culture as exemplified by the house ruins. The pottery, however, of this district is very characteristic, and differs from that of any other part of the Southwest. Large lots of it are to be found in several museums, but they are unfortunately for the most part commercial collections, accompanied by few or no data, so that we know nothing as to the circumstances of discovery or of the exact provenience of the specimens. It seems certain, however, that the bulk of the material came from ruins in the San Francisco drainage.

There are three wares: corrugated, black-on-white, and red. The corrugated appears in the form of large ollas of fairly good workmanship, but as I have never seen a whole vessel I can say nothing as to the shape. Another type of

3. Hales, 1893, p. 537.
4. Hough, 1907, p. 44.

corrugated ware is, however, very abundant in collections. It is made of a high grade paste which allows the production of very fine work. The commonest forms are rather flat-bottomed bowls eight to ten inches in diameter. The interiors of these bowls are of a deep black color and highly polished (pl. 44, m-p). The black gloss was evidently obtained by the process in vogue today among the potters of Santa Clara pueblo, by smothering the fire toward the end of the burning with an application of pulverized fuel. The blacking, however, in the case of the Tularosa bowls was only produced on the interior, the exterior surfaces being brown or red-brown. In rare instances the exteriors are smooth, but usually they are wholly or partly covered with exceedingly fine corrugation, often tastefully patterned with decorative indentations (pl. 44, m-p). The coils in most Southwestern corrugated ware are relatively broad, running three to five to the inch; in the Tularosa bowls there are often as many as twelve to the inch. This fine corrugation may extend over the entire outside of the specimen, or may be confined to a narrow, fillet-like band just under the rim.

Black-on-white pottery is well-made, the slip bright, and the paint a sharp, clear black. Ollas have not been recovered, the only forms that appear in collections being pitchers, bowls, ladles, and eccentrically shaped pots. By far the commonest type is the pitcher, a round-bodied vessel with cylindrical neck and with a handle which extends from below the rim to the upper side of the body (pl. 44, i-l). A common feature of Upper Gila pitchers, occurring in forty to fifty per cent of all specimens, is the modification of the handle into the crudely modelled form of a small animal. The entire body of the animal may be shown (pl. 44, j), or the handle may be reduced to a small protuberance representing the head and neck (pl. 44, c, d, f).

Black-on-white bowls (pl. 44, a, b) are relatively rare,

their place having been taken, apparently, by the fine corrugated bowls. The few specimens that I have seen are decorated only in the inside, have rather steeply rising sides, and plain rims. Ladles, also, are uncommon; they are all of the bowl-and-handle variety. Bird-shaped, double-lobed, doughnut-like, and other small vessels of eccentric form occur in considerable numbers.

The decoration of the black-on-white ware is elaborate and in most cases well painted. The most typical design is an involved interlocking device in contrasted black and hatching that is applied very skillfully to the rounded bodies of pitchers. It may be either angled (pl. 44, k, l) or curvilinear (pl. 44, i, j). The necks of pitchers are usually ornamented with interlocking key figures in solid black (pl. 44, d-f, i, j, l). Other characteristic motifs are close-set small key figures so arranged as to cover large areas (pl. 44, c), and fine herringbone work in black lines (pl. 44, e, f).

Redware is so rare in collections that I cannot give any adequate description of it. It seems, however, to appear in the form of bowls and pitchers, decorated with dull black paint.

Pottery of the above types is commonly known as "Tularosa," from the fact that most of the collections have come from the ruins in the valley of that river. While its headquarters was doubtless there and in the other tributaries of the Upper Gila, it had a considerably greater range, and trade pieces are found in ruins at great distances from the home area.

Ruins producing nothing but Tularosa pottery occur on the San Francisco from mouth to source, and on its tributaries, the Blue and the Tularosa. The numerous sites that are presumably to be found on the Upper Gila proper, north of Silver City, may also be expected to contain the same wares. I have been told by cattlemen that there are many ruins in the vicinity of Magdalena, New Mexico, and from their descriptions of the pottery it would seem to belong to the Tularosa type, which may thus be expected to occur as far east as the Rio Grande and to extend along that stream from Socorro south to Elephant Butte. I have no evidence of its extension east of the Rio Grande.

To the south Tularosa ware appears not to have penetrated the valley of the Mimbres; nor to the southwest is it found, as far as I know, on the Gila below Solomonsville.[5] In the northwest and north, however, the conditions are different. The White Mountain country, the Zuñi district, and the Little Colorado contain, according to Spier, ruins which show an admixture of Tularosa wares. This admixture is strong in the Black-on-white ruins, may last into the early Glaze period, but disappears in later times.[6] Tularosa polished black bowls have been found by Morris at Aztec,[7] and Nelson has recorded fragments of the same sort of vessels from the upper layers of the Pueblo Bonito refuse heap.[8]

The chronological relation between the Upper Gila culture and the groups to the north and west of it is fairly clear. It was contemporaneous with the later Black-on-white periods in the San Juan and Little Colorado and may even have lasted long enough to be coexistent with the early Glaze period in the latter district. How it compares in age with the Mimbres, Chihuahua, and Lower Gila cultures is not known, but the fact that bowls with polished black interiors are found only in the Upper Gila and Lower Gila cultures seem to show some connection

5. Fewkes figures some corrugated ware from Solomonsville that shows strong Upper Gila influence (1904, pl. 67).

6. Spier, 1919, p. 372. One site has only Tularosa pottery. See also Hodge, 1923, pl. 22, a, showing a Tularosa bowl from a Black-on-white site in Zuñi Valley.

7. Morris, 1919, p. 73.

8. In Pepper, 1920, p. 384.

a   b

c   d   e   f   g   h

PLATE 44. Black-on-white and corrugated wares of Upper Gila type.

between the two. My guess would be that the Upper Gila antedated the Lower Gila, and passed on to it certain elements of pottery technique.[9]

Of remains earlier than the Tularosa in the Upper Gila district we have but one definite instance. In the vicinity of Luna, in the San Francisco Valley, Hough discovered a group of about one hundred pit houses. Upon excavation these proved to be circular structures about fourteen feet in diameter by five feet deep, and apparently to have had conical roofs of logs and earth supported by low, wattled sidewalls.[10] The pottery was neck-coiled dark ware and black-on-white of a sort quite different from the Tularosa type and somewhat resembling the pre-Pueblo black-on-white of the San Juan. The primitive nature of these pit houses and of the artifacts found in them would alone be quite sufficient to indicate that they antedate the true pueblo ruins of the neighborhood, but this was proved beyond question by Hough's discovery of similar pit dwellings underlying a rectangular pueblo in the Los Lentes Valley.[11] Although the still older Basket Maker culture has not been certainly identified in this region, a number of Hough's cave specimens have a suspiciously Basket Maker look.[12]

BIBLIOGRAPHY OF THE UPPER GILA

Bandelier, 1892, pp. 359–65.   Lyon, 1906.
Hales, 1893.   Hough, 1907*; 1914*; 1917;
Heister, 1894.   1918; 1919*; 1923.
Duff, 1897.

   * Major contribution.

9. Since the above was written this guess has been practically confirmed by Hodge's find of a Lower Gila polychrome bowl in a grave that lay *above* rubbish containing an Upper Gila corrugated vessel (Hodge, 1923; and see p. 272).

10. Hough, 1919.

11. Hough, 1907, p. 63 and fig. 28; and Hough 1919, p. 409.

12. For example, an atlatl; see Hough, 1914, pl. 20, fig. 2.

The Mimbres

The Mimbres River rises in the Black Mountains of south-eastern New Mexico and flows southward toward the Mexican border (fig. 24). Although it is tributary to the inland drainage system of northern Chihuahua, its waters sink into the sand on emerging from the mountains, and its lower course consists, except in times of exceptional flood, of an underflow which only appears here and there in the form of seep springs. The upper river, however, is a fine running stream bordered by willows and cotton-woods. Its narrow valley contains many patches of easily irrigable and very fertile land; lower down toward the city of Deming, New Mexico, the country opens out into great barren flats and much of it is practically desert.

Both Bandelier and Hough[1] mention ruins in the Mimbres Valley, but no adequate descriptions of them were published until the appearance of a series of articles by Webster in the *Archaeological Bulletin*.[2] The very extraordinary pottery of this district was brought to the knowledge of students by Fewkes less than ten years ago.[3]

Ruins in the Mimbres extend from an unknown distance below Deming to the headwaters of the river, and also occur in its western tributaries which drain the country about Silver City and Fort Bayard. Passing over for the present certain ruins that belong to another culture, we may say that the typical Mimbres sites are small stone-built pueblos of from five or six to forty or fifty rooms. They are situated, as are those of the Tularosa region, on ridges, or knolls, or slight swells in the valley bottoms,

1. Bandelier, 1892, p. 350; Hough, 1907, p. 83.
2. Webster, 1912a.
3. Fewkes, 1914.

and show no particular desire on the part of their builders
for defensive locations. The houses are in all cases badly
preserved, but from the ground plan of the Swarts ruin
given by Webster [4] and from a hasty personal examination
of several others, it seems to me that these dwellings are
typically puebloan, for they are composed of closely set
rectangular rooms grouped about courts, and both Webster and Duff believe that some of the houses were more
than one story high.[5] Further relationship to the northern
pueblos is to be seen in the presence of the underground
kiva. The important discovery that the kiva was in use
by the ancient Mimbreños was made by Mr. and Mrs.
C. B. Cosgrove of Silver City. Ardent archaeologists, the
Cosgroves have done everything in their power to preserve
the fast disappearing ruins of their neighborhood; and
have purchased and themselves carefully excavated a site
near their home. In it they found a sunken rectangular
room with firepit and ventilator, an undoubted kiva, by
far the southernmost example of such a structure yet
recorded.[6]

The burial customs of the Mimbreños were peculiar.
The bodies were placed, closely flexed, in excavations
under the floors of living rooms. Over the head in almost
every case was put a pottery bowl so inverted as to cover
the skull closely. In the bottom of each such bowl a small
round hole was broken in order to "kill" it ceremonially.

Because so little excavation has been done the details
of the Mimbres culture are practically unknown.[7] We are
accordingly forced, as so often elsewhere in the Southwest,

4. 1912a, pl. 25.
5. Webster, 1912a, p. 113; Duff, 1902, p. 397.
6. Cosgrove, 1923.
7. An expedition sponsored by the Chino Copper Co., and directed by
W. Bradfield of the New Mexico State Museum, has begun excavations in
the Mimbres. A brief preliminary report indicating the great importance
of the work has been issued (Bradfield, 1923). When Mr. Bradfield's complete results are published, they will throw much light on this interesting
culture.

to rely upon the evidence of pottery for our knowledge of distribution and exterior relationships. Of Mimbres pottery there is fortunately a large amount in our museums, but the collections, having been made in all cases by commercial diggers, are inadequately labelled and few or no data accompany them.

The wares are of two sorts, black-on-white and corrugated. Decorated red ware very seldom occurs in pure Mimbres sites. The corrugated ware appears in the form of small pitchers and large full-bodied ollas with slightly flaring rims. The corrugations are narrow and therefore close-set; they are never, so far as I can tell from the sherds that I collected in 1922 from Mimbres sites, sharply notched or indented, being merely waved or roughly punched. Even this amount of decoration is uncommon. Before the pots were sun-dried, the corrugation was usually more or less worked over with some sort of smoothing tool which has given the surfaces a "wiped" appearance.

The standard black-on-white ware form is the bowl, ollas being unusual to judge by the sherds. A few small, narrow-mouthed vessels were made,[8] but apparently no pitchers resembling those of Tularosa, or ladles of any sort. The bowls are relatively deep, run up to as much as fourteen or fifteen inches in diameter, and have rather steeply rising sides. The rim is usually straight (i.e., with no in- or out-curve), square topped, and well finished. Some bowls are slipped with white on both exterior and interior, but the majority have slip only within. The slip is a clear chalky white in most specimens, but it is very often overfired (?) to a yellowish shade. In these cases the normally black paint of the decoration has turned to a bright red.[9] The paint when not so affected is a sharp, clear black.

8. Fewkes, 1914, pl. 8.

9. That this flushing to yellow of the slip and to red of the paint is due to some peculiarity in firing seems proved by the fact that it often occurs on certain parts of pieces the rest of whose surfaces are normal black-on-white.

In bowls the ornamentation is confined to the interior. The rim is usually painted black. Below the rim comes a series of framers, either one or two wide lines, or a set of several very fine lines drawn close together. Under the framers there is often a band of geometric decoration which leaves according to its width a larger or smaller open space in the bottom.

The geometric decorations are extraordinarily well executed, with a delicacy of line and an accuracy of spacing unequalled in Southwestern ceramic art. Only a limited use is made of the key figure, the bulk of the patterns being based on opposed dentate elements in contrasted hatching and solid black. The nature of the geometric designs alone would be sufficient to distinguish Mimbres ware from all others, but it is further characterized by a most amazing profusion of naturalistic drawings. These range from strange composite creatures, evidently mythical, to figures of animals, birds, fishes, insects, and human beings; and there are also many cases of true narrative depiction, such as hunting and trapping scenes, dances, and ceremonial observances. The figures are sometimes interwoven to a certain extent with the geometrical patterns under the bowl rims, but are more commonly set clear in the large round spaces left in the bottoms of the bowls. A few examples are here shown (pl. 45), but to get a true idea of the richness and variety of the work one should consult the excellent pictures in Fewkes's publications on Mimbres pottery.[10]

True naturalism is so rare a phenomenon in all Southwestern pottery decoration, particularly in the early phases marked by black-on-white wares, that its very high development here is most puzzling. When one takes into consideration the superlative excellence of the geometrical work on the same pieces, it must be granted that the ancient Mimbreños were the most remarkable artists of

10. Fewkes, 1914; 1916c; 1922; 1923a; 1923c.

a

b

c

d

e

f

g

h

PLATE 45. Mimbres pottery. Interior designs of black-on-white bowls.

the Pueblo area, not even excepting the yellow-ware potters of Sikyatki. In the case of the Mimbres, there is no question of the intrusion of a foreign art, for no such art exists elsewhere; and furthermore the Mimbres pottery is surely a development of the old stock wares of the Southwest, the black-on-white and the corrugated. In such an instance as this one is almost forced to see the influence of some forgotten individual genius, whose work so stimulated her contemporaries and successors as to result in the founding of a local school or tradition in pottery design.

As the Mimbres culture is at present known to us only by its pottery, we cannot as yet say what its exterior affiliations may be in other respects; but the appearance of the ruins (and the general nature of the pottery as well) would lead us to identify it with the Pueblo civilization, and to place it chronologically in middle Black-on-white times. It does not seem to have been exactly contemporaneous with the Tularosa culture, for, so far as I know, no Mimbres specimens have turned up in Tularosa collections, or vice versa, in spite of the fact that the two districts lie close together.[11] We have so far but a few bits of relative chronological evidence.

It will be remembered that in the third paragraph of this section certain ruins in the Mimbres country were mentioned that belonged to another culture. These are sites about Deming (the Black Mountain ruin is the only one which I have visited) that without question are of Lower Gila affiliation, the pottery being preponderantly of Lower Gila types.[12] Now at the Black Mountain pueblo there is also a very strong admixture of Chihuahua (Casas Grandes) sherds, but no Mimbres ware at all, although typical Mimbres ruins lie within a few miles of the place. Some sixty miles northwest, on Duck Creek, a tributary

11. Mr. Cosgrove informs me that he has never found Tularosa sherds at any of the Mimbres ruins he has examined.
12. See Fewkes, 1914, p. 13.

Courtesy Bureau of Ethnology

After Fewkes

PLATE 46. The Casa Grande ruin.

of the Gila, is an unnamed ruin, one or two rooms of which had at the time of my visit been recently partly cleared out. The sherds on the slopes below this site were a mixture of Lower Gila and Mimbres wares. On examining the excavated rooms, however, it was seen that the sherds protruding from the earth still left in them were mostly Lower Gila with a few Chihuahua specimens, but those embedded *in the adobe of the walls* were straight Mimbres. All of which of course indicates that the houses were built by Mimbreños and later occupied by people of Lower Gila culture. Lower Gila and Chihuahua being approximately contemporaneous, these data practically prove that Mimbres preceded them both.

The pottery of the Mimbres has, as I pointed out several years ago,[13] certain points of resemblance to that of Chihuahua; the likeness is to be seen in the use, by artists of both areas, of negative drawing, and in the forms of certain bird and serpent heads. As the Mimbres ware is without much doubt earlier than the Chihuahua, the above similarities must be accounted for, I think, by Mimbres influence on the formative stages of the Chihuahua culture, which, as will be shown below, appears to be a mixture of Pueblo and Mexican elements.

I have gone into these matters at length in order to bring out the fragmentary nature of our present knowledge and the need of careful stratigraphic and analytical studies. Data to settle these questions positively are to be had; it is merely necessary to do more field work and to keep the problems constantly in mind.

We have as yet no evidence as to the presence of antecedent cultures, pre-Pueblo or earlier, from the Mimbres.

13. Kidder, 1916, p. 268.

BIBLIOGRAPHY OF THE MIMBRES

Henshaw in Putnam, 1879, pp. 370–71.

Bandelier, 1892, pp. 350–58.

Taylor, 1898.

Duff, 1902.

Hough, 1907, pp. 83–89.

Webster, 1912; 1912a*.

Fewkes, 1914*; 1915; 1916b; 1916c; 1922; 1923a*; 1923c*.

Bradfield, 1923*.

Cosgrove, 1923.

* Major contribution.

The Lower Gila

The country we are about to consider comprises the valley of the Gila from Solomonsville, Arizona, west to Gila Bend; it also includes the lower valley of the Gila's great northern tributary, the Salt, and that of its southern affluents, the Santa Cruz and the San Pedro (fig. 25). This is a very large stretch of territory and is in many respects different from any which we have so far taken up. The average elevation of the land is much less, there is little rainfall, the winters are mild and the summers exceedingly hot. Vegetation is correspondingly scanty, and many southern desert growths appear. In spite of the general barrenness of the country much of the soil along the rivers is very rich, and where water can be got upon it is of amazing fertility.

The archaeological remains are also unlike those of any of our other districts, and are in some ways so aberrant that, were it not for the pottery, we should be forced to consider that we had overstepped the limits of the Southwestern culture area. Although little is known of the ruins, they all seem to have certain features in common. It is wisest, therefore, to consider first one of the few sites that has been carefully studied. The best known ruin of the Lower Gila region is Casa Grande (pl. 46), a site discovered in the early historic period, frequently described by explorers and archaeologists, and recently excavated by Fewkes.[1] It consists of a large five-room central structure forty feet long by sixty feet wide. The massive walls are of adobe and formerly extended to a height of at least three stories. About it are lower buildings, also of adobe, made up of large but not uniformly sized rectangular

1. For early accounts of Casa Grande, see Fewkes, 1912, pp. 53–81.

rooms. The whole is surrounded by a heavy adobe wall
probably once seven or eight feet high; this forms a rectangular enclosure some 420 feet long by 230 feet wide
(pl. 47). Fewkes has very aptly termed groups of this sort
"compounds." There are several others in the immediate

FIG. 25. The Lower Gila area.

vicinity, smaller than Casa Grande, but closely similar to
it. In one of them, "Compound B," are both adobe buildings and the remains of less solidly made houses, the walls
of which consisted of upright stakes covered with mud.[2]
Some of these houses were congregated on large, low,

2. Fewkes, 1912, pl. 26.

pyramidal substructures. The method of erecting adobe
walls in the various Casa Grande buildings much resembles
modern concrete work. To quote Mindeleff:

> The walls are composed of huge blocks of earth, three
> to five feet long, two feet high, and three to four feet
> thick. These blocks were not molded and placed in
> situ, but were manufactured in place. The method
> adopted was probably the erection of a framework of
> canes or light poles, woven with reeds or grass, form-
> ing two parallel surfaces or planes, some three or four
> feet apart and about five feet long. Into this open box
> or trough was rammed clayey earth obtained from the
> immediate vicinity and mixed with water to a heavy
> paste. When the mass was sufficiently dry, the frame-
> work was removed along the wall and the operation
> repeated.[3]

The rectangular compound as seen at Casa Grande is
evidently the unit of Lower Gila architecture. A village
might have consisted of one or several compounds, each
having a large central building, a number of smaller
houses, and a heavy surrounding wall. The exact function
of the different elements is unknown, but it seems likely
that the large central structure was a sort of temple. The
smaller houses may have been ceremonial in nature, resi-
dences of priests, or, less probably, the dwellings of the
people. Most observers, however, seem to believe that the
commoners lived in more perishable quarters, perhaps
such log-walled houses as were found in Fewkes's Compound B. In any case the whole conception of a Lower
Gila community of the Casa Grande type is radically unlike that of a Southwestern pueblo, which has no single
dominating structure, either religious or residential, and
in which the living rooms of all the people are identical in
size and construction. The Casa Grande groups seem to

3. Mindeleff, 1896a, p. 310.

have been laid out on lines very similar to those of Central Mexican communities, and the resemblance is still further heightened by the pyramidal substructure seen in Compound B.

Sociological conditions are always strongly reflected in architecture and village planning; hence it is to be inferred that the people of the Lower Gila were organized on a different and probably a less democratic basis than were the true Pueblos. The result of this may perhaps be seen also in the extraordinarily elaborate irrigation works executed in the district, works so extensive as to hint at the existence of a strongly centralized form of government.[4]

In such of the Lower Gila ruins as have been excavated evidence of two kinds of mortuary customs have come to light: cremation and inhumation. Cremation would appear to have been the commoner method. The bodies were burned on large "pyral mounds," and what fragments of bones were left unconsumed were enclosed in jars and buried in the edges of the mounds. Offerings of ceremonially broken ("killed") pottery were frequently placed about the cinerary urns.[5] Inhumation seems to have been less regularly practiced; in most such cases the body was placed in a hole dug in the floor, or even in the wall, of a house or temple structure and carefully mudded in, thus occupying a sort of adobe sarcophagus. Mortuary pottery with such burials was seldom "killed." Cushing believed that these two methods of disposal indicated a difference in the rank of the dead; the common people being cremated, the priestly class interred.[6] Although this is, of course, quite possible, and indeed the general layout of the Lower Gila settlements seems to suggest that a sociologic system involving strong differentiation between

4. See Hodge, 1893.
5. Cushing, 1890, p. 172.
6. Cushing, 1890, p. 174.

classes and masses was in force in that district, yet it is perhaps even more likely that the two sorts of mortuary customs represent a change in culture, and accordingly a more or less considerable lapse of time. As will be brought out in the discussion of the pottery, two distinct groups of wares come from the Lower Gila ruins, wares so unlike as to raise the suspicion that they may even have been manufactured at different periods. The accounts of both Cushing and Fewkes, the only investigators who have done any excavation in these sites, indicate that there are large deposits of refuse at and about the ruins, and it is unfortunate that neither of them were able to make any stratigraphic studies. It is certain that important chronological information could be obtained from the Lower Gila.

Although the architectural remains of the Lower Gila communities present many non-Southwestern features, the culture of the district is in certain respects surely allied to that of the Pueblos. This is illustrated most clearly by the pottery. Lower Gila vessels, although aberrant in certain respects, are in shape and in technology very similar to those of the country to the north and east; and in the decoration many typical Southwestern elements are to be recognized.

There are three principal wares: plain red, polychrome red, and red-on-gray. Very little corrugated pottery appears in collections from these ruins; and when it does, it is in the form of small sherds.

The plain red pottery occurs in three varieties: (1) unslipped pieces of a light brick-red color; (2) slipped pieces of a richer red with black firing clouds; (3) large-mouthed pieces (bowls, dippers, etc.) with polished black interiors.

The base clay of all these is reddish gray and of rather coarse texture, thickly but not grossly tempered with finely ground particles of quarts or some other silicious rock. The second and third classes differ from the first only in the

After Fewkes

PLATE 47. The Casa Grande ruin excavated. Photograph of a model showing the main structure, the groups of smaller rooms, and the enclosing wall. The whole forms a typical Lower Gila "compound."

addition of a slip, which in both of them is rich turkey red and often contains a considerable amount of powdered mica. The surfaces of both are well smoothed and in some cases made glossy by means of the rubbing stone.

The most interesting specimens are the bowls and dippers with polished black interiors, as they remind us of like wares from the Upper Gila, the Chihuahua basin, and modern Santa Clara. The exteriors are always red, some with and some without firing clouds; the interiors are a deep jet black, often bluish or greenish in certain lights.

FIG. 26. Lower Gila vessel shapes.

The surface is very highly polished, smooth, even, and glossy (pl. 48, b).

Bowls are all straight rimmed; there is never any in- or out-curve, bevel, or thickening. The largest examples are shallow, with a flat base and flaring sides (fig. 26, a). From this they shade gradually off into smaller and relatively deeper types (pl. 48, b; fig. 26, b), and so pass into tiny handleless cups (fig. 26, g).

Cups and mugs (pl. 48, a; fig. 26, i) occur in great variety both of size and shape. Apart from the difference in color they are quite unlike the mug form of Mesa Verde black-

on-white ware in that the handle never runs to the bottom
of the side. Some of them are not over one and one-half
inches high by two inches in diameter, and are shaped almost exactly like modern teacups. From this form they run
up through larger replicas of the same to mugs (fig. 26, i),
the biggest examples being ten inches to twelve inches high.
None of them have constricted necks like the pitchers of
other regions. The handles are heavy, being composed of a
solid round bar of clay. They run from just below the rim
to a point about halfway down the side. A few examples
of the taller types are not provided with handles.

Dippers (fig. 26, e, f) are so called to distinguish them
from the ladles of other regions, although they doubtless
served the same functions. They have no true handles and
are thus really bowls, modified by having part of one side
somewhat elongated and bent outward and made into a
sort of "tab" by which the piece can be lifted. A few of
them distantly resemble the "half-gourd" ladle, but the
shape of the majority is very distinctive. The inner surface
of these dippers is almost always polished black. Bird- or
foot-shaped pots are very common (fig. 26, d).

Ollas vary a great deal, but there seem to be two main
types with a number of intermediate examples between
them. The first may be called the "high-necked" olla (fig.
26, h). It has a rounded, sometimes recurved, underbody,
a very wide and sharp shoulder, and a straight cylindrical
neck, which is usually between one-third and one-half of
the total height of the vessel. Most of these ollas are from
fifteen to twenty inches high.

The second class, "round-bodied" ollas (fig. 26, j), are
less uniform in shape, the variations being produced by the
raising or lowering of the point of greatest diameter. In
general these ollas are smaller than the "high-necked"
variety, but in the Peabody Museum collection fragments
are preserved of a vessel of this form which was apparently
about six feet in circumference and two and a half feet

high. Some modern storage jars reach proportions comparable to this, but I know of nothing in ancient pottery to approach it.

Polychrome redware is the typical pottery of the Lower Gila. The base clay and general technology are exactly the same as in the plain red, but the pieces are more carefully finished. The black firing clouds, which in the plain red seem not to have been guarded against, or perhaps even to have been intentionally produced for their decorative qualities, are rarely seen on the polychrome. The visible surfaces bear a clear red slip, well polished, and upon this are applied bands and other fields of white slip, upon which, in turn, are painted the decorations in black. The majority of designs are in black alone, but red is occasionally introduced to set off or complement some element of the main black device (pl. 49, c). It is never used, I think, in producing independent figures.

Polychrome bowls fall into two classes: (1) those with rounded sides (fig. 26, b); (2) those with sides more or less vertical, with outcurving (fig. 26, c) or straight lip. In both cases the whole interior is slipped with white, and the black, or black and red, design applied over it. The decoration usually takes the form of an "all-over" figure (pls. 48, d, e; 49, d, e); less commonly it is a band leaving a round empty space in the bottom. Bowls of Class 1 are plain red on the exterior. Class 2 bowls, however, bear an encircling band of white slip about the upper half or two thirds of the exterior, and this space is further elaborated with decoration in black, or black and red. The rims of both classes are generally left red, although in a few cases they are slipped with white (either wholly or in sections) and ticked with black.

Cups, mugs, dippers, and bird-shaped pots do not differ greatly in shape from the like forms in plain red ware described above. Polychrome dippers are much rarer than plain red ones, there being no perfect examples in the Peaa b c

d e

f g

PLATE 48. Lower Gila pottery.

body Museum collection. All these pieces have decorated zones of white slip.

Ollas (pl. 48, f, g) are the handsomest examples of the polychrome technique. In shape they form a somewhat less sharply defined type than do the high-necked plain red ollas; the shoulder is rounder, the neck lower and less cylindrical, and the underbody is not so flat.

The bottom is uniformly red, and is cut off from the main decorative band by a broad black line, broken as a rule by an "exit space" (pl. 48, g). The two zones of ornamentation are, as usual, white with black, or black and red, figures. One encircles the body, another the neck. The two are almost always separated from each other by a band of red.

The decoration is usually in black, but, as was stated above, red counterelements are sometimes introduced. The designs are strictly geometric; life forms, either plant, animal, or symbolic are entirely wanting. While curvilinear elements are common (pls. 48, d, f; 49, b, c), angled patterns predominate, and chief among these are various modifications of the ubiquitous key figure (pls. 48, e, g; 49, e). Bands consist of a series of repeated units, often worked into a current design by means of decorative connections between the units; interlocking scrolls with toothed backs occur again and again (pl. 49, c). A characteristic feature of Lower Gila art is the use of small triangles set along lines or on the margins of painted areas to produce a sawtooth edge (pls. 48, e; 49, d).

In the case of bowl interiors where an all-over decoration is applied, it often takes the form of a dual balanced design in black or in black opposed to hatching (pls. 48, d, e; 49, d, e).

We now come to the red-on-gray pottery. Judging from the small number of whole pieces of this ware in the Peabody Museum collections, it might seem to have been rather uncommon, but an examination of the sherds from the ruins excavated shows that this was not the case. The base clay is reddish yellow, containing a moderate amount of tempering material, some of which is crushed quartz and some a substance which may be either ground-up potsherds or tiny bits of tufaceous rock. The visible surfaces are treated with a grayish or buff-colored slip so thin as to be almost a wash. In it can be made out small particles of mica. The surfaces are well smoothed but are never polished, the finishing was done with an implement that has left numerous faint scratches and striations in the slip. The rubbing stone was obviously never used.

The paint of the ornamentation is usually a sort of faded chocolate-red; it is dark crimson in certain examples that seem to have been particularly thoroughly fired. This pigment does not stand out sharply from the surface of the ware, but appears to have sunk into it, giving a flat, dull look to the designs. This is due, probably, both to the porosity of the ware and to the thinness and lack of body of the paint itself.

Little can be said of the shapes of red-on-gray pottery, as so few whole pieces are available. A sort of globular cup with a single handle seems to have been a common form, and small ollas with very flat bases also occur. There are sherds of bowls and larger ollas in the collection. The former were apparently dish-like, with flat bases and flaring sides (a type not seen elsewhere among ancient Southwestern pottery); the latter seem to have been more round in the body than polychrome or plain red examples. Scoops or dippers are not represented.

In decoration red-on-gray ware is strikingly different, not only from the polychrome of this region, but also from all other groups of pottery in the Southwest. The principal difference lies in the fact that the designs, instead of consisting of repetitions of bold geometric units, coherently arranged in bands, squares, or other definite zones and areas, are made up of series of tiny independent units, most of them evidently produced by a single stroke or "quirk" of the brush, and these are used as fillers of zones, or to give a sort of "texture" to the zone, rather than as elements of a coherent ornament. I give a selection of these little elements (fig. 27). All of them are seen again and again on the sherds, arranged in series of lines, horizontal, vertical, and oblique. There are simple dots and dashes, crosses, an infinite variety of squiggles of all sorts, little crude swastika-like figures, and, most singular of all, numerous

FIG. 27. Lower Gila red-on-gray designs.

sets of small animal-like things (fig. 27, h) that pursue each other around and around the sides of bowls, ollas, and globular cups.

All of these units are characterized by hasty, offhand brush work; they appear to have been scribbled on the pots with an eye more to general textural effect than to the achievement of true designs. They represent the impressionist school in ancient Southwestern art, and break very radically from the rigid formality that in general characterizes it.

The same dash and lack of convention characterize also

a

b

c

d   e

PLATE 49. Designs of Lower Gila polychrome ware.

a rarer category of red-on-gray designs, some examples of which are shown (fig. 27, i, j). These consist of meanders, current motifs, interlocking units, and waved and stepped lines. The circle and the spiral are of very common occurrence; but terraced elements in general and the key figure in particular seem to be entirely absent.

I have gone to this great length in considering the wares of the Lower Gila, because no adequate description of them has been published, nor are illustrations of representative pieces available in any book. The red-on-gray ware is especially interesting because, as was said above, it is so radically unlike the polychrome and, indeed, so unlike all other Southwestern pottery, that it gives rise to the suspicion that it may be the result of an intrusion from some hitherto unlocated centre; or may represent an early or a late period of local work. Careful excavation can be counted upon to clear up these points.

In the minor arts the people of the Lower Gila turned out a number of objects not made, or at least not commonly found, in other areas. Their stone axes, for example, are of a peculiar type, with straight back, and three-quarter groove; they are fashioned from hard black stone, and are beautifully shaped. Another peculiar class of objects are miniature effigies of frogs, birds. and animals cut from shell or from thin flakes of stone. Shell was much used for bracelets, finger rings, and pendants.[7] Flat, rectangular slate palettes with decorated borders are also found at Lower Gila sites; never, as far as I am aware, in other parts of the Southwest.

The Lower Gila culture had an extensive range. The easternmost ruin of which I have knowledge is in the Mimbres Valley, at Black Mountain near Deming, N. M.[8] The pottery of this site is typical of the Gila, as Fewkes

7. Axes are well illustrated by Fewkes (1912, pls. 49–56); effigies (ibid., pl. 75, b; and Moorehead, 1906, fig. 47); bracelets (Fewkes, 1912, fig. 48); rings (ibid., pl. 75, a, and fig. 49).

8. Fewkes, 1914, p. 13; and p. 294 above.

points out; but the building itself, as far as I could tell
from surface indications, was a rectangular adobe structure
made up of a double or triple tier of cell-like rooms surrounding a large plaza; I could not make out, nor does
Fewkes mention, any large central "temple." Hence this
ruin seems to be more like a pueblo than a true Gila compound. No red-on-gray ware appeared on the mounds, but
I noticed a considerable admixture of sherds of Chihuahua
(Casas Grandes) type.

Some seventy-five miles to the west, however, in the
Pueblo Viejo Valley near Solomonsville, Arizona, on the
Gila, there are evidently real compounds. The ruins
mentioned here by Fewkes are large, are enclosed by walls,
and contain great central structures; they produce typical
Lower Gila polychrome ware, but seem to contain no red-
on-gray. Both cremation and inhumation occur.[9] For the
next seventy-five miles downstream we have no data for the
Gila, but from a little east of Florence, Arizona, and thence
almost if not quite to Gila Bend, the valley contains a considerable number of typical compounds, including the
famous Casa Grande ruin itself. In the San Pedro Valley,
which enters the Gila from the south between Solomonsville and Florence, are ruins apparently of compound type,
and there are many others in the Santa Cruz drainings,
notably near Tucson.[10] Lastly, the great group of ruins
investigated by the Hemenway Expedition under Cushing
lies in the valley of the Salt, fifteen to twenty miles above
its junction with the Gila.[11]

The culture represented by these enormous adobe constructions, and by the easily recognizable types of pottery
that seem always to accompany them, is a most interesting
one, and it is a pity that we know so little in detail with
regard to it. Fewkes's work at Casa Grande was hampered

9. Fewkes, 1904, pp. 168–87.
10. The Gila, San Pedro, and Santa Cruz sites are described by Fewkes,
1909a.
11. Baxter, 1888; Cushing, 1890.

by the necessity of repairing the buildings, so that he was unable to devote himself to the purely archaeological problems encountered; and Cushing's excavations were very inadequately published. The pressing need is for stratigraphic research, to determine whether or not there is any chronological distinction between the polychrome wares and the remarkable red-on-gray group. Reconnaissance should also be carried out in the Gila country, in order to ascertain if it was ever occupied by makers of black-on-white pottery. At present there is no evidence that this ware, so typical of the earlier phases of Southwestern development, occurs in the Lower Gila.

As to the age of the compounds we have some hints. We know that the characteristic polychrome pottery is later than that of the Mimbres (see p. 296), and we suspect the Mimbres wares to have been made in the middle Black-on-white times. Lower Gila polychrome vessels have been found in Little Colorado sites, as at Stone Axe ruin, where was also found buffware of probably late prehistoric date; but Tularosa type vessels also came from this ruin or group of ruins, as well as red vessels with white exterior decoration, which appear to be earlier than the buffware, so that it is uncertain just where the Gila pieces fit into the Little Colorado series.[12] Hodge, however, has discovered Gila ware at Hawikuh, in the Zuñi country, in association with pottery of his Class C, a fairly late prehistoric ware (see p. 272).

The chronological relation between the Lower Gila and the Chihuahua (Casas Grandes) culture is clear enough. Their contemporaneity is established by many cross-finds of pottery,[13] and by the mixture of the characteristic wares of the two cultures at several sites in southern New Mexico, for example, at the Black Mountain ruin. While neither the Lower Gila nor the Chihuahua

12. Hough, 1903, pls. 57–64.
13. Kidder, 1916, p. 267.

cultures can yet be positively correlated in time with any of the groups we have previously considered, I feel sure that they were in their prime toward the end of the prehistoric period, perhaps at about Glaze 1 times in the Rio Grande, and after most if not all of the pure Black-on-white cultures had passed away.

Belonging geographically to the Gila drainage are the many ruins of pueblos, cliff houses, and caveate lodges that occur in the Verde Valley. I have never had the opportunity of visiting these sites, and the descriptions given by Mindeleff and Fewkes[14] are derived almost exclusively from surface observations. For this reason they contain so little information as to the details of Verde archaeology (the pottery, for example, is nowhere properly described) that it seems wiser not to attempt to classify these sites at present. The pottery, according to Fewkes,[15] is principally black-on-white and corrugated. This would appear to indicate early occupancy and northern, possibly Kayenta, affinities.

BIBLIOGRAPHY OF THE LOWER GILA[16]

Bartlett, 1854, vol. 2, pp. 272–77.
Burr, 1880.
Baxter, 1888.
Cushing, 1890.*
Bandelier, 1892, chaps. 10, 11.*
Fewkes, 1892; 1904, pp. 168–92; 1909a*; 1912.*
Hodge, 1893.
Matthews, 1894.
Mindeleff, 1896a.*

Moorhead, 1898; 1906.
Patrick, 1903.
Huntington, 1914, chap. 7.

VERDE DISTRICT

Mearns, 1890.
Hall, 1895.
Mindeleff, 1896.*
Fewkes, 1896; 1898, pp. 536–76*; 1912a.
Spier, 1919.

* Major contribution.

14. Mindeleff, 1896; Fewkes, 1898, pp. 536–76.
15. 1898, p. 70.
16. For early accounts of Casa Grande, see Fewkes, 1912, pp. 53–81.

The Chihuahua Basin

This, the last great area of specialization definitely associable with the Southwestern culture, lies in the northern part of the Mexican state of Chihuahua (fig. 11, p. 163). Bounded on the west by the high chain of the Sierra Madre, and on the east by lower mountain ranges, is a long, wide valley. The waters which drain into it from the Sierra Madre have no outlet to the sea, but flow into a series of salt lakes, such as the Lago de Guzman and the Lago de Santa Maria; the Mimbres also, geographically speaking, empties into this basin; but actually goes dry far to the north of it. The eastern and northeastern part of the plateau is largely desert, but its southern and western slopes are beautiful rolling uplands, covered with long grass, well watered, and forming one of the finest cattle ranges to be found anywhere.

The archaeological remains are situated for the most part in the western side of the basin. They consist of mound ruins and cliff houses. The mound ruins extend from about the American border to an undetermined distance southward. The majority of them have become reduced to low, inconspicuous piles of adobe, and only one survived into the last century in anything approaching a good state of preservation. This ruin is the so-called Casas Grandes group, which lies on the Casas Grandes River, a southern tributary of the Ascension.[1] Although Casas Grandes was in fair condition when it was examined by Bartlett in the early 1850's, as well as when Bandelier saw it some thirty-five years later, it has recently been so badly destroyed

1. There is a confusing similarity in the names of the principal ruin groups of the Lower Gila and Chihuahua areas. Casa Grande is the Lower Gila ruin, Casas Grandes the Chihuahua site.

that when I visited it in 1922 only a few fragments of wall remained standing. The outlines, however, of the structures described by the earlier writers could still be made out, and the ground plans of certain rooms were plainly discernible.

Casas Grandes was a massive adobe building standing to a height of at least three stories. The walls were built of puddled adobe blocks cast in place in movable frames by the same method that was employed at Casa Grande on the Gila. The rooms were large and rectangular, and were grouped together to form a great central structure with lower buildings about it. Were it not for the absence of a surrounding wall, the ruin would closely resemble a Lower Gila compound.

The other mound sites in the Chihuahua basin are, as was said above, so reduced by decay that little can be learned from a surface examination of them, and none have so far been thoroughly excavated. From Lumholtz's descriptions, however, and from the few observations I was able to make on the sides of pothunters' diggings, it appears that the buildings which once occupied these sites were much less massive and less extensive than Casas Grandes. The walls of all of them are of adobe, but they are generally not more than a foot in thickness, as against three or four feet in some of the Casas Grandes walls. The rooms, too, are smaller, and seem to have been built in rows about square or rectangular courtyards, thus approximating the pueblo arrangement.

It would seem, then, that the practice of "great house" building was less developed in the Chihuahua basin than on the Lower Gila, and that Casas Grandes was an exceptional rather than a typical structure.[2] That it was at least approximately contemporaneous with the smaller settlements is proved by the fact that the pottery from

2. Blackiston, however, mentions some larger ruins which may possibly have been great houses (1906b).

Casas Grandes and from the small sites is about the same. I say "about" advisedly, for there do appear to be slight differences in wares from Casas Grandes and from some of the less conspicuous sites, and in one mound near Corralitos I found evidence in an old pothunter's hole, of a cruder style underlying the later and finer wares of the upper levels. The data, however, are insufficient.

The burial customs of this region were apparently very uniform. Cremation was not practiced. The bodies were flexed tightly and disposed of in holes under the hard adobe floors of the rooms, usually in the corners and often four or five together. With the dead were placed offerings of shell and turquoise beads, as well as the beautiful pottery vessels that have caused the mounds to be so thoroughly ransacked.

Chihuahua pottery or, as it is more commonly called, Casas Grandes pottery, is represented by large collections in several museums, but unfortunately it is mostly unlocated, as the bulk of it was dug by Mexican peons and sold to traders and ranchers. It is very fine, harmonious in color, and in accuracy of line work is not surpassed by any other class of Southwestern ceramics. There are five styles: rough darkware, corrugated ware, polished blackware, redware, and polychrome painted ware.

Of the rough darkware only sherds are known. They indicate olla-shaped vessels of considerable size. Corrugated ware also is only represented by fragments. The bulk of the pieces are of reddish paste, poorly coiled and with the indentations wiped over and nearly obliterated while the clay was still soft.[3] Polished blackware occurs in the form of bowls and small jars. It is excellently made and the glossy black surfaces are as fine as those of the best old Santa Clara pieces. Redware was used for a great variety of

3. Corrugated is not mentioned in my paper on Casas Grandes pottery (Kidder, 1916), as no specimens were in the collections then available for study.

vessels, such as little bowls, medium-sized jars, and many odd-shaped pieces. The redware is occasionally painted with large fret designs in black, but is more commonly decorated by incision, gouging, scraping, or some other sort of surface texturing.[4]

The typical Casas Grandes pottery is the polychrome painted ware. It is a warm yellow color with decoration in black and red. The standard form is the jar (pl. 50), a gracefully shaped vessel seven or eight inches high. There are also many effigy pots made by adding animal, bird, or human heads to the sides and rims of jars (pl. 50, nos. 5, 7, 8, 9); and a few effigies of more realistic type.[5]

While the decoration is elaborate, only a few design elements are used, and of these a considerable number are non-Southwestern in appearance. The ubiquitous key-figure, however, is present, as well as the triangle and the scroll (pl. 50). "Negative," or background, drawing is much used to produce life designs such as birds and human figures. Altogether, Casas Grandes decoration is less Puebloan than is any other class with which we have had to deal. It has obviously assimilated a number of Mexican elements, but its basic structure is nevertheless Southwestern.

Aside from the pottery we have little knowledge of the minor arts of the builders of the adobe mound ruins. They produced large quantities of fine shell beads and bracelets, but did not apparently make the little shell and stone carvings that were turned out so commonly on the Lower Gila. The metate, according to Lumholtz,[6] was provided with four legs, thus differing from all other Southwestern metates and recalling the Mexican type. The stone axe is common, and is beautifully made. It has the same

4. For illustrations of the above wares, see Kidder, 1916.
5. See Kidder, 1916, pl. 3; and Lumholtz, 1902, p. 89.
6. Lumholtz, 1902, vol. 1, p. 88; Bartlett illustrates one (1854, vol. 1, p. 362).

PLATE 50. Pottery of the Chihuahua basin.

straight back and three-quarter groove possessed by Lower
Gila axes. This kind of axe is not found elsewhere in the
Pueblo region, except sporadically on the Little Colorado,
where its presence is probably to be ascribed to Gila
influence.

As to the range of the Chihuahua basin culture we have
no precise information. It extended northward to the
American border and perhaps even a short way into New
Mexico. On the west it only here and there managed to
work through the barrier of the Sierra Madre into Sonora.[7]
For the east we have no data at all, and for the south little
more, although Hewett states that there are no "pueblos"
south of the Babicora plains.[8]

Something may be gleaned as to the exterior relationships of the culture. In architecture it is surely allied to
the civilization of the Lower Gila, and that the two were at
least approximately contemporaneous is proved by cross-
finds of traded pottery. It is connected in some way with
the Mimbres, as is shown by similarities in design elements,
and the use of negative painting; but the finds at the Duck
Creek ruin (see pp. 294–95) seem to show that the Mimbres
culture was the older. There is need for much more work
in this most interesting area: first, reconnaissance to determine the range of the sites; secondly, excavation to find
out whether or not there is evidence of a succession of types
in the district; and thirdly, analytical studies of the remains, to enable us to ascertain which elements are Southwestern and which are Mexican.

Another important question that should be investigated
is the relation between the cliff houses that occur in the
Sierra Madre west and southwest of Casas Grandes, and
the mound ruins of the open country. These houses are
built in caves, are constructed of adobe, and bear a super-

7. What appears to be Chihuahua-type pottery is described by Bandelier
from Huachinera (1892, p. 517).
8. Hewett, 1908, p. 76.

ficial likeness to the cliff dwellings of the north. At present
we have no idea whether they are earlier or later than the
mound ruins; or, indeed, whether they were made by the
same people at all. Of their pottery we know nothing, but
Blackiston states that it is different from that of Casas
Grandes.[9]

BIBLIOGRAPHY OF THE CHIHUAHUA BASIN

Bartlett, 1854, vol. 2, chap. 35.
Bandelier, 1892, chap. 14.*
Lumholtz, 1891; 1891a; 1902, vol. 1.*

Saville, 1894.
Hewett, 1908, chap. 8.
Blackiston, 1905; 1906; 1906a; 1906b; 1908; 1909.
Kidder, 1916.

* Major contribution.

9. Blackiston, 1905, p. 361. The cliff houses are described in that paper;
also in Lumholtz, 1902, vol. 1, chap. 5; and in Blackiston, 1906, 1909.

Conclusions

The data, so far as we can summarize them at present, are now before us. It remains to combine them into some sort of coherent whole. This can best be done in the form of an historical reconstruction, but it must be remembered that such a reconstruction is merely a working hypothesis, designed to correlate our information, and to indicate more clearly the needs of future study. We must have no hesitation in abandoning our conclusions, partly or *in toto,* if contradictory evidence appears.

To begin with, it is safe enough to postulate the former presence in the Southwest of a more or less nomadic people, thinly scattered over the country, ignorant of agriculture and of pottery-making. Their life must have resembled closely that of the modern Digger tribes of the Plateau; that is to say, they dwelt in more or less makeshift houses, and subsisted principally on small game: rabbits, prairie dogs, and doves; and on such wild vegetable products as grass seeds, berries, and roots. As to their language, it is less safe to speculate; but from the fact that peoples of Uto-Aztecan speech seem to have formed the basic population of the highlands from Montana far south into Mexico, it is quite likely that they belonged to that group.[1] Whoever they were, there could not have been many of them, for the natural food resources of the Southwest were probably, even in those ancient times, not sufficient to support more than a very small population. Remains of these aborigines have not yet been discovered, nor will they be easy to distinguish from those of such modern nomads as the Apache and Paiute, unless they are found buried below the relics of later cultures.

1. See Goddard, 1920.

These supposedly original Southwesterners eventually acquired the knowledge of corn-growing; they took up farming in a more or less haphazard way, but its practice did not at first react very strongly upon their way of life; for the Basket Makers, as we call the earliest agriculturists, apparently had no permanent houses, nor did they make pottery. As to the date of the introduction of corn we are still ignorant, but it is possible to make certain deductions.

Corn was originally brought under cultivation in the highlands of Mexico or Central America. This general locality is indicated by the identification of the probable wild ancestor of corn, a heavy-seeded grass which grows only in that region.[2] How long ago Mexican agriculture began is unknown; the remains indeed, of the first farmers, the Mexican Basket Makers so to speak, still await discovery. Corn, however, is a very highly specialized cereal, a fact which would seem to indicate great antiquity. Be that as it may, corn-growing was without any question the factor which made possible the development of all the higher American civilizations, and so the discovery of agriculture must have long antedated their rise. Now the Maya, apparently the oldest and certainly the most brilliant of these civilizations, was at its zenith during the sixth century of the Christian era; and its complex calendar system, which we must suppose to have taken several centuries to develop, had undoubtedly been perfected by the year 1 A.D.[3] It is, therefore, not rash to guess that the Maya began to differentiate themselves from the other archaic corn-growing peoples as long ago as 1000 B.C. Judging by the rate of progress made by nascent civilizations elsewhere in the world, it seems safe to allow at least two thousand years more for the period that elapsed be-

2. Harshberger, 1893.

3. Since the above was written Spinden has announced in the press the discovery that the Maya calendar was in use as early as the seventh century before Christ.

tween the time of the first cultivation of corn (say at about 3000 B.C.) and the beginnings of the Maya culture.[4] During these two millenniums we must allow for the early, localized practice of agriculture in the highlands; and the subsequent very extensive diffusion of the primitive corn-growing, pottery-making complex known as the Archaic Mexican culture.[5]

All this somewhat speculative time reckoning does not help us directly in our attempt to arrive at an approximate date for the introduction of farming in the Southwest, and the consequent springing up there of the Basket Maker culture; but it does give us a certain sense of perspective, and makes it seem quite possible that the Basket Makers as we know them lived as long ago as fifteen hundred or two thousand years before Christ. I believe, indeed, because of the simple and undifferentiated nature of Basket Maker corn, that the practice of corn-growing may have spread into the Southwest in the pre-Archaic period of Mexico, and that the influence of the developed Archaic is perhaps to be seen in the pottery and crude figurines of the post-Basket Makers.

There is still another set of considerations which bear on the question of chronology, namely, the problem of whether the entire development of the Pueblo civilization was an autochthonous one, or whether it consisted of a series of cultural leaps stimulated from without. If the second supposition be true, the post-Basket Maker stage might have grown up elsewhere and imposed itself directly on the antecedent Basket Maker, the pre-Pueblo on the post-Basket Maker, and the true Pueblo on the pre-Pueblo. Such a process would not necessarily have required a great stretch of time, for the long developmental stages of each culture might have taken place in other areas.

When our knowledge of Southwestern archaeology was

4. In this connection see Wissler, 1919, p. viii.
5. For a valuable discussion of the Archaic, see Spinden, 1922, chap. 1.

less full than it is today, transition stages between the main periods were not recognizable, and a theory of development by jumps or influxes seemed necessary to account for the observed facts. Now that transitions are beginning to be found, it is becoming increasingly evident that the Southwest owes to outside sources little more than the germs of its culture, and that its development from those germs has been a local and almost wholly an independent one. This being the case, the time required must have been long, and the postulated date of Basket Maker origin of 1500 to 2000 B.C. does not seem at all improbable.

At some early time, then, the Southwestern nomads took up the practice of corn-growing; but at first their agriculture sat lightly upon them; their crops were not of sufficient importance, nor had their methods of cultivation become intensive enough, to tie them very closely to their fields. Eventually, however, better care brought fuller harvests, and it became necessary to provide storage places for the garnered grain. Where caves were available they were used, holes being dug in the floors for caches. The population undoubtedly increased, and the leisure acquired from the possession of surplus foodstuffs, and the consequent partial release from the exacting requirements of the chase, allowed the people to work at, and to perfect, their arts, and to lavish time upon elaborate sandal weaves, fine basketry, and carefully made implements. But they were as yet ignorant of pottery.

Such were the Basket Makers. Their range is known to have covered south-central and southeastern Utah and northeastern Arizona (fig. 28); but from the fact that the knowledge of agriculture and the seeds of corn reached them from the south, it is probable that tribes of similar culture occupied parts of New Mexico and southern Arizona, and stretched southward well into Mexico. It seems likely, however, that Basket Maker culture reached its highest and most characteristic development in the San

Juan, for the cultures which appear to have developed from it, and which ultimately spread out and gave rise to the later Pueblo civilization, had their origin, as will be shown presently, in that country.

In the course of time the Basket Makers, becoming more

FIG. 28. Distribution of Basket Maker sites as known at the present time.

and more dependent upon their crops, and correspondingly more sedentary in habit, either discovered for themselves, or (more probably) learned from tribes to the south, that vessels fashioned from clay, dried in the sun, and finally fired, were easier to make, and more suitable for holding water and for cooking, than the baskets that had hitherto served these purposes. At about the same period they began to enlarge their storage cists into dwellings, to wall them higher with slabs, and to provide them with pole-and-brush roofs. These two great advances mark the opening of the post-Basket Maker period. That its culture

FIG. 29. Distribution of post-Basket Maker sites as known at the present time.

was merely a developed phase of the Basket Maker there can be little doubt, the headform of the people remained the same, several old Basket Maker arts, such as twined-woven bag making, held on in degenerate form, and the territory occupied includes most of the known Basket Maker country. Post-Basket Maker remains occur throughout the whole San Juan drainage and also appear in the northern parts of the Little Colorado watershed (fig. 29).

Guernsey has found indications that the pottery of certain post-Basket Maker sites is much cruder than that of others, and Morris's Long Hollow settlements with their well-decorated black-on-white ware would seem to represent a late phase of the culture little inferior to the pre-Pueblo.[6] Thus we have a hint that the post-Basket Maker period was a long one, during which a steady evolution in all the arts went on.

There now comes one of the apparent breaks in continuity which formerly made it seem that Southwestern growth must have advanced in leaps stimulated from without the area. To be explicit: the pre-Pueblo, the next stage of which we have knowledge, shows a population with an entirely different headform. Furthermore, the houses began to be grouped into more or less compact communities.

It must be remembered that pre-Pueblo remains were known long before the discovery of the post-Basket Maker stage, and the gap between pre-Pueblo and Basket Maker was accordingly so very wide that it was hard to see any relationship between the two. With the post-Basket Maker culture now becoming understood, however, the break is being narrowed; we have the post-Basket Maker slab-walled house standing between the Basket Maker cist and the pre-Pueblo dwelling, and the crude and advanced styles of post-Basket Maker pottery to indicate a local growth in that art. The new and so far unexplained elements in the pre-Pueblo complex are the presence of the bow and arrow, the use of cotton, and particularly the practice of skull deformation.

The skulls of the Basket Makers and post-Basket Makers are dolichocephalic and undeformed; those of the pre-Pueblo are, as far as we know, always artificially flattened

6. Morris, 1919, p. 194, and review of same by Kidder and Guernsey (1920).

posteriorly (pl. 33). This flattening renders it difficult to
tell what the natural form of the head might have been,
and it is possible that the mere introduction of hard-
bedded cradles (a not very radical cultural change) might
have caused this effect, and that the pre-Pueblos were
really as long-headed as their predecessors. My feeling is,
however, that the pre-Pueblo were actually of a different
physical type, naturally brachycephalic, and that their
broad-headedness was merely accentuated by deformation.[7]

It seems, therefore, that we must recognize the arrival in
the Southwest of a new race, which eventually became
the preponderating one, to the submergence of the old
dolichocephalic strain. But (and this point deserves emphasis) the new people, if such they were, introduced no
new cultural elements except cotton and perhaps the bow
and arrow. The really vital traits, agriculture, pottery,
and semipermanent houses, were already in the possession
of the post-Basket Makers. The broad-heads, then, merely
took over the old way of life and added certain improvements; but in general carried it on in a perfectly normal
course of development.

The pre-Pueblo period saw some increase in the agricultural population of the Southwest and a considerable en-
largement in the territory occupied. Pre-Pueblo sites are
found throughout the entire San Juan country, as well as
in parts of the Rio Grande, the Little Colorado, and the
Upper Gila (fig. 30). Wherever this culture penetrated it
resulted in the introduction of more or less permanent
settlements and in the manufacture of black-on-white and
neck-coiled pottery. It is probable that as the houses became more solidly built, more drawn together, and more
commonly above ground, there was evolved a rudimentary
type of kiva, a ceremonial survival of the subterranean and

7. For a discussion of the relation between skull deformation and headform, see Hooton, Peabody Museum Papers, vol. 8, no. 1, pp. 85–89.

semisubterranean dwellings of former days. Such rooms
have been found in association with pre-Pueblo ruins in
northeastern Arizona and southwestern Colorado,[8] both
sites in the San Juan drainage. The San Juan, indeed,
appears to have been the breeding ground and place of

FIG. 30. Distribution of pre-Pueblo sites as known at the present time.

dissemination of all the traits typical of the pre-Pueblo
culture, for it is there that the remains are most abundant
and most highly specialized; and as one goes out from the
San Juan one seems to find the pre-Pueblo culture considerably less advanced.

8. Kidder-Guernsey, 1919, p. 43; Morris, 1919, p. 186.

At the present time we possess enough data as to pre-Pueblo ruins to enable us to characterize them fairly accurately. We also have abundant data as to the developed Pueblo culture. But the small pueblo-like ruins that presumably were built during the transition period between the two are, as Morris observes,[9] practically unknown. I use the term "transition" advisedly, for it is evident that there was no sharp break, either in culture or in race between pre-Pueblo and Pueblo. It is most important, then, that these small ruins be sought out and excavated, because in them we should find the germs of all the traits that were later developed and combined to form the classic Pueblo culture.

Lacking these data, we are forced to proceed with our reconstruction on the basis of very scanty information. All we know is that scattered over almost the entire Southwest are little ruins built of horizontally coursed masonry, or of adobe, with closely grouped rectangular rooms and containing corrugated and black-on-white pottery. All such sites I class together as belonging to the early Pueblo period, for wherever they are even cursorily investigated they prove to have antedated the larger pueblos. The limits of their enormous range (fig. 31) extend from southern Nevada east and north to Great Salt Lake in Utah, east again to Colorado, down the edge of the Rockies to the headwaters of the Rio Grande, east again around the southern end of the Rockies practically to the Texas border, thence southwest across New Mexico to the neighborhood of El Paso, along the southern border of New Mexico, south of the headwaters of the Gila and Salt, along the southern base of the Mogollons, thence across to the edge of the western Arizona desert and so northwest to southern Nevada. The only parts of the Southwest in which so far no remains of the small-house, black-on-white

9. Morris, 1921.

pottery people of the early Pueblo period have been found, are the Lower Gila and the Chihuahua basin.

Thus it appears that the early Pueblo culture spread far and wide over country which had not previously been occupied by pre-Pueblos. I speak of it with considerable confidence as a spreading, for it is virtually out of the question that so uniform a culture could have sprung up simultaneously and independently in several districts. We must, therefore, search, for the point of origin, and all the information we now have points toward the San Juan drainage.

It may, of course, be due to the fact that the San Juan has been more thoroughly worked than other areas, but it is nevertheless very suggestive, that the most abundant and most highly developed exemplifications of the early cultures (the Basket Maker, post-Basket Maker, and pre-Pueblo) have been found in or near that country. And when we consider the early Pueblo remains we seem to see the same state of affairs. Early Pueblo ruins are very abundant in the San Juan, and they possess the traits most characteristic of Pueblo culture in greater perfection than do the early ruins in any other area. To be explicit: corrugated ware is at this period of marked excellence in the San Juan, and becomes progressively cruder as we proceed outward; the same is true, though perhaps to a less extent, in the case of black-on-white; the kiva also reaches an early high specialization in the San Juan, and becomes less common and less specialized the further away we get. As to other architectural traits we cannot yet speak, our data being still too scanty, but as will be shown in the consideration of a later period, the typical pueblo style of building also seems to have worked outward from the San Juan.

Somewhere, then, in the San Juan, probably in the northern tributaries, the pre-Puebloans had begun to build their houses of horizontally coursed masonry and to work their rooms into rectangular form. In so doing they were faced by the necessity of keeping certain round chambers, already used for ceremonies, separate from the house clusters. These took on more and more the aspect of places apart, became specialized in construction and in function, and so finally developed into what we call kivas. At the same time the methods of pottery-making were improved; the neck coils of the pre-Pueblo water jars and cooking pots were found to be pleasing, and possibly also of practical value in increasing evaporation or the conduction of heat; they were accordingly extended to cover the entire bodies of the vessels. Black-on-white decoration became more varied. The above improvements in architecture and ceramics were taken over by neighboring groups, and having, so to speak, a head start over most of pre-Pueblo culture, did not encounter the resistance of competition by other localized improvements. They accordingly spread very easily. How rapidly they spread we have at present no means of knowing, but from the fact that great territorial expansion involved very little change, it would seem that the process must have been a relatively quick one.[10] At all events the early Pueblo culture ultimately diffused itself well beyond the former range of the pre-Pueblo, and became planted, as has been said, in territory not hitherto occupied by sedentary peoples. I think that this was not due to actual migration, but rather to a taking over of the culture by tribes who were already semi-agricultural, and therefore ready to embrace the manifest advantages of the new form of life. A certain increase in population, however, must have been brought about by the greater ease of existence and security of food supply; and this increase would naturally have been most rapid at the original point of diffusion, and so would have caused more or less outward pressure therefrom.

10. A parallel phenomenon is seen in the wide and uniform extension of the Archaic culture in middle America (see Spinden, 1922, chap. 1).

I have tentatively located the center of diffusion in the San Juan, and believe that because of the early advantage thus gained by the inhabitants of the San Juan, they continued for a long time to be the leaders in the development of Southwestern culture. They seem to have evolved, late in this period, the unit-type dwelling, a compact and eminently practical home for a small farming community, and one which, as Prudden originally suggested, appears to have had a very important influence on the form of all later pueblo structures.

In assigning all small ruins containing true corrugated ware and more or less unspecialized black-on-white pottery to the early Pueblo period, I may of course be in error, it is wholly possible that some of the examples in the outlying regions may be peripheral survivals into much later times; but, as will be shown presently, the forces that tended to break up this early widespread population, and to concentrate it into more compact groups, would have been particularly unfavorable for the persistence of small isolated settlements along the borders.

The small sites show, as a general rule, little provision for defense against enemies. The villages are seldom large, nor do they often occupy protective sites. Gradually, however, we begin to see the working of the forces mentioned in the last paragraph which were ultimately to bring about the concentrations typical of the later prehistoric and the historic Pueblo periods. To what this integration may have been due cannot be stated definitely, but I am inclined to see in it the result of hostile pressure from without rather than the effect of climatic change. To begin with, many of the districts which were shortly to be abandoned are still among the most favorable as to water supply in the entire Southwest; secondly, many peripheral ruins (as in western Utah and eastern New Mexico) were seemingly deserted at an early time; lastly, the more recent villages are larger, and stronger, and occupy more easily defensible sites, than the older ones.

From the very beginning of agricultural life in the Southwest there must have been strife between the farmers and the hunting tribes. Even the Basket Makers probably had their difficulties with wilder neighbors. But, as has been said before, the Southwest is a land too poor in game to have supported a large nonagricultural population, and the first sedentary people presumably had few foes to trouble them. As the early Pueblos, however, increased in prosperity, and began to extend their sphere of influence outward from the point of origin, they presumably came in contact with the more powerful hunting tribes of the Great Plains, of the Rocky Mountains, and of the northern Plateau. Attacks by these hunters brought the latter rich stores of garnered corn, and they soon came to realize that by raiding the practically defenseless small towns they could supplement their food supply and so maintain themselves in territory not hitherto open to them because of lack of game.

It is not necessary to postulate any great incursion of nomads. A few bands working in here and there and adopting a semiparasitic existence might well have been sufficient to bring about the observed results. But when such a process was started, even in a small way, it must have had the most far-reaching consequences. The parasite ultimately destroys its host, and is then forced to seek new prey; and the nomad once blooded, so to speak, by the sack of frontier settlements, had to push farther in to gratify his new tastes. Ruined farmers, too, their crops destroyed or stolen, might themselves have turned hunter-raiders and so increased the inward pressure. Wars between village and village, or between stock and stock, may also have occurred, but as yet we have little evidence of such feuds.

There is reason to believe that the region north of the

Colorado River was first given up, although some settlements evidently held out for a time along the Grand Canyon and in the Virgin Valley. In the northern San Juan the unit-type villages began to bunch together to form somewhat larger aggregations; the same thing appears to have gone on in the Mesa Verde country and south of the San Juan. In the Kayenta region there seems at first to have been less trouble. In the Rio Grande, the Little Colorado, and the Upper Gila and Salt there was also little or no change from the easy, small-village life of earlier times.

Until this stage the danger from the postulated nomads seems to have come from the north, and the outlying Pueblos were pushed in, or destroyed. Now, however, wild tribes appear to have infiltrated from all sides. They spread out over the San Juan basin, and carried their incursions well to the south. The result was that the small towns of the San Juan had to be abandoned; but instead of giving up the struggle, their inhabitants gathered together in large communities, and these large communities became more or less isolated from each other. Thus their enemies seem to have forced the Pueblos into that very form of life which, by fostering communal effort, was to permit them to attain their highest cultural achievements.

I stress here, as before, the influence of the nomadic enemy; for this appears to me best to explain the observed facts of Pueblo history. The same facts, however, may also be, and indeed have been, explained in accordance with the theory of a progressive desiccation of the Southwest.[11] During the discussion of the Chaco Canyon certain arguments opposed to the desiccation theory were presented, and these apply equally well to the situation in other parts of our area. Although the question is still an open one, the bulk of the evidence now available seems to me to indicate that as far back as the time of the Basket Makers

11. Hewett, Henderson, and Robbins, 1913; Huntington, 1914.

the climate was much the same as it is today; and that aridity, comparable to that of the present, has from the very beginning been one of the most vital factors in shaping Southwestern culture. I find it, therefore, hard to believe in a progressive drying up of the country during the period of its occupancy by man.

Whatever the causes may have been, whether aridity, the attacks of savage enemies, or a combination of the two; the Pueblos gave up great stretches of outlying territory, began to congregate into large communities, and entered that stage of their history which we may call the Great Period, or the Period of Specialization (see fig. 31).

In the San Juan it was indeed a Great Period, for it saw the building of the Chaco Canyon towns, the Mesa Verde cliff houses and canyon-head fortresses, as well as the imposing cliff dwellings of the Kayenta country. In the south, compact pueblos sprang up on the Rio Grande, on the Little Colorado, and even on the Upper Gila and Salt. Still further to the south in northern Chihuahua, and to the southwest on the Lower Gila, there were coming into being the great adobe "casas grandes." The archaeology of the latter regions is too little understood to permit much speculation as to the origin and growth of their cultures; but though their peculiar architecture has no recognized prototype in the Southwest, their pottery is definitely puebloan in style. My feeling is that these two related and contemporaneous civilizations were rather rapidly achieved results of an amalgamation of Mexican Indians, forced northward, with Pueblos forced or strayed south. At all events it is probable that the Chihuahua-Gila cultures were just beginning to get under way at the time that the maximum development was taking place in the Chaco and on the Mesa Verde.

The underlying causes for the Great Period are not hard to discern. Pressure of one sort or another had forced the Pueblos to draw together into large aggregations, where community of interest stimulated community of effort. The difficulties confronting them were sufficient to spur them to their best endeavors, but not great enough to stunt their progress. Life was not too easy, nor yet too hard. They

FIG. 31. Distribution of population during the various periods of Pueblo history. Early Period (unshaded). Great Period (oblique shading). Late Prehistoric Period (horizontal shading). Period of the Conquest (black). Present-day Pueblo villages (white dots).

had reached that vital moment in their history when opportunity and necessity were evenly balanced. And, as before, the San Juan was the seat of the highest development; the achievements of its people in architecture, in the arts, and probably also in social and religious organization, were obviously of great importance in determining the development of the peoples to the south of them. This is most clearly seen in the spread of the massed-terraced style of building which during the Great Period began to come into vogue in the Rio Grande and the Little Colorado.

It was fortunate for the persistence of Pueblo culture that these tendencies did work southward, for the time of the San Juan was at hand. In spite of all they could do, the people of this region were finally forced to give up the struggle; but that they made a hard fight of it is witnessed by the strongly fortified nature of the latest dwellings, and the protective sites chosen for them, particularly in the frontier districts of the north.[12] But eventually Chaco Canyon was abandoned; then the Mesa Verde; lastly the Kayenta plateau; and from that time on the San Juan ceased to play any significant part in Pueblo history.[13]

As to the date of the desertion of the San Juan we have no information; but from the fact that pottery of Toltecan type has been found at Pueblo Bonito, it would seem that these ruins must have been inhabited at some time between 800 and 1100 A.D.[14] Their abandonment can hardly have been much later than 1100, for, as will be shown below, a considerable length of time must have elasped between that event and the arrival of Europeans in 1540.

At the same time as the giving up of the San Juan, or shortly after, their inhabitants left the villages of the Upper Gila. At a somewhat later date the Lower Gila and Chihuahua basin settlements were abandoned. What caused this wholesale exodus of the Pueblos from their former homes we do not know. Many diverse factors

12. For example, the system of watchtowers evolved in the McElmo-Yellowjacket country (see Morley and Kidder, 1917, p. 43).

13. The occupation of the Gobernador-Largo district after the revolt of 1680 (see Kidder, 1920) and the possible use of Canyon de Chelley by the Hopi (see Fewkes, 1906) were merely temporary.

14. For a discussion of Toltecan dating, see Spinden, 1922, p. 155; the pottery mentioned above is referred to on p. 167.

doubtless operated; but from the fact that the process was merely a continuation of the concentration toward the geographical center of the Southwest which began at the close of the early Pueblo period, it seems likely that the same cause, pressure by nomads, was again responsible.[15] The result in deserted territory is obvious, but what the effect upon the actual size of Pueblo population may have been, is harder to gauge. There must have been a considerable shrinkage, but it is not likely that the entire population of the abandoned regions was riped out. Although I am disinclined to allow any great degree of historical accuracy to the Hopi and Zuñi clan migration stories, they do seem to indicate that both communities received increments of population from the north and the south. The best argument for a movement of people from the peripherae toward the center is provided by the marked increase in the number and size of pueblo ruins of relatively late date in and near that center. During the early Pueblo period and even in the Great Period that had just closed, the Rio Grande and the Little Colorado were not very densely populated. The towns of those times (i.e., the Black-on-white sites) were small when numerous, and few when they became larger; now, however, just as the northern and southern districts were being abandoned, villages became much more abundant and much greater in size. As examples of this we may name the great pueblos of the Rio Grande from Socorro to the headwaters of the Chama, and the many new towns that sprang up in the Zuñi country, along the Little Colorado, and about the Hopi mesas.

I think the connection between the two sets of phenomena, abandonment of the outlying districts and sudden increase in population in the central areas, cannot be mistaken. The puzzling thing about it is that the incoming people brought with them so little of their local cul-

15. This is also Nelson's opinion (1919, fig. 1.).

tures. No adobe "casas grandes" were built in the Little
Colorado, no towns of the Mesa Verde or Chaco types were
erected in the Rio Grande. The old styles of pottery became extinct, or were altered so rapidly and completely
that the transitional stages have escaped identification. It
would seem as if the transference of people must have been
by small groups, rather than by whole communities, an
infiltration rather than a migration. Each successive in-
crement became amalgamated with the resident group
that it joined, adopted the local culture, probably stimulated and strengthened it, possibly influenced it to a
certain extent, but seldom, if ever, succeeded in changing
it radically, or in turning its course of development sharply
away from the channels in which it was already running.

As to the date of this era of redistribution we are as yet
ignorant, but we must consider that it took place some
centuries before 1540, because we have to allow time for
the rise, development, and partial decline of the glazed
pottery technique between the end of the Great Period
and the coming of the Spaniards. It is reasonably certain
that Glaze 1 of the Rio Grande series did not originate
until after the abandonment of the Chaco ruins, for no
Glaze 1 pottery, or its accompanying biscuit wares, have
ever been found at a Chaco site; nor has any Chaco Black-
on-white turned up in Glaze 1 Rio Grande settlements.
As, however, the actual dating of many prehistoric ruins
may be expected during the next few years, it is not necessary or even advisable at the present time to indulge in
dating by guesswork.

When the redistribution had become well advanced,
the entire Pueblo population was concentrated in the
limits indicated on the map (see fig. 31). The shrinkage in
territory held, and probably also to some extent in actual
numerical strength, was not yet over, for many districts
were abandoned between this time and the conquest. For
example, a great number of large towns on the Chama and

its tributaries, on the Pajarito plateau, and further south along the Rio Grande were certainly deserted before 1540. The same is true of many settlements in the Zuñi country, along the Little Colorado, and in the Hopi region. In this we seem to see merely a continuation of the pressure that had been felt ever since the early days of the true Pueblo period, rather than the working of new factors. The upshot of it was that in 1540 the entire population was gathered together in sixty or seventy towns, strung out along the Rio Grande from Socorro to Taos, and running westward in a narrow, interrupted line through Acoma and Zuñi to the Hopi villages. The still further shrinkage in the seventeenth and eighteenth centuries, the giving up of the Piro and Tano areas, and the concentration of many groups of other stocks into a smaller number of communities, are matters of documentary record. It should be noted that the extermination of the Piro was largely due to the persecution of the Apache.

To recapitulate, the Pueblo civilization owed its origin to stimuli from without, but once well on its feet it developed in its own peculiar way. It passed through an early phase of wide territorial expansion marked by great uniformity of culture. It then drew in upon itself and enjoyed a period of efflorescence characterized by strong specialization in its different branches. Finally it underwent great hardship, suffered a further diminution of territory, and in 1540 was waging a hard fight for mere existence.

Few races have gone as far toward civilization as did the Pueblos while still retaining the essential democracy of primitive life. Most other peoples, as they advanced from savagery, have first set up for themselves, and later fallen under the domination of, rulers temporal or religious; aristocracies or theocracies have sprung up, and the gap between the masses and the classes has become wider and wider. But among the Pueblos no such tendency ever made headway; there were neither very rich nor very poor, every family lived in the same sort of quarters, and ate the same sort of food, as every other family. Pre-eminence in social or religious life was to be gained solely by individual ability and was the reward of services rendered to the community.

In the sixteenth century the Pueblos had fallen upon hard times; they had been forced from many of their old ranges, were reduced in numbers, and had lost something of their former skill in material accomplishments. But their customs had not changed, and they still held out undismayed among their savage enemies. There can be little doubt that had they been allowed to work out their own salvation, they would eventually have overcome their difficulties, and might well have built up a civilization of a sort not yet attempted by any group of men. It is the tragedy of native American history that so much human effort has come to naught, and that so many hopeful experiments in life and in living were cut short by the devastating blight of the white man's arrival.

The sketch of Pueblo history which has just been presented is the merest outline. Great bodies of data have been lumped together, and no account has been taken of various complexities which are known to be present in some of the regions discussed. Many of the correlations made between one area and another are also unsatisfactorily vague, and some of them rest on the unreliable evidence of surface finds. Many corrections will have to be made, some of them, perhaps, fundamental. But whether or not our working hypothesis can stand the severe tests which we hope to apply to it in the future, it has shown how much still remains to be done. Nevertheless, we are far enough along in our studies to realize that the problems of any given district can be solved, and that accurate correlations between the different districts can eventually be made, so that in the end we shall surely be able to reconstruct with surprising fullness the history not only of the Pueblo culture in its perfected form, but also that of the early cultures from which it originated. The material is remarkably abundant, and, thanks to the dry climate of the Southwest, extraordinarily well preserved. I know of no other area in the Americas, with the possible exception of Peru, where all the steps in the development of a people from nomadic savagery to a comparatively high degree of civilization, can be traced so accurately and with such a wealth of detail.

When the long task is finished, we shall be able to tell a most interesting story, but the aim of our researchers is, or should be, a much broader one than that. We must use our results for the solution of those general problems of anthropological science without a true understanding of which we can never hope to arrive at valid conclusions as to the history of mankind as a whole.

Anthropologists, particularly those who have concerned themselves with the various manifestations of human culture, have reasoned very loosely, have been prone to draw inferences from fragmentary data, to evolve theories which fit well with preconceived ideas. In no science is the need for empirical study more keenly felt. We have had much writing upon culture growth, trait transmission, divergent and convergent evolution, the tendencies of primitive art, the influence of environment on culture, and the like. But when one examines these writings closely, one finds all too often that they are based on data insufficient in quantity or even historically incorrect.

The Southwest alone cannot, of course, give us final answers to any of these broader problems, for the Southwest was only occupied for a relatively short time by a single small branch of the human race. But as to that time, and as to that people, we can learn a great deal; and we shall have, for this area at least, full data which are also historically correct. As chronology is the basis of history, information bearing on the age of Southwestern remains is diligently to be sought for, and we must be constantly on the lookout for new methods of obtaining it.

One such new method is that of tree-ring study, devised by Professor A. E. Douglass of the University of Arizona, for determining the chronological sequence of ruins.[16] His system is based on the fact that in arid countries like the Southwest all vegetable life has a stern struggle for existence. When rainfall is adequate, growth is normal; but during, the frequent dry years growth is checked in proportion to the severity of the drought. Douglass has shown that this irregularity of growth, conditioned by irregularity of rainfall, is clearly and accurately recorded in the width of the annual rings of trees. In a favorable year a broad, easily recognizable ring will be produced; in a bad year an equally characteristic narrow ring. Now let us suppose for example that six good years are followed by three rather poor ones, then by one very bad, one good, and one very good. A sequence such as this leaves a clear record in the rings added to a given tree during those years and one which is exceedingly unlikely ever to be exactly duplicated. Douglass has further proved that all, or practically all, the trees over a whole district will register in exactly the same way. He has also determined that the weather conditions which produced the observed variations in ring growth extended over very considerable areas, trees as much as two hundred miles apart often showing exactly parallel peculiarities of ring growth. To illustrate the application of this method, we will say that one examines and counts the rings in a section of a tree cut in 1922 in Flagstaff, Arizona, and finds that eighty-four rings (i.e., years) in from the bark there ended a peculiar sequence of exceptional years, producing a peculiar and easily recognizable sequence of rings. This sequence must therefore have ended in 1922 minus 84, or in other words

16. See Douglass, 1921, 1922, 1922a; Wissler, 1921.

in 1838. One now examines in section a log used, say, as a roofbeam in an old house in Santa Fe, New Mexico, and discovers that the same peculiar sequence of rings occurs twenty rings in from the bark; thus it is shown that the Santa Fe log was cut in 1838 plus 20, i.e., in 1858. Extending his investigations, Douglass has employed the same process for trees not actually datable, and has studied sections from the roof beams of prehistoric ruins. Through the cooperation of the American Museum of Natural History he was enabled to examine sections of beams from the great Aztec ruin, and recognized in each of them certain peculiar and characteristic groups of rings which allowed him to determine the relative dates of the cutting of the logs. To express these dates conveniently he assigned an arbitrary date, R.D. (Relative Date) 500 to a certain easily recognizable ring and expressed all dates with reference to that year. He found that most of the beams examined had been cut during two periods, namely, in R.D. 524–525, and in R.D. 528. The next series of beams to be examined came from Pueblo Bonito, some sixty-five miles to the south, and in these he recognized the same characteristic ring groups that he had found at Aztec. By counting from them he was able to determine that the Bonito logs had been cut between forty and fifty years earlier than those at Aztec (i.e., in about R.D. 484).

When it is remembered how much material in the way of roof beams, terracing logs, and other woodwork is still preserved in the ruins of the Southwest, it can readily be realized what vast possibilities have been opened up by Douglass's remarkable discovery; for example, we shall undoubtedly be able to make out the exact order of erection of many of the great Mesa Verde cliff houses, and even determine the relative date of building of parts of structures, such as single rooms, kivas, etc. The prospect is fairly dazzling.

In discussing the archaeological evidence, and in con-

sidering Douglass's method as well, we have confined ourselves to the relative dating of remains of man in the
Southwest. It has been shown, I hope, that the outlook is
bright, and that patient work will eventually enable us to
arrange in approximately their proper order all the ruins
that we know at the present time, or shall find in the
future. We must not, however, allow ourselves to evade
the issue of absolute chronology; for if we could apply
dates, even if only approximate ones, to the main stages
of Southwestern development, our historical perspective
would not only be greatly sharpened, but we should also
have acquired data of the utmost value for the solution
of many of the broader problems of anthropology, such
problems, for example, as those of the rate of acceleration
in culture, the rapidity of the spread of culture traits, etc.

For arriving at the age of the basic stages of Southwestern culture, such as the Basket Maker, we have as yet
no reliable evidence whatever. No way of applying geological methods to the problem has been discovered. Help
might be derived from a correlation of the Basket Maker
period with some stage in the history of Mexican culture,
but the actual chronology of early Mexico is by no means
clear.[17] We must for the present, therefore, be content to
work back through the Pueblo and pre-Pueblo periods
from our historic datum of 1540 A.D. Two lines of research seem promising: tree-ring studies, and correlation
with the known chronology of the Maya area.

It has been shown above that the relative dating of
prehistoric sites in the Southwest may be accomplished
by Douglass's method of tree-ring study. This line of investigation has also been extended to include the great
sequoias of the Pacific Coast. It has been found that in
the annual rings of these exceedingly long-lived trees

17. If there is a single problem of outstanding importance for American
archaeology, it is that of dating the origin of corn-growing and the rise
of the Archaic culture in the highlands of Mexico.

there are preserved weather records, so to speak, reaching back for 3,000 years,[18] and it is possible that certain of the more marked peculiarities in tree-ring growth may be due to weather conditions so widespread as to have affected regions as far distant as the Southwest, and that beams used in prehistoric pueblos and cliff houses may yet be actually dated by comparing their rings with those of the sequoias.

Even should the sequoias fail us as a time index, the tree-ring method may yet, it seems to me, be used for ascertaining the actual date of many prehistoric ruins. For example, there are in the New Mexico mission churches many large beams which were cut in the early and middle parts of the seventeenth century; some of these bear carved dates, but all of them should be accurately datable by comparing their outer rings with the inner rings of the three and four hundred years old pines still growing today in the nearby mountains. We may next compare the inner rings of the mission beams with the outer rings of beams from such ruins as stratigraphic studies of the pottery show to have been inhabited during the later stages of prehistoric times. This process may be pursued indefinitely, and it is not beyond the bounds of possibility that we may eventually be able to establish reliable series of overlapping tree growths extending from the present day back to the time when the ancestors of the Pueblos first began to use large timbers in the construction of their houses.[19]

While Douglass's method gives us our best hope for absolute chronology, we must not fail to undertake a second line of investigation which, although it cannot provide us

18. Huntington, 1913.

19. There are few Southwestern ruins from which some beam material cannot be recovered by careful work. Professor Douglass informs me that he has secured useful data from badly decayed, and even from charred, logs. It is evident that no opportunity for the collection of such specimens should be overlooked.

with more than approximate dates, may still serve to throw light on the age of many Southwestern ruins, and act as a cross-check on such results as may be attained by the Douglass system. This second line of investigation must consist in an attempt to determine the time correlation between the ruins of the Southwest and those of the Maya culture of Central America. This may appear a far cry, but one bit of evidence is already at hand, and much more may confidently be expected.

The Maya people, as is well known, erected monuments bearing a wealth of contemporary dates which not only are decipherable, but have been correlated with considerable precision with the years of our own system of chronology.[20] This of course provides for students of Maya archaeology an excellent basis for working out the development of Maya pottery, lapidary work, etc. Hence it should eventually be possible to date with fair accuracy any given Maya pot, jade ornament, or other specimen. Aboriginal trade having been surprisingly active and far-reaching, it is reasonable to suppose that datable Maya objects will be found in, say, central Mexican sites. A few such finds would fix the approximate date of those sites beyond reasonable doubt. Objects characteristic of the thus datable central Mexican cultures may be expected from northern Mexico, northern Mexican specimens from southern New Mexico, and so on. Such dating naturally becomes less and less accurate as we recede from the starting point, for many as yet unassessable factors enter, such as the rate of travel for trade objects, the persistency of objects among a people as heirlooms, etc. Nevertheless much may be done, and the technological and artistic studies necessary for carrying out the attempt are in themselves well worthwhile.

As was said above, there is already one bit of evidence at hand. From Pueblo Bonito, Pepper collected sherds of

20. Spinden, 1922, p. 129.

a certain type of cloisonné pottery characteristic of one phase of the Toltec culture. Fragments of the same, or a closely allied, ware have been found at a Maya site, Chichen Itza, in Yucatan. While it cannot yet be stated just how old the Toltec ruins (which are the headquarters of this pottery) may be, there is no question but that their age will in the near future be ascertained with reasonable accuracy, and then it will be possible to give an approximate date for the occupation of Pueblo Bonito. That anything so fragile as pottery should have been carried in aboriginal trade all the way from central Mexico to northern New Mexico is very surprising. It is also encouraging, for it gives rise to the hope that many other Mexican objects less difficult of transportation will yet be found in Southwestern sites.

We have briefly summarized the data at present available for the study of Southwestern archaeology; have made an attempt to fit these data together into a historical reconstruction; and, finally, have pointed out the need for further chronological information, both relative and absolute. The place of Pecos in the general archaeological scheme is now clear, for of all the stratified sites in the Southwest, Pecos is the largest and was the longest inhabited. If a single outstanding fact has become apparent in our survey, it is the great value of stratigraphy, first for determining the sequence of local types and for solving local problems, secondly for the possibilities that it holds out for providing cross-finds of contemporaneous non-local types and so for solving the broader and more important problems of inter-area chronology. It is by work of this sort that we shall eventually be enabled to piece together the story of the Pueblos and of their ancestors, and by an extension of it shall ultimately recover the history of all the higher American civilizations.

Bibliography

ANONYMOUS
  1918 Excavations at Hawikuh. *El Palacio,* vol. 5, no. 11, pp. 180–84. Santa Fe.
AYER, E. A. B.
  1916 The memorial of Fray Alonso de Benavides, 1630. Chicago.
BANDELIER, A. F.
  1881 Historical introduction to studies among the sedentary Indians of New Mexico. Report on the ruins of the pueblo of Pecos. *Papers of the Archaeological Institute of America. American Series,* no. 1. Boston.
  1890 Final report of investigations among the Indians of the southwestern United States, part 1. *Papers of the Archaeological Institute of America. American Series,* no. 3. Cambridge.
  1890a Contributions to the history of the southwestern portion of the United States. *Papers of the Archaeological Institute of America. American Series,* no. 5. Cambridge.
  1890b The delight makers. New York.
  1892 Final report of investigations among the Indians of the southwestern United States, part 2. *Papers of the Archaeological Institute of America. American Series,* no. 4. Cambridge.
  1892a An outline of the documentary history of the Zuñi tribe. *Journal of American Ethnology and Archaeology,* vol. 3, pp. 1–115. Cambridge.
  1910 Documentary history of the Rio Grande Pueblos of New Mexico. *Archaeological Institute of America; Papers of the School of American Archaeology,* no. 13. Santa Fe.
BANCROFT, H. H.
  1889 History of Arizona and New Mexico. San Francisco.

BARBER, E. A.

1876   The ancient pottery of Colorado, Utah, Arizona and New Mexico. *American Naturalist,* vol. 10, pp. 449–64. Cambridge.

1877   Stone implements and ornaments from the ruins of Colorado, Utah and Arizona. *American Naturalist,* vol. 11, pp. 264–275. Cambridge.

BARTLETT, J. R.

1854   Personal narrative of explorations and incidents in Texas, New Mexico, California, Sonora and Chihuahua. New York.

BAXTER, S.

1888   The old New World. Reprinted from *Boston Herald* of April 15, 1888. Salem.

BEAM, G. L.

1909   The prehistoric ruin of Tsankawi. *National Geographic Magazine,* vol. 20, no. 9, pp. 807–22. Washington.

BICKFORD, F. T.

1890   Prehistoric cave-dwellings. *Century Magazine,* October, 1890, pp. 896–911. New York.

BIERBOWER, S.

1905   Among the cliff and cavate dwellings of New Mexico. *Records of the Past,* vol. 4, pp. 227–33. Washington.

BIRNIE, R.

1875   Report on certain ruins visited in New Mexico. *Annual Report of the Geographical Explorations and Surveys West of the 100th Meridian,* pp. 178–80. Washington.

BLACKISTON, A. H.

1905   Cliff dwellings of northern Mexico. *Records of the Past,* vol. 4, pp. 355–61. Washington.

1906   Cliff ruins of Cave Valley, northern Mexico. *Records of the Past,* vol. 5, pp. 5–11. Washington.

1906a Casas Grandian outposts. *Records of the Past,* vol. 5, pp. 142–47. Washington.

1906b Ruins on the Cerro de Montezuma. *American Anthropologist,* n.s., vol. 8, no. 2, pp. 256–61. Lancaster.

1908   Ruins of the Tenaja and the Rio San Pedro. *Records of the Past,* vol. 7, pp. 282–90. Washington.

1909   Recently discovered cliff-dwellings of the Sierras Madres. *Records of the Past,* vol. 8, pp. 20–32. Washington.

BLAKE, W. P.

1899   Aboriginal turquoise mining in Arizona and New Mexico. *American Antiquarian,* vol. 21, no. 5, pp. 278–84. Chicago.

BLOOM, L. B.

1922   The West Jemez culture area. *El Palacio,* vol. 12, no. 2, pp. 18–25. Santa Fe.

1923   The Jemez expedition of the School. Summer of 1922. *El Palacio,* vol. 14, no. 2, pp. 13–20. Santa Fe.

BOLTON, H. E.

1916   Spanish exploration in the Southwest, 1542–1706. New York.

BRADFIELD, W.

1921   Economic resources of Chaco Canyon. *Art and Archaeology,* vol. 11, nos. 1–2, pp. 36–38. Washington.

1923   Preliminary report on excavating at Cameron Creek site. *El Palacio,* vol. 15, no. 5, pp. 67–73. Santa Fe.

BURR, R. T.

1880   Ruins in White River Cañon, Pima county, Arizona. *Annual Report of the Smithsonian Institution for 1879,* pp. 333–34. Washington.

CHAPIN, F. H.

1890   Cliff-dwellings of the Mancos cañons. *American Antiquarian,* vol. 12, no. 4, pp. 193–210. Chicago.

1892   The land of the cliff dwellers. Boston.

CHAPMAN, K. M.

1921   What the potsherds tell. *Art and Archaeology,* vol. 11, nos. 1–2, pp. 39–44. Washington.

1922   Life forms in Pueblo pottery decoration. *Art and Archaeology,* vol. 13, no. 3, pp. 120–22. Washington.

COLTON, H. S.

1920   Did the so-called cliff dwellers of central Arizona also build "hogans"? *American Anthropologist,* n.s., vol. 22, no. 3, pp. 298–301. Lancaster.

COLTON, M. R. F. and H. S.

1918   The little-known small house ruins in the Coconino forest. *Memoirs American Anthropological Association,* vol. 5, no. 4, pp. 101–26. Lancaster.

COPE, E. D.

1875   Report on the remains of population observed on and near the Eocene plateau of northwestern New Mexico *Annual Report of the Geographical Explorations and Surveys West of the 100th Meridian,* pp. 166–73. Washington.

COSGROVE, C. B.

1923   Two kivas at Treasure Hill, *El Palacio,* vol. 15, no. 2, pp. 18–21. Santa Fe.

CROTSENBURG, C. N.

1900   Cliff-dweller's ruins. *American Antiquarian,* vol. 22, no. 6, pp. 400–01. Chicago.

CUMMINGS, B.

1910   The ancient inhabitants of the San Juan Valley. *Bulletin of the University of Utah,* 2nd Archaeological number, vol. 3, no. 3, pt. 2. Salt Lake City.

1915   Kivas of the San Juan drainage. *American Anthropologist,* n.s., vol. 17, no. 2, pp. 272–82. Lancaster.

CUSHING, F. H.

1886   A study of Pueblo pottery as illustrative of Zuñi culture growth. *Fourth Report of the Bureau of Ethnology,* pp. 467–521. Washington.

1890   Preliminary notes on the origin, working hypothesis and primary researches of the Hemenway Southwestern Archaeological Expedition. *Congrès International des Américanistes, Compte-rendu de la septième session;* pp. 151–94. Berlin.

1901   Zuñi folk-tales. New York.

1920   Zuñi breadstuff. *Museum of the American Indian, Heye Foundation; Indian Notes and Monographs,* vol. 8. New York.

DONALDSON, T.

1893   Moqui Indians of Arizona and Pueblo Indians of

New Mexico. *11th Census of the United States, extra census bulletin.* Washington.

DOUGLASS, A. E.

1921 Dating our prehistoric ruins. *Natural History,* vol. 21, no. 1, pp. 27–30. New York.

1922 Some aspects of the use of the annual rings of trees in climatic study. *Scientific Monthly,* vol. 15, no. 1, pp. 5–22. Utica.

1922a Some topographic and climatic characters in the annual rings of the yellow pines and sequoias of the Southwest. *Proceedings American Philosophical Society,* vol. 61, no. 2, pp. 117–22. Philadelphia.

DUFF, U. F.

1897 The prehistoric ruins of the Rio Tularosa. *American Geographical Society Journal,* vol. 29, pp. 261–70. New York.

1902 The ruins of the Mimbres Valley. *American Antiquarian,* vol. 24, pp. 397–400. Chicago.

1904 Some exploded theories concerning southwestern archaeology. *American Anthropologist,* n.s., vol. 6, no. 2, pp. 303–06. Lancaster.

DUFFIELD, M. S.

1904 Aboriginal remains in Nevada and Utah. *American Anthropologist,* n.s., vol. 6, no. 1, pp. 148–50. Lancaster.

EMORY, W. H.

1848 Notes of a military reconnaissance from Fort Leavenworth, in Missouri, to San Diego, in California, etc., 30th Congress, 1st sess., Senate, ex. doc. no. 7. Washington.

FEWKES, J. W.

1891 Reconnaissance of ruins in or near the Zuñi reservation. *Journal of American Ethnology and Archaeology,* vol. 1, pp. 93–133. Boston.

1892 A report on the present condition of a ruin in Arizona called Casa Grande. *Journal of American Ethnology and Archaeology,* vol. 2, pp. 176–93. Cambridge.

1893 A-wa-to-bi; an archaeological verification of a Tusayan legend. *American Anthropologist,* vol. 6, no. 4, pp. 363–76. Washington.

1896   Two ruins recently discovered in the Red Rock country, Arizona. *American Anthropologist,* vol. 9, no. 8, pp. 263–83. Washington.

1896a The prehistoric culture of Tusayan. *American Anthropologist,* vol. 9, no. 5, pp. 151–73. Washington.

1896b Southern extension of prehistoric Tusayan. *American Anthropologist,* vol. 9, no. 7, p. 253. Washington.

1896c Pacific coast shells from prehistoric Tusayan pueblos. *American Anthropologist,* vol. 9, no. 11, pp. 359–67. Washington.

1896d Studies of Tusayan archaeology. *Internationales Archiv für Ethnographie,* vol. 9, pp. 204–05. Leiden.

1898   Archaeological expedition to Arizona in 1895. *Seventeenth Report of the Bureau of American Ethnology,* pt. 2, pp. 519–742. Washington.

1898a The feather symbol in ancient Hopi designs. *American Anthropologist,* vol. 11, no. 1, pp. 1–14. Washington.

1898b Preliminary account of an expedition to the pueblo ruins near Winslow, Arizona in 1896. *Annual Report of the Smithsonian Institution for 1896,* pp. 517–39. Washington.

1900   Pueblo ruins near Flagstaff, Arizona. *American Anthropologist,* n.s., vol. 2, no. 3, pp. 422–50. New York.

1904   Two summers' work in pueblo ruins. *Twenty-second Report of the Bureau of American Ethnology,* pt. 1, pp. 3–195. Washington.

1906   Hopi ceremonial frames from Cañon de Chelly, Arizona. *American Anthropologist,* n.s., vol. 8, no. 4, pp. 664–70. Lancaster.

1907   Excavations at Casa Grande, Arizona, in 1906–07. *Smithsonian Miscellaneous Collections,* vol. 50 (quarterly issue, vol. 4, pt. 3), pp. 289–329. Washington.

1908 Ventilators in ceremonial rooms of prehistoric cliff-dwellings. *American Anthropologist,* n.s., vol. 10, no. 3, pp. 387–98. Lancaster.

1909 Antiquities of the Mesa Verde National Park: Spruce-tree House. *Bulletin 41, Bureau of American Ethnology.* Washington.

1909a Prehistoric ruins of the Gila Valley. *Smithsonian Miscellaneous Collections,* vol. 52 (quarterly issue, vol. 5, pt. 4), pp. 403–36. Washington.

1909b Ancient Zuñi pottery. *Putnam Anniversary Volume,* pp. 43–82. New York.

1910 Cremation in cliff-dwellings. *Records of the Past,* vol. 9, pt. 3, pp. 154–56. Washington.

1910a Report on the excavation and repair of Cliff Palace, Mesa Verde National Park, Colorado, in 1909. *Reports of the Department of the Interior for 1909,* vol. 1, pp. 483–503. Washington.

1910b A new type of Southwestern ruin. *Records of the Past,* vol. 9, pt. 6, pp. 291–97. Washington.

1911 Preliminary report on a visit to the Navaho National Monument, Arizona. *Bulletin 50, Bureau of American Ethnology.* Washington.

1911a Antiquities of the Mesa Verde National Park; Cliff Palace. *Bulletin 51, Bureau of American Ethnology.* Washington.

1912 Casa Grande, Arizona. *Twenty-eighth Report of the Bureau of American Ethnology,* pp. 25–179. Washington.

1912a Antiquities of the Upper Verde River and Walnut Creek valleys, Arizona. *Twenty-eighth Report of the Bureau of American Ethnology,* pp. 181–220. Washington.

1914 Archaeology of the lower Mimbres Valley, New Mexico. *Smithsonian Miscellaneous Collections,* vol. 63, no. 10. Washington.

1915 Prehistoric remains in New Mexico. *Smithsonian Miscellaneous Collections,* vol. 65, no. 6, pp. 62–72. Washington.

1916   Excavation and repair of Sun Temple, Mesa Verde
        National Park. *Department of the Interior*. Wash-
        ington.

1916a   The cliff-ruins in Fewkes Cañon, Mesa Verde
        National Park, Colorado. *Holmes Anniversary Vol-
        ume*, pp. 96–117. Washington.

1916b   Prehistoric remains in Arizona, New Mexico and
        Colorado. *Smithsonian Miscellaneous Collections,*
        vol. 66, no. 3, pp. 82–98. Washington.

1916c   Animal figures on prehistoric pottery from Mimbres
        Valley, New Mexico. *American Anthropologist*, n.s.,
        vol. 18, no. 4, pp. 535–45. Lancaster.

1916d   The relation of Sun Temple, a new type of ruin
        lately excavated in the Mesa Verde National Park,
        to prehistoric "towers." *Journal of the Washington
        Academy of Sciences*, vol. 6, no. 8, pp. 212–21. Wash-
        ington.

1916e   A Sun Temple in the Mesa Verde National Park.
        Art and Archaeology, vol. 3, no. 6, pp. 341–46.
        Washington.

1917   Prehistoric remains in New Mexico, Colorado and
        Utah. *Smithsonian Miscellaneous Collections*, vol.
        66, no. 17, pp. 76–92. Washington.

1917a   Archaeological investigations in New Mexico, Colo-
        rado and Utah. *Smithsonian Miscellaneous Collec-
        tions*, vol. 68, no. 1. Washington.

1917b   A prehistoric Mesa Verde pueblo and its people.
        *Annual Report of the Smithsonian Institution for
        1916*, pp. 461–88. Washington.

1918   Prehistoric ruins in southwestern Colorado and
        southeastern Utah. *Smithsonian Miscellaneous Col-
        lections*, vol. 68, no. 12, pp. 108–33. Washington.

1919   Prehistoric villages, castles, and towers of south-
        western Colorado. *Bulletin 70, Bureau of American
        Ethnology*. Washington.

1919a   Designs on prehistoric Hopi pottery. *Thirty-third
        Report of the Bureau of American Ethnology*, pp.
        207–84. Washington.

1920   Field-work on the Mesa Verde National Park, Colorado. *Smithsonian Miscellaneous Collections,* vol. 72, no. 1, pp. 47–64. Washington.

1921   Field-work on the Mesa Verde National Park. *Smithsonian Miscellaneous Collections,* vol. 72, no. 6, pp. 75–94. Washington.

1922   Archaeological field-work on the Mesa Verde National Park. *Smithsonian Miscellaneous Collections,* vol. 72, no. 15, pp. 64–83. Washington.

1923   Archaeological field-work on the Mesa Verde National Park, Colorado. *Smithsonian Miscellaneous Collections,* vol. 74, no. 5, pp. 89–115. Washington.

1923a   Designs on prehistoric pottery from the Mimbres Valley, New Mexico. *Smithsonian Miscellaneous Collections,* vol. 74, no. 6. Washington.

1923b   The Hovenweep National Monument. *American Anthropologist,* n.s., vol. 25, no. 2, pp. 145–55. Menasha, Wis.

1923c   Additional designs on prehistoric Mimbres pottery. *Smithsonian Miscellaneous Collections,* vol. 76, no. 8. Washington.

GODDARD, P. E.

1920   The cultural and somatic correlations of Uto-Aztecan. *American Anthropologist,* n.s., vol. 22, no. 3, pp. 244–47. Lancaster.

1921   Indians of the Southwest. *American Museum of Natural History, Handbook Series,* no. 2, 2nd ed. New York.

GREGG, J.

1845   Commerce of the prairies, 2nd ed. New York.

GREGORY, H. E.

1916   The Navajo country, a geographic and hydrographic reconnaissance of parts of Arizona, New Mexico and Utah. *United States Geological Survey,* Water-supply paper 380. Washington.

GUERNSEY, S. J. AND KIDDER, A. V.

1921   Basket-Maker caves of northeastern Arizona. *Papers of the Peabody Museum of American Archaeology and Ethnology,* vol. 8, no. 2. Cambridge.

GUNCKEL, L. W.

1897   Ruins and picture writings in the cañons of the
       McElmo and Hovenweep. *American Antiquarian,*
       vol. 19, pp. 223–26. Chicago.

GUTHE, C. E.

1917   The pueblo ruin at Rowe, New Mexico. *El Palacio,*
       vol. 4, no. 4, pp. 33–39. Santa Fe.

"H"

1894   Recent finds in Utah. *The Archaeologist,* vol. 2, no.
       5, pp. 154–55. Waterloo, Ind.

HALES, H.

1893   Prehistoric New Mexican pottery. *Annual Report of
       the Smithsonian Institution for 1892,* pp. 535–54.
       Washington.

HALL, S. M.

1895   The cliff-dwellings of the lower Verde Valley,
       northern Arizona. *The Archaeologist,* vol. 3, no. 5,
       pp. 119–22. Columbus, Ohio.

HARRINGTON, J. P.

1916   The ethnogeography of the Tewa Indians. *Twenty-
       ninth Report of the Bureau of American Ethnology.*
       Washington.

HARSHBERGER, J. W.

1893   Maize: a botanical and economic study. *Contri-
       butions from the Botanical Laboratory of the Uni-
       versity of Pennsylvania,* vol. 1, no. 2. Philadelphia.

HEISTER, A. L.

1894   Pueblo graves. *The Archaeologist,* vol. 2, no. 5, pp.
       153–54. Waterloo, Ind.

HEWETT, E. L.

1904   Studies on the extinct pueblo of Pecos. *American
       Anthropologist,* n.s., vol. 6, no. 4, pp. 426–39. Lan-
       caster.

1904a Archaeology of Pajarito Park, New Mexico. *Ameri-
       can Anthropologist,* n.s., vol. 6, no. 5, pp. 629–59.
       Lancaster.

1905   A general view of the archaeology of the Pueblo
       region. *Annual Report of the Smithsonian Insti-
       tution for 1904,* pp. 583–605. Washington.

1905a Prehistoric irrigation in the Navajo desert. *Records of the Past*, vol. 4, pt. 11, pp. 322–29. Washington.

1905b Historic and prehistoric ruins of the Southwest and their preservation. *Department of the Interior.* Washington.

1906 Antiquities of the Jemez Plateau, New Mexico. *Bulletin 32, Bureau of American Ethnology.* Washington.

1908 Les communautés anciennes dans le désert américain. Geneva.

1909 The excavations at Tyuonyi, New Mexico, in 1908. *American Anthropologist,* n.s., vol. 11, no. 3, pp. 434–55. Lancaster.

1909a The excavations at El Rito de los Frijoles in 1909. *American Anthropologist,* n.s., vol. 11, no. 4, pp. 651–73. Lancaster.

1909b The Pajaritan culture. *American Journal of Archaeology,* 2nd series, vol. 13, no. 3, pp. 334–44. Norwood, Mass.

1909c Archaeology of Rio Grande Valley. *Out West,* vol. 31, no. 2, pp. 692–719. Los Angeles.

1920 The cliff maiden. *El Palacio,* vol. 8, nos. 5–6, p. 109. Santa Fe.

1921 The Chaco Canyon and its ancient monuments. *Art and Archaeology,* vol. 11, nos. 1–2, pp. 3–28. Washington.

1922 The Chaco Canyon in 1921. *Art and Archaeology,* vol. 14, no. 3, pp. 115–31. Washington.

HEWETT, E. L. HENDERSON, J., ROBBINS, W. W.

1913 The physiography of the Rio Grande Valley, New Mexico, in relation to Pueblo culture. *Bulletin 54, Bureau of American Ethnology.* Washington.

HODGE, F. W.

1893 Prehistoric irrigation in Arizona. *American Anthropologist,* vol. 6, no. 3, pp. 323–30. Washington.

1895 The first discovered city of Cibola. *American Anthropologist,* vol. 8, no. 2, pp. 142–52. Washington.

1897 The Enchanted Mesa. *National Geographic Magazine,* vol. 8, no. 10, pp. 273–84. Washington.

1897a The verification of a tradition. *American Anthropologist*, vol. 10, no. 9, pp. 299–302. Washington.

1904   Hopi pottery fired with coal. *American Anthropologist*, n.s., vol. 6, no. 4, pp. 581–82. Lancaster.

1914   Archaeological explorations in western New Mexico. *Smithsonian Miscellaneous Collections*, vol. 63, no. 8, pp. 53–58. Washington.

1918   Excavations at Hawikuh, New Mexico. *Smithsonian Miscellaneous Collections*, vol. 68, no. 12, pp. 61–72. Washington.

1920   Hawikuh bonework. *Museum of the American Indian, Heye Foundation; Indian notes and monographs*, vol. 3, no. 3. New York.

1921   Turquois work of Hawikuh, New Mexico. *Leaflets of the Museum of the American Indian, Heye Foundation*, no. 2. New York.

1922   Recent excavations at Hawikuh. *El Palacio*, vol. 12, no. 1, pp. 1–11. Santa Fe.

1923   Circular kivas near Hawikuh, New Mexico. *Contributions from the Museum of the American Indian, Heye Foundation*, vol. 7, no. 1. New York.

HOFFMAN, W. J.

1878   Report on the Chaco cranium. *Tenth Annual Report of the U. S. Geological and Geographical Survey of the Territories, 1876*, pp. 453–57. Washington.

HOLMES, W. H.

1878   Report on the ancient ruins of southwestern Colorado, examined during the summers of 1875 and 1876. *Tenth Annual Report of the U. S. Geological and Geographical Survey of the Territories, 1876*, pp. 383–408. Washington.

1886   Pottery of the ancient Pueblos. *Fourth Report of the Bureau of Ethnology*, pp. 257–360. Washington.

1905   Notes on the antiquities of Jemez Valley, New Mexico. *American Anthropologist*, n.s., vol. 7, no. 2, pp. 198–212. Lancaster.

HOUGH, W.

1902   Ancient peoples of the Petrified Forest of Arizona.

Harper's Magazine, vol. 105, November, 1902, pp. 897–901. New York.

1903 Archaeological field-work in northeastern Arizona, the Museum-Gates expedition of 1901. *Annual Report of the U. S. National Museum for 1901*, pp. 279–358. Washington.

1907 Antiquities of the Upper Gila and Salt River valleys in Arizona and New Mexico. *Bulletin 35, Bureau of American Ethnology*. Washington.

1914 Culture of the ancient Pueblos of the Upper Gila River region, New Mexico and Arizona. *Bulletin 87, U. S. National Museum*. Washington.

1915 The Hopi Indians. *Little Histories of North American Indians*, no. 4. Cedar Rapids.

1917 Archaeological investigations in New Mexico. *Smithsonian Miscellaneous Collections*, vol. 66, no. 17, pp. 99–103. Washington.

1918 Ancient pit dwellings in New Mexico. *Smithsonian Miscellaneous Collections*, vol. 68, no. 12, pp. 72–74. Washington.

1919 Exploration of a pit house village at Luna, New Mexico. *Proceedings U. S. National Museum*, vol. 55, pp. 409–31. Washington.

1920 Archaeological excavations in Arizona. *Smithsonian Miscellaneous Collections*, vol. 72, no. 1, pp. 64–66. Washington.

1923 Pit dwellings and square kivas of the Upper San Francisco River. *El Palacio*, vol. 15, no. 1, pp. 3–9. Santa Fe.

HULL, D.

1916 Castaño de Sosa's expedition to New Mexico in 1590. *Old Santa Fe Magazine*, vol. 3, no. 12, pp. 307–32. Santa Fe.

HUNTINGTON, E.

1912 The physical environment of the Southwest in pre-Columbian days. *Records of the Past*, vol. 11, no. 3, pp. 128–41. Washington.

1913 The secret of the big trees. *Department of the Interior*. Washington.

1914   The climatic factor as illustrated in arid America. *Publications of the Carnegie Institution of Washington*, no. 192. Washington.

JACKSON, W. H.
1876   Ancient ruins in southwestern Colorado. *Annual Report of the U. S. Geological and Geographical Survey of the Territories, 1874*, pp. 367–81. Washington.
1878   Report on the ancient ruins examined in 1875 and 1877. *Annual Report of the U. S. Geological and Geographical Survey of the Territories, 1876*, pp. 411–50. Washington.

JEANCON, J. A.
1911   Explorations in Chama basin, New Mexico. *Records of the Past*, vol. 10, pt. 2, pp. 92–108. Washington.
1912   Ruins of Pesedeuinge. *Records of the Past*, vol. 11, pt. 1, pp. 28–37. Washington.
1919   Preliminary report of the excavations at Po Shu Ouinge, near Abiquiu. *El Palacio*, vol. 7, no. 4, pp. 66–69. Santa Fe.
1921   Archaeological explorations in New Mexico. *Smithsonian Miscellaneous Collections*, vol. 72, no. 6, pp. 120–25. Washington.
1922   Archaeological research in the northeastern San Juan basin of Colorado during the summer of 1921. *State Historical and Natural History Society of Colorado and the University of Denver*. Denver.
1923   Excavations in the Chama Valley, New Mexico. *Bulletin 81, Bureau of American Ethnology*. Washington.

JUDD, N. M.
1917   Evidence of circular kivas in western Utah ruins. *American Anthropologist*, n.s., vol. 19, no. 1, pp. 34–40. Lancaster.
1917a   Archaeological reconnaissance in western Utah. *Smithsonian Miscellaneous Collections*, vol. 66, no. 17, pp. 103–08. Washington.
1917b   Notes on certain prehistoric habitations in western Utah. *Proceedings 19th International Congress of Americanists*, pp. 119–24. Washington.

1918 Archaeological work in Arizona and Utah. *Smithsonian Miscellaneous Collections*, vol. 68, no. 12, pp. 74–83. Washington.

1919 Archaeological investigations at Paragonah, Utah. *Smithsonian Miscellaneous Collections*, vol. 70, no. 3. Washington.

1920 Archaeological investigations in Utah and Arizona. *Smithsonian Miscellaneous Collections*, vol. 72, no. 1, pp. 66–69. Washington.

1922 The Pueblo Bonito expedition of the National Geographic Society. *National Geographic Magazine*, vol. 41, no. 3, pp. 322–31. Washington.

1922a Archaeological investigations at Pueblo Bonito, New Mexico. *Smithsonian Miscellaneous Collections*, vol. 72, no. 15, pp. 106–17. Washington.

1923 Archaeological investigations at Pueblo Bonito, New Mexico. *Smithsonian Miscellaneous Collections*, vol. 74, no. 5, pp. 134–43. Washington.

KENDALL, G. W.
1844 Narrative of the Texan Santa Fe expedition. New York.

KIDDER, A. V.
1910 Explorations in southeastern Utah in 1908. *American Journal of Archaeology*, 2nd ser., vol. 14, pp. 337–59. Norwood, Mass.

1915 Pottery of the Pajarito plateau and of some adjacent regions in New Mexico. *Memoirs American Anthropological Association*, vol. 2, pt. 6, pp. 407–62. Lancaster.

1916 The pottery of the Casas Grandes district, Chihuahua. *Holmes Anniversary Volume*, pp. 253–68. Washington.

1916a Archaeological explorations at Pecos, New Mexico. *Proceedings of the National Academy of Sciences*, vol. 2, pp. 119–23. Baltimore.

1916b The pueblo of Pecos. *Archaeological Institute of America; Papers of the School of American Archaeology*, no. 33. Santa Fe.

1917 Prehistoric cultures of the San Juan drainage. *Pro-

ceedings 19th International Congress of American-ists, pp. 108–13. Washington.

1917a The old north pueblo of Pecos. *Archaeological Institute of America; Papers of the School of American Archaeology*, no. 38. Santa Fe.

1917b A design-sequence from New Mexico. *Proceedings of the National Academy of Sciences*, vol. 3, pp. 369–70. Baltimore.

1919 Review of Spier, "An outline for a chronology of Zuñi ruins." *American Anthropologist*, n.s., vol. 21, no. 3, pp. 296–301. Lancaster.

1920 Ruins of the historic period in the upper San Juan Valley, New Mexico. *American Anthropologist*, n.s., vol. 22, no. 4, pp. 322–29. Lancaster.

KIDDER, M. A. AND A. V.

1917 Notes on the pottery of Pecos. *American Anthropologist*, n.s., vol. 19, no. 3, pp. 325–60. Lancaster.

KIDDER, A. V. AND GUERNSEY, S. J.

1919 Archaeological explorations in northeastern Arizona. *Bulletin 65, Bureau of American Ethnology*. Washington.

1920 Review of Morris, "Preliminary account of the antiquities of the region between the Mancos and La Plata rivers in southwestern Colorado." *American Anthropologist*, n.s., vol. 22, no. 3, pp. 285–88. Lancaster.

1921 Peabody Museum Arizona exploration, 1920. *Proceedings of the National Academy of Sciences*, vol. 7, pp. 69–71. Easton, Pa.

KROEBER, A. L.

1916 Zuñi culture sequences. *Proceedings of the National Academy of Sciences*, vol. 2, pp. 42–45. Baltimore.

1916a Zuñi potsherds. *Anthropological Papers of the American Museum of Natural History*, vol. 18, pt. 1. New York.

1917 Zuñi kin and clan. *Anthropological Papers of the American Museum of Natural History*, vol. 18, pt. 2. New York.

LOEW, O.

1875   Report on the ruins of New Mexico. *Annual Report of the Geographical Explorations and Surveys West of the 100th Meridian*, pp. 174–78. Washington.

LUMHOLTZ, C.

1891   Report of explorations in northern Mexico. *Bulletin of the American Geographical Society*, no. 3, pp. 386–402. New York.

1891a   Explorations in the Sierra Madre. *Scribner's Monthly Magazine*, November, 1891, pp. 532–48. New York.

1902   Unknown Mexico. New York.

LUMMIS, C. F.

1889   Mysterious ruins, a visit to the Pueblo Alto. *San Francisco Sunday Chronicle*, January 27.

1906   The land of *poco tiempo*. New York.

1910   Pueblo Indian folk-stories. New York.

LYON, M. W.

1906   Mammal remains from two prehistoric village sites in New Mexico and Arizona. *Proceedings U. S. National Museum*, vol. 31, pp. 647–49. Washington.

MARTIN, H. T.

1909   Further notes on the pueblo ruins of Scott County. *Kansas University Science Bulletin*, vol. 5, no. 2, pp. 11–22. Lawrence.

MATTHEWS, W.

1894   Explorations in the Salado Valley. *The Archaeologist*, vol. 2, no. 12, pp. 351–66. Waterloo, Ind.

MEARNS, E. A.

1890   Ancient dwellings of the Rio Verde Valley. *Popular Science Monthly*, October, 1890, pp. 745–63. New York.

MINDELEFF, C.

1895   Cliff ruins of Canyon de Chelly, Arizona. *American Anthropologist*, vol. 8, no. 2, pp. 153–74. Washington.

1896   Aboriginal remains in Verde Valley, Arizona. *Thirteenth Report of the Bureau of Ethnology*, pp. 179–261. Washington.

1896a   Casa Grande ruin. *Thirteenth Report of the Bureau of Ethnology*, pp. 289–319. Washington.

1897   The cliff ruins of Cañon de Chelly, Arizona. *Sixteenth Report of the Bureau of American Ethnology*, pp. 73–198. Washington.

1898   Origin of the cliff dwellings. *Bulletin of the American Geographical Society*, vol. 30, no. 2, pp. 111–123. New York.

MINDELEFF, V.

1891   A study of Pueblo architecture: Tusayan and Cibola. *Eighth Report of the Bureau of Ethnology*, pp. 3–228. Washington.

MONTGOMERY, H.

1894   Prehistoric man in Utah. *The Archaeologist*, vol. 2, nos. 8, 10, 11, pp. 225–34, 298–306, 335–42. Waterloo, Ind.

MOONEY, J.

1893   Recent archaeologic find in Arizona. *American Anthropologist*, vol. 6, no. 3, pp. 283–84. Washington.

MOOREHEAD, W. K.

1898   Some objects from the Salado Valley, Arizona. *American Archaeologist*, vol. 2, no. 8, pp. 207–210. Columbus, Ohio.

1902   The field diary of an archaeological collector. Andover.

1906   A narrative of explorations in New Mexico, Arizona, Indiana, etc. *Bulletin of Phillips Academy, Dept. of Archaeology*, no. 3. Andover.

1908   Ruins at Aztec and on the Rio La Plata, New Mexico. *American Anthropologist*, n.s., vol. 10, no. 2, pp. 255–63. Lancaster.

MOOREHEAD, W. K. AND GUNCKEL, L. W.

1892   In search of a lost race. *Illustrated American*, vol. 10, no. 116; vol. 11, nos. 119, 121, 122, 124–30. New York.

MORGAN, L. H.

1880   On the ruins of a stone pueblo on the Animas River in New Mexico. *Reports of the Peabody Museum*, vol. 2, pp. 536–56. Cambridge.

1881 Houses and house life of the American aborigines. *Contributions to North American Ethnology*, vol. 4. Washington.

MORLEY, S. G.

1908 The excavation of Cannonball ruins in southwestern Colorado. *American Anthropologist*, n.s., vol. 10, no. 4, pp. 596–610. Lancaster.

1910 The South House, Puyé. *Southwest Society, 6th Bulletin*. Los Angeles.

MORLEY, S. G. AND KIDDER, A. V.

1917 The archaeology of McElmo Canyon, Colorado. *El Palacio*, vol. 4, no. 4, pp. 41–70. Santa Fe.

MORRIS, E. H.

1915 The excavation of a ruin near Aztec, San Juan county, New Mexico. *American Anthropologist*, n.s., vol. 17, no. 4, pp. 666–84. Lancaster.

1917 The place of coiled ware in Southwestern pottery. *American Anthropologist*, n.s., vol. 19, no. 1, pp. 24–29. Lancaster.

1917a Discoveries at the Aztec ruin. *American Museum Journal*, vol. 17, no. 3, pp. 169–79. New York.

1917b Explorations in New Mexico. *American Museum Journal*, vol. 17, no. 7, pp. 461–71. New York.

1918 Further discoveries at the Aztec ruin. *American Museum Journal*, vol. 18, no. 7, pp. 603–10. New York.

1919 Preliminary account of the antiquities of the region between the Mancos and La Plata rivers in southwestern Colorado. *Thirty-third Report of the Bureau of American Ethnology*, pp. 155–206. Washington.

1919a The Aztec ruin. *Anthropological Papers of the American Museum of Natural History*, vol. 26, pt. 1. New York.

1921 Chronology of the San Juan area. *Proceedings of the National Academy of Sciences*, vol. 7, pp. 18–22. Easton, Pa.

1921a The house of the great kiva at the Aztec ruin. *Anthropological Papers of the American Museum of Natural History*, vol. 26, pt. 2. New York.

NELSON, E. W.

1884   Explorations in southern Arizona. *Annual Report of the Smithsonian Institution for 1884*, pp. 20–24. Washington.

NELSON, N. C.

1913   Ruins of prehistoric New Mexico. *American Museum Journal*, vol. 13, no. 2, pp. 63–81. New York.

1914   Pueblo ruins of the Galisteo basin, New Mexico. *Anthropological Papers of the American Museum of Natural History*, vol. 15, pt. 1. New York.

1916   Chronology of the Tano ruins, New Mexico. *American Anthropologist*, n.s., vol. 18, no. 2, pp. 159–80. Lancaster.

1917   Archaeology of the Tano district, New Mexico. *Proceedings 19th International Congress of Americanists*, pp. 114–18. Washington.

1917a Excavation of the Aztec ruin. *American Museum Journal*, vol. 17, no. 2, pp. 85–99. New York.

1919   The archaeology of the southwest: a preliminary report. *Proceedings of the National Academy of Sciences*, vol. 5, pp. 114–20. Baltimore.

1919a The Southwest problem, *El Palacio*, vol. 6, no. 9, pp. 132–35. Santa Fe.

NEWBERRY, J. S.

1876   Report of the exploring expedition from Santa Fe, New Mexico, to the junction of the Grand and Green rivers of the Great Colorado of the West, in 1859. *U. S. Engineering Dept.* Washington.

NORDENSKIOLD, G.

1893   The cliff-dwellers of the Mesa Verde. Translated by D. Lloyd Morgan. Stockholm.

NUSSBAUM, J. L.

1922   A Basket-Maker cave in Kane County, Utah; with notes on the artifacts by A. V. Kidder and S. J. Guernsey. *Museum of the American Indian, Heye Foundation; Indian Notes and Monographs* (no. 29). New York.

PALMER, E.

1876   Exploration of a mound in Utah. *American Naturalist*, vol. 10, pp. 410–14. Cambridge.

1880 Cave dwellings in Utah. *Reports of the Peabody Museum*, vol. 2, pp. 269–72. Cambridge.

PALMER, F. M.

1905 A land of mystery. *Out West*, vol. 23, no. 6, pp. 525–38. Los Angeles.

PATRICK, H. R.

1903 The ancient canal systems and pueblos of the Salt River Valley, Arizona. *Phoenix Free Museum Bulletin*, no. 1. Phoenix.

PEPPER, G. H.

1899 Ceremonial deposits found in an ancient Pueblo estufa in northern New Mexico. *Monumental Records*, vol. 1, no. 1, pp. 1–6. New York.

1902 The ancient Basket Makers of southeastern Utah. *American Museum Journal*, vol. 2, no. 4, suppl. New York.

1905 Ceremonial objects and ornaments from Pueblo Bonito, New Mexico. *American Anthropologist*, n.s., vol. 7, no. 2, pp. 183–97. Lancaster.

1905a The throwing-stick of a prehistoric people of the Southwest. *International Congress of Americanists, 13th Session, New York, 1902*, pp. 107–30. Easton, Pa.

1906 Human effigy vases from Chaco Canyon, New Mexico. *Boas Anniversary Volume*, pp. 320–34. New York.

1909 The exploration of a burial room in Pueblo Bonito, New Mexico. *Putnam Anniversary Volume*, pp. 196–252. New York.

1920 Pueblo Bonito. *Anthropological Papers of the American Museum of Natural History*, vol. 27. New York.

PRUDDEN, T. M.

1897 An elder brother to the cliff-dweller. *Harper's Monthly Magazine*, vol. 95, June, 1897, pp. 56–63. New York.

1903 The prehistoric ruins of the San Juan watershed in Utah, Arizona, Colorado and New Mexico. *American Anthropologist*, n.s., vol. 5, no. 2, pp. 224–88. Lancaster.

1914   The circular kivas of small ruins in the San Juan watershed. *American Anthropologist*, n.s., vol. 16, no. 1, pp. 33–58. Lancaster.

1918   A further study of prehistoric small house ruins in the San Juan watershed. *Memoirs American Anthropological Association*, vol. 5, no. 1, pp. 3–50. Lancaster.

PUTNAM, F. W. AND OTHERS.

1879   Reports upon archaeological and ethnological collections from the vicinity of Santa Barbara, Cal., and from ruined pueblos in Arizona and New Mexico, and certain interior tribes. *Report of the U. S. Geographical Surveys West of 100th Meridian*, vol. 7, Archaeology. Washington.

REAGAN, A. B.

1917   The story of Jemez and Zia. *El Palacio*, vol. 4, no. 2, pp. 24–72. Santa Fe.

1919   The ancient ruins in Lower and Middle Pine River Valley, Colorado. *El Palacio*, vol. 7, nos. 9–12, pp. 170–76. Santa Fe.

1922   Additional notes on the Jemez-Zia region. *El Palacio*, vol. 12, no. 9, pp. 120–21. Santa Fe.

ROBERTS, F. J. J. JR.

1922   Report on the work of the 1922 season in the Piedra Parada archaeological field. *University of Denver Bulletin*, vol. 23, no. 9. Denver.

SAPIR, E.

1916   Time perspective in aboriginal American culture; a study in method. *Geological Survey of Canada, Anthropological Series*, no. 13. Ottawa.

SAUNDERS, C. F.

1912   The Indians of the terraced houses. New York.

SAVILLE, M. H.

1894   The plumed serpent in northern Mexico. *The Archaeologist*, vol. 2, no. 10, pp. 291–93. Waterloo, Ind.

SIMPSON, J. H.

1850   Journal of a military reconnaissance from Santa Fe, New Mexico, to the Navajo country. Reports of the

Secretary of War, 31st Congress, 1st sess., Senate, ex. doc. 64, pp. 56–139. Washington.

SPIER, L.

1917   An outline for a chronology of Zuñi ruins. *Anthropological Papers of the American Museum of Natural History*, vol. 18, pt. 3. New York.

1918   Notes on some Little Colorado ruins. *Anthropological Papers of the American Museum of Natural History*, vol. 18, pt. 4. New York.

1919   Ruins in the White Mountains, Arizona. *Anthropological Papers of the American Museum of Natural History*, vol. 18, pt. 5. New York.

SPINDEN, H. J.

1922   Ancient civilizations of Mexico and Central America. *American Museum of Natural History, Handbook Series*, no. 3, 2nd ed. New York.

STARR, F.

1900   Shrines near Cochiti, New Mexico. *American Antiquarian*, vol. 22, no. 4, pp. 219–23. Chicago.

STEVENSON, J.

1883   Illustrated catalogue of the collections obtained from the Indians of New Mexico and Arizona in 1879. *Second Report of the Bureau of Ethnology*, pp. 307–422. Washington.

1883a   Illustrated catalogue of the collections obtained from the Indians of New Mexico in 1880. *Second Report of the Bureau of Ethnology*, pp. 423–65. Washington.

1884   Illustrated catalogue of the collections obtained from the pueblos of Zuñi, New Mexico, and Wolpi, Arizona, in 1881. *Third Report of the Bureau of Ethnology*, pp. 511–94. Washington.

1886   Ancient habitations of the Southwest. *Bulletin American Geographical Society*, no. 4, pp. 329–42. New York.

TAYLOR, W.

1898   The pueblos and ancient mines near Allison, New Mexico. *American Antiquarian*, vol. 22, no. 5, pp. 258–61. Chicago.

TWITCHELL, R. E.
  1911   The leading facts of New Mexican history. Cedar
         Rapids, Iowa.
  1914   The Spanish archives of New Mexico. Cedar Rapids,
         Iowa.
WALTER, P. A. F.
  1916   The cities that died of fear. *El Palacio*, vol. 3, no. 4,
         pp. 12–73. Santa Fe.
WEBSTER, C. L.
  1912   Some burial customs practiced by the ancient people
         of the Southwest. *Archaeological Bulletin,* vol. 3, no.
         3, pp. 69–78. Madison, Ind.
  1912a Archaeological and ethnological researches in south-
         western New Mexico. *Archaeological Bulletin*, vol.
         3, no. 4; vol. 4, nos. 1, 2; vol. 5, nos. 2, 3. Madison,
         Ind., and Ottawa, Kansas, 1912, 1913, 1914.
WETHERILL, L. W. AND CUMMINGS, B.
  1922   A Navaho folk tale of Pueblo Bonito. *Art and
         Archaeology*, vol. 14, no. 3, pp. 132–36. Washington.
WETHERILL, R.
  1894   Snider's well. *The Archaeologist*, vol. 2, no. 9, pp.
         288–89. Waterloo, Ind.
WILLISTON, S. W.
  1899   Some prehistoric ruins in Scott County, Kansas.
         Kansas University Quarterly, vol. 7, no. 4, pp. 109–
         14. Lawrence.
WILSON, L. L. W.
  1916   Excavations at Otowi. *El Palacio*, vol. 3, no. 2, pp.
         28–36. Santa Fe.
  1916a A prehistoric anthropomorphic figure from the Rio
         Grande basin. *American Anthropologist*, n.s., vol.
         18, no. 4, pp. 548–51. Lancaster.
  1918   Hand sign or avanyu, a note on a Pajaritan biscuit-
         ware motif. *American Anthropologist*, n.s., vol. 20,
         no. 3, pp. 310–17. Lancaster.
WINSHIP, G. P.
  1896   The Coronado expedition, 1540–1542. *Fourteenth
         Report of the Bureau of Ethnology*, pt. 1, pp. 329–
         613. Washington.

WISSLER, C.

1919   The Archer M. Huntington survey of the Southwest. Zuñi district. General Introduction. *Anthropological Papers of the American Museum of Natural History,* vol. 18, pp. i-ix. New York.

1921   Dating our prehistoric ruins. *Natural History,* vol. 21, no. 1, pp. 13–26. New York.

1922   Pueblo Bonito as made known by the Hyde expedition. *Natural History,* vol. 22, no. 4, pp. 343–54. New York.